UNITAS

UNITAS

Building Healing Communities for Children

SECOND EDITION

by

Edward P. Eismann

FORDHAM UNIVERSITY PRESS
New York
1996

Library of Congress Cataloging-in-Publication Data

Eismann, Edward P.
   Unitas—building healing communities for children / by Edward P.
Eismann — 2nd ed.
      p.   cm.
   Rev. ed., originally published: Bronx, N.Y. : Hispanic Research
Center, Fordham University, 1982.
   Includes bibliographical references (p.).
   ISBN 0-8232-1686-1
   1. Therapeutic communities—Handbooks, manuals, etc.   2. Child
psychotherapy—Study and teaching—Handbooks, manuals, etc.
3. Unitas (Bronx, New York, N.Y.)—Handbooks, manuals, etc.
4. Social work with children—New York (State)—New York—Handbooks,
manuals, etc. I. Title.
RJ505.T53E37   1996
362.2—dc20   96-16790
                                                          CIP

DEDICATION

To all those who love children

. . . by consanguinity

. . . by adoption

. . . by friendship

CONTENTS

Foreword

This monograph is a sequel to the ethnographic documentation of the Unitas Therapeutic Community published by the Hispanic Research Center in 1981 as Monograph No. 6 -- *Unitas: Hispanic and Black Children in a Healing Community,* written by Anne Farber and Lloyd H. Rogler. As readers of that monograph will know, Unitas is an outreach therapeutic program serving Hispanic and Black children in the South Bronx, a national symbol of urban decay. It is a complicated institutional structure based upon philosophical, psychological, and sociological views of how interpersonal relations can be shaped in the interest of a child's healthy social and emotional life. To achieve what Unitas calls the healing of a child's "brokenness," the program has created a network of symbolic families composed of children and teenagers living in the same neighborhood. The teenagers play the roles of symbolic parents and become the caretakers and, indeed, therapists of the younger children.

In Keeping with one central objective of Fordham University's Hispanic Research Center (HRC), that of focusing its research to inform public policy and practice, the findings and recommendations in the Farber and Rogler report were widely disseminated. Almost without exception, the response to our research on Unitas was enthusiastic. The attention of readers of the monograph was caught by the innovativeness of the Unitas therapeutic community operating in the South Bronx; its work with emotionally distressed Hispanic and Black children living in deteriorated neighborhoods; its mobilization, recruitment, and training of teenagers from such neighborhoods to serve both as surrogate parents and as therapists to the children; the ingenious use of the concepts of fictive nuclear and extended families as the foundation of the program's social organization; the diverse ways in which the rituals enacted at Unitas' meetings, so deeply absorbing to the participating children, provide institutional meaning to the Unitas pattern of mutual help; the commitment to heal the psychological wounds resulting from a disadvantaged childhood; the cost-effectiveness of the Unitas program at a time of depleting budgets for inner city programs; and, the vision of the founder and director of Unitas, Dr. Edward Eismann. Under his leadership, Unitas grew out of the grassroots of the South Bronx, to serve the emotional well-being of the neighborhood's children. All of this evoked the interest of those who through our research became familiar with Unitas.

The purpose of the present study is twofold. First, in conducting the earlier ethnographic documentation of Unitas, Dr. Farber and I had worked necessarily from the viewpoint of the outside observer. The present monograph, however, presents Unitas from a different viewpoint -- that of the insider. Therefore, this study can be viewed as a forum from which the central actor of Unitas, namely, its founder and director, Dr. Edward Eismann, speaks as the "main insider." As such, he provides us with a very rich, first-hand account of how he went about mobilizing the youngsters who would later become the core of the Unitas program, of the reasons why these teen-agers were attracted to the Unitas program and what motivated them to be-come the surrogate parents of the younger children in their neighborhoods, and some of the ideas in the social science and therapeutic literature which influenced the shaping of the Unitas program.

The second purpose of the present study is to present a series of training modules for persons interested in replicating certain aspects or dimensions of the Unitas program in other settings. In these training mod-ules, Dr. Eismann offers the reader an understanding of the basic knowledge and skills he has developed and used for the training of Unitas teenagers.

The first three parts of this monograph, therefore, are an insider's ac-count of how Unitas was pieced together as a healing community. The information presented in these sections, by its very nature, cannot be reduced to training modules, nor can the shaping of a healing modality be packaged into predigested units. However, the reader will find that by under-standing the history of Unitas' early mobilization efforts, the motivation of the teenagers, and the ideas which influenced the creation of the program, the training modalities, presented in the fourth part of the monograph, will be-come more meaningful.

A subsequent monograph, *Unitas: Evaluating a Preventive Program for Hispanic and Black Youth,* by Mary E. Procidano and David S. Glen-wick, HRC monograph #13, is a psychotherapeutic evaluation of Unitas which attempts to examine how children who participate in the program change as a result of their Unitas experience. Indeed, it was the need for such a study which first brought Edward Eismann to the HRC and Unitas to our attention. The three Unitas studies—one an ethnographic outsider's account, the second an insider's view, and the third an experimental re-search evaluation—provide a comprehensive, well-rounded evaluation of the Unitas experience. Together these studies provide a new multifaceted, multi-perspective view of an exciting and innovative therapeutic approach.

Although the present study can be read and utilized in its own right, the reader will find it of value to consult the earlier ethnographic account of the Unitas program for a more comprehensive understanding of Unitas' goals and methods.

We hope that the skills and knowledge imparted in this monograph will be of value to all persons interested in the emotional, psychological, and so-cial well-being of children.

Lloyd H. Rogler
Albert Schweitzer University Professor of the Humanities
Fordham University
September 1995

ACKNOWLEDGEMENTS

This monograph would not have been written were it not for the invitation extended to me by Dr. Lloyd H. Rogler, former director of the Hispanic Research Center, to become a Research Associate for seven months at the Center for the purpose of writing this manual. Lynn Stekas, administrator of Unitas, worked out an equitable arrangement for my absence three days a week during those months, assuming all administrative responsibilities for the program, in order for me to take advantage of the opportunity extended to me by Dr. Rogler. To both these people, I am deeply grateful.

My thanks to the Hispanic Research Center antedate the writing of this manual. In the spring of 1980 the Hispanic Research Center published the first of a series of studies on the Unitas therapeutic program, its sixth monograph titled *Unitas: Hispanic and Black Children in a Healing Community,* written by Anne Farber and Lloyd H. Rogler. Indeed, the present manual is not only a companion to this earlier publication, but also a result of it. Through that publication, the Hispanic Research Center brought Unitas a great amount of publicity and national recognition, and Dr. Rogler, personally, was instrumental in linking me with the vast mental health network that exists on a national level. Subsequent to these two publications, a third monograph, *Unitas: Evaluating a Preventive Program for Hispanic and Black Youth*, was published by the Center, forming a comprehensive and in-depth view of Unitas as an innovative model of mental health care rooted in classical concepts of therapeutic community.

I am grateful for the assistance and cooperation of many hardworking staff members of the Hispanic Research Center who contributed expert administrative, secretarial, and typing skills to this work. Stasia Madrigal had the monumental task of editing and honing down hundreds of pages of manuscript into manageable size, assisted by Elizabeth Collado, who also typed a great deal of the manuscript, together with Magdalena Porrata and Mercedes Rivera. Elizabeth Ospina arranged a comfortable social context for me at the Center where my work would be uninterrupted. When the manuscript neared completion, the professional advice I received from Dr. Beth Grossman, clinical psychologist, and Dr. Caroline Manuele, educational psychologist, enabled me to organize the entire work in a more readable and clinically precise way. This was particularly true regarding the organization of the training modules in Part IV of the monograph.

Taping the dialogue of all the teenagers and transcribing these tapes into written form for analysis was a monumental task. I am indebted to all those teenagers who sat with me during the summer of 1981, some of whose names are mentioned in Part II of this work. I am equally indebted to my very special friends Eileen Morel, Anthony Rosario, Wilson Martinez, and Richard Sherman, who assisted me voluntarily in writing out verbatim the contents of all those tapes; Martha Anderson, who shared in the typing of the transcriptions; and to Eric Cox, who creatively captured the cover photo at a timely moment from a tenement rooftop.

Revising and updating the contents of this second edition involved invaluable organizational contributions from Tony Vera, Executive Director of Unitas; Patria Jimenez, a keyboard wizard who retyped essential changes in the text; Laura Lewandowski, who redeveloped the cover photo for present use. Special thanks to Dean Marianne Quaranta, Associate Dean Bertram Beck, and Professor Rosa Perez-Koenig from the Graduate School of Social Services, Fordham University, for their endorsement and support in the formal publication of this work.

I would like to particularly acknowledge Marjane Cloke of the Mutual Life Insurance Company of New York (MONY) whose enthusiasm and belief in Unitas' work with children of the South Bronx has made her a devoted friend. She arranged that the typesetting of this book be done at and by MONY as a contribution of that organization to disseminating the methods of Unitas to a reading public. For this invaluable contribution of Marjane and MONY, I am deeply grateful.

Finally, to my son Ben, I am grateful, for it must indeed have been intolerable at times to have lived with a book writer.

New York City   Edward P. Eismann
1996

INTRODUCTION

The Unitas Therapeutic Community is a mental health treatment and prevention program for youth in the South Bronx, New York City. Based on theories of therapeutic community and social psychology, Unitas stresses psychological methodologies which cultivate the healing potential present in all interpersonal relationships -- dyadic, group, and communal.

Unitas has developed training techniques which integrate existing knowledge about interpersonal healing processes on individual, group, and communal levels, and it applies this knowledge to natural social contexts. For example, a classroom of students constitutes a natural social context. Unitas methodology would first recognize that contained in this social setting are the individuals who themselves can be psychological and educational helpers to each other. Armed with this basic belief, a skilled psychological or educational facilitator would then utilize specific techniques to activate the dormant healing qualities naturally possessed by the students in their existing relationships with each other to come to bear on one another. Thus, behavioral or educational growth would occur as a result of the skillful promotion of such interactions rather than as a result of promotion of educator/student or therapist/client interactions alone. These techniques of activating existing but dormant healing characteristics of people in their natural relationships with one another can be used in individual, group, family, and community contexts. Once learned, the techniques may be applied to almost all social contexts.

In the spring of 1981, the Hispanic Research Center at Fordham University published a two-year ethnographic study of Unitas, examining its organizational structure and interpersonal processes. The study described and analyzed the composition of Unitas' program elements; its staff and the participating children; its concepts of psychological healing, therapeutic systems and techniques; its history in the context of the community mental health movement; its elaborate symbolic family structure; its impact on the lives of its teenage symbolic "parents" and children; and, finally, the success of Unitas as a mental health program and the desirability of replicating it.

The conclusions of this ethnographic study were published in the monograph *Unitas: Hispanic and Black Children in a Healing Community* written by Dr. Anne Farber and Dr. Lloyd H. Rogler.[1] One of the major questions raised as a result of this appraisal was that of the program's replicability. If a program successfully reaches and changes the lives of problem children in the South Bronx, where serious social problems of poverty, unemployment, and housing exacerbate psychological stress, is it possible to transport its techniques to other settings?

The Hispanic Research Center's ethnographic study concluded that it was feasible and valid to replicate the Unitas program. The findings viewed

[1]Farber, Anne and Rogler, Lloyd H. *Unitas: Hispanic and Black Children in a Healing Community.* Bronx, New York: Hispanic Research Center, Fordham University, 1981.

total replication of the program as difficult, but possible, and partial replication as more likely to succeed, with both total and partial replication depending on the institution's willingness to commit itself to enter into the very life of naturally existing social organizations such as a cultural group, a family, a classroom, a gang, or a parish committee, and to mobilize the indigenous strengths contained therein in the direction of mental health goals.

The guidelines suggested by the study, within which Unitas might be totally or partially replicated, together with the study's conclusions concerning the validity of such replication, coincided with one of my own primary considerations as Unitas developed over the years, namely, to keep its methods and techniques universal enough to be used either as a total program approach (as in Unitas itself) or as treatment components within larger organizational structures (as in groups within settlement houses, classrooms within schools, or therapies within mental health structures). Encouraged, therefore, by the scientific conclusions of the study and recognizing many of the difficulties involved in the replication process, I began to feel the urgency of putting the system and methods of Unitas down in writing.

The decision to think through and write up a "foundation manual" was imperative. In the spring of 1980 the Coalition of Hispanic Social Service and Mental Health Organizations (COSSMHO) in Washington, D.C., conducted a mental health research seminar on mental health service innovations and knowledge transfer. The seminar attracted clinical personnel from all over the United States as well as from the various divisions of the National Institute of Mental Health. The Unitas concept, its theoretical framework, and innovative practices were presented at that seminar. Soon after this presentation, COSSMHO published an account of the seminar in its newsletter and Unitas then received letters and phone calls in response to this discussion and publication. There were so many inquiries that I had to begin to think of a way to deal with requests for consultation, training, workshops, lectures, and publications. COSSMHO itself pledged to come to the South Bronx and provide the needed monies to sponsor a workshop on Unitas methodology and to make the arrangements to bring together the people who had responded to its article.

In the midst of this response, one problem was paramount. Up to this point, the methodology of Unitas was a tradition handed down by myself, by clinical interns who had received training at Unitas over the years, and by the children themselves who had grown up in Unitas and absorbed the values and methods of the organization, and who as teenagers passed these on to younger children. I saw that it was necessary to articulate the Unitas methods in writing.

It was immediately after the publication of the Hispanic Research Center's monograph that the opportunity to begin the present manual was given me through the center's director, Dr. Lloyd H. Rogler. Dr. Rogler had invested philosophically and professionally in the Unitas concept from the days when we first met four years ago and began to collaborate on a plan for conducting the ethnographic documentation which culminated in the monograph. He offered me a period of employment to compose a logistics manual, a companion to the monograph. The present manual is the product of this effort.

The purpose of this manual is twofold:

1. To describe the steps taken, historically, together with the methods and techniques used in the creation of Unitas as a healing community for children.

2. To offer a substantive example of a training curriculum that simulates the training given to Unitas teenagers and clinical staff.

The manual attempts to present Unitas techniques in a sequential and integrative manner. While sections could be understood and used as separate modules in their own right, the intention is integrative. Thus, understanding the process of therapeutic community as applied to classroom management would necessitate an experiential understanding of dyadic bonding, then small group dynamics, and finally large group influences. Again, multiple family group interventions would follow a similar format: bonding on dyadic levels, then fostering the healing forces of the small nuclear family group to come to bear on one another, and finally utilizing large group influences to instill controls and nurturance toward one another as would occur naturally in an extended family.

The training curriculum is a logical sequel to the monograph. Its aim is to inform readers of the monograph about the clinical logistics involved in setting up similar programs within their own social contexts. However, this is not a "how-to-do-it-yourself" manual with step-by-step instructions for easy replication. Descriptions of methods for effecting psychological change on individual, group, and community levels abound in the literature. There are quick skills courses, training kits, short seminars, the "fast food" phenomena of the day. They represent simplistic prescriptions to complex mental health needs. This manual should not be used in this way. Its intent is to serve as an educational tool to be used in conjunction with supervised training, whether that supervision occurs within Unitas in the South Bronx, or on the work site of any organization interested in replicating the Unitas program or parts of it.

If the goal is to replicate the program in a substantive part or in its entirety, direct participation in the program beforehand is probably necessary. Direct participation yields knowledge which is not entirely reducible to explicitly rendered sets of prescriptions on how to accomplish therapeutic goals. Direct participation also provides a clinical sense of the expressive components of the healing process, and the clear recognition of the need for the commitment to an ethic of helping other persons, whether that ethic be rooted in religious, humanistic, or psychotherapeutic beliefs.

This manual is divided into four parts. Part I is descriptively logistical. If someone were to ask me how to set up a community mental health program modeled after Unitas, I could not provide a bureaucratic blueprint of how to go about doing it. And so without giving such instruction, I describe to the reader the path I took 15 years ago as I struggled to break out of a system of psychiatric care that gave no evidence of touching the lives of troubled neighborhood youth.

Part II describes the components involved in building a caretaker system of neighborhood teenagers available to each other and neighborhood children in need. Although this section describes teenagers as the designated helpers, the process by which this network is built is similar to the building of networks in general. I have attempted to let the teenagers speak for themselves as they consider the major components involved in the building of this healing network.

Part III describes the theoretical framework of Unitas in philosophical, sociological and psychological formulations. Operationalizing those theories in an integrative manner seemed to produce a profound climate of healing among children and teenagers, unearthing a "therapeutic community" which had been there all along.

While Parts I, II and III describe the creation of a therapeutic community, focusing on how teenagers were mobilized into a network of helpers of children, Part IV of the manual contains the training program itself. As such, it constitutes a book in its own right and assumes the presence of people already mobilized for training. The training program teaches specific skills to help children become more effective, happy, and cooperative. Its purpose is to impart skills needed to build children's self-esteem and feelings of competence; to understand and communicate more effectively with children on individual, group, and communal levels by developing skills in encouragement, empathy, problem solving, conflict resolution, group process, and therapeutic community. Together with a humanely disposed personality, the mastery of these skills is a requisite for effective healing and a *sine qua non* for the building of a healing or "therapeutic community."

UNITAS

PART I
BUILDING A SYMBOLIC FAMILY
FOR NEIGHBORHOOD CHILDREN

In the winter of 1967 I took employment as a clinician in the Lincoln Community Mental Health Center in the South Bronx, New York. The center had just received a two million dollar grant to operate a program of psychiatric care for residents within its catchment area. During the years prior to its funding, the center's parent body, the Albert Einstein College of Medicine of Yeshiva University, had collected epidemiological data measuring the extent of the social and psychiatric pathology rampant within the catchment boundaries, data which served to justify the monies requested and granted through the Community Mental Health Centers Act of Congress of 1964. Top names in the mental health field were involved in establishing the contact with the National Institute of Mental Health and setting up the machinery for the operation of the program. It seemed exciting to become part of a well-designed, carefully researched, expertly planned, well-administered, and innovative community mental health center.

Actually it was a disastrous experience! During my first year in that center, politics, racism, internal accusations of mismanagement, and the influence of radical groups within and without the center resulted in massive work stoppages, strikes, manifestations of professional and paraprofessional megalomania, support of gross worker incompetencies and bitter persecution of administrators in key positions. In the midst of this administrative chaos, I became more and more disillusioned, angry, and depressed. In six months I had received only two requests for consultation and had conducted two mini-workshops.

In the summer of 1968, on the brink of resigning from this job situation of apathy and administrative upheaval, I began to take long walks on the streets of the South Bronx. As I walked down certain streets with regularity over a period of weeks, I began to see the same faces of children, the same huddled groups of teenagers, the invariable presence of garbage, broken glass, wine bottles, and beer cans. I stopped and watched games, sat on curbs, waved and smiled at children from a distance, caught a ball that missed its bat, and threw out comments here and there. At first, I kept my distance and did not dally in any one place; I moved on and left "trails of crumbs" -- expressions of support, acknowledgement, affirmation, and nurturance -- throughout the streets that were becoming my forest trail.

As I maintained my daily ritual down Beck Street, around Kelly Street, down to Longwood and onto Fox, I slowed down to sit and to talk with the youngsters I saw: on car fenders, curbs, stoops, and in schoolyards and alleyways. When I talked to one child, he would introduce me to his friends, and these friends to their friends, their brothers and sisters, even their mothers and fathers. I found that the language of empathy, conflict resolution, clarifying and reframing open hostilities that were erupting in front of me had as valid application in the street as it did in my clinic office.

There were some of my very early friends -- Santos, Ismael, Luis, Jojo, and Orlando -- climbing in an abandoned house across the street from the schoolyard. I climbed around with them, listening to their conversations with one another. Most of the talk was braggadocio, an attempt to impress me and each other of their superlative skills in scaling, balancing, jumping, and hiding. Casually, I made it known that I passed by that spot during the week around lunchtime and that I would look for them each time. Over the weeks we began having lunch together, and gradually the small group expanded to nine persons.

After a few weeks of meeting informally with Santos and the eight other boys, I learned that a rival gang was after Luis because he had cut one of their members with a knife. It was a tense situation. Luis and his cohorts were anxious about the consequences and about saving face in the event Luis should be attacked. They thought they should all carry knives to prepare for the anticipated attack of Luis' rival. I commented that they were "right"; if they believed they would be attacked they "needed defenses" and that "it was good to have a knife to protect yourself with," but that "there were other ways to protect yourself too." Then they began talking of other ways such as using broken bottles and hardening the callouses on their knuckles. As I continued to foster the idea of alternatives, I kept my eye open for natural groups of older teenagers in the same schoolyard, groups with whom I had made friendly alliances over the weeks. These were non-hostile groups of teens with good common sense. I beckoned to some of these teens to come over where we were. Three of these teens saw Luis' knife and started to tell him of the trouble he could get into. I commented that "they sounded like they knew what they were talking about." Two of the boys recounted the trouble they had experienced with the police and the courts, and their eventual detention in a state training school for a year. Luis listened carefully. At the right moment, I commented on the suggestions made by the boys about ways of protecting themselves. The older teens gave all the boys, particularly Luis, advice on "other ways," and agreed to help out Luis in the school gym where equipment for hardening his fists was available. Luis handed over his knife to me and I said that I would "mind it" for him.

The following day, Santos, Luis, and some of the other boys were sitting in the usual spot waiting for me. As we were eating lunch, Santos spotted Angel, the boy whom Luis had cut up a few weeks ago. There were whispers and eye-crossing among the group. I mentioned that they were "scared about something." Santos referred to the presence of Angel. "Call him over," I said. They hesitated. I urged. Santos called to Angel. Angel came and sat away from Luis. I said to Angel, "You were cut with a knife a few weeks ago. How did it happen?" He described the incident saying that "that punk" (pointing to Luis) had thrown a knife in his direction and as he (Angel) had thrown down his arm, the knife had cut him. I reflected his anger at Luis, saying "maybe it was an accident, maybe not, but a knife wound hurts." I listened to both boys relate their defensive versions of the event; then commented to both of them that they had really been thinking a lot about what had happened and must have felt afraid of each other after the incident; perhaps even sorry it had happened at all. "Had they known each other before the incident?"

Each one unwillingly said yes. I said it almost did not seem that way, so I would introduce them to each other. I immediately threw the dialogue into play form and introduced one to the other as kings of different empires. Humor and recognition of their "royalty" broke the barriers of their negative feelings.

The boys then began to talk of trips they had taken in the past with the Boy Scouts. Angel had never had that experience. I encouraged Luis to tell the group about things he had done with the Scouts. He mentioned the Scout Master, saying that he worked nearby. I suggested we go there and meet him together. On the walk to the Scout Center and then back to the boy's neighborhood, Angel and Luis were talking to each other as though they were old friends, and were even planning to be in the same Scout unit so they could camp out together. I found out that although Luis and Angel lived on the same street, and in nearby buildings, Angel was a member of a gang from a different turf. It appeared now that Angel had found a new bond, to Luis especially, and to the group itself, into whose membership I was slowly inserting him.

Luis introduced me to his mother who was standing on the stoop. I said hello to some neighbors along the way who smiled at me and the boys. Santos said to me, "If you keep on saying hello to people, soon you'll know everyone." I said, "It seems that way, doesn't it? It's a good feeling when people really know each other in friendly ways."

When the group broke up, each going his own way for the day, I sat on the stoop with Santos for a few minutes, and told him I was going to tell him a secret. The other day he had said to me that I should try to help Luis, did he remember? He said he did, and he said that Luis needed a lot of help. Well, I said, it seemed that he, Santos, had helped Luis more today than I or anyone else could. With a few hints, he saw what I meant, namely, that Luis and Angel had been enemies until today when Santos brought them together to be friends. It was he who had called Angel over in the first place; it was he who had introduced the subject of the Boy Scouts; it was he who had taken us to the Scout Center. Did he notice how they walked along together and had been planning their scout activities? Santos' face lit up and he was so pleased that he said he was going to ask Luis about this. I said that he could if he wanted to, but that it was really something that at least the two of us knew and were happy about.

From the relationship established with each member of this natural group of boys and within the group as a whole, a fearful and drifting collective of youngsters became a small support community for helping one another, thinking through important issues related to self-esteem and handling enemies. Dealing with enemies through shared dialogue and recognition of common interests was for them a unique experience. In addition, a lonely, isolated boy, an apparent "enemy" of the group, had been absorbed into it.

This experience, occurring so naturally, yet requiring a skill and understanding of individual and group forces at least equal to those needed in any clinic setting, provided me with a sense of personal and professional pleasure. I understood that I had moved the healing forces in several natural social networks to come to bear on the lives of a group of boys who had been drifting into a defensive, useless way of life. My personal bond with the boys was the first step. With a nurturing relationship established, the movement toward constructive action came primarily through the skill I had used in stirring up the helping, but dormant, "charisms" possessed by the peer group itself, the older teen peer group (to whom the younger boys looked as models), the neighbors, a Boy Scout troop and a school. Using interpersonal skills directly in the open setting where a group of boys lived their actual lives, I was able, within a few days, to tap the healing forces of four social systems to influence the thinking and actions of a group of trouble-prone youngsters and one alienated boy in particular. It is questionable that such a conclusion would have occurred in any context removed from the reality itself.

The story of my friendship with Eddie, Martin, Joey, Nelson, Willy, Edgar, Raphael and Gil has equal poignancy. These boys, aged 7 to 11 at the time, looked forward eagerly to my daily visit when I sat for an hour or two each day on their stoop listening to their incessant, almost compulsive talk, a desperate need for communication born of a hunger for attention, approval, and recognition. They liked the stoopside chats so much that they often brought along other friends as needy and confused as they were. These boys brought me their personal and family problems and the chats with them were the beginnings of a group therapy of the street. The boys talked of their fears of being hexed by enemies, anxieties connected with superstitions imposed on them: the women in Puerto Rico who smear tears of dogs on men and turn them into unicorns; the headless man who rides forever through Puerto Rico on horseback, ravaging the area where he appears; the burning of dolls representative of enemies in order to destroy those enemies. Interposed between this outpouring of fright were the realities they had experienced or lived in fear of: Edgar who was "fucked by two older punks at knifepoint"; "Pothead," a glue sniffer who lived on the rooftops and whose violence frightened the boys into hiding at the very word of his appearance on the street; Willy, who in panic abandoned his baby sister whom he was minding when he saw Pothead coming down the fire escape of his building; Robert, who tells of Joey being mashed in the head by two other "punks" who took his racing car.

Always, my question to them was: How did they help each other? They began to give examples of how they defended each other. I said that was really important, that's what friends were for, that's what we were all about together here, to have friends you could depend on. The theme of listening to each other and helping each other was maintained from day to day. One day I asked them, "Do you have a name for your friendship group?" Joey said they had a couple of names: The Dragon Flies, The Musketeers, the King's Men. I told them I had another name that described them: The Protectors. Robert's face lit up and he said, "Yeah, that's right."

One day the boys were playing tag and at a certain point in their game they started to hurl rocks and stones at the "enemy." I could not see their enemy, but they said it was the "niggers" from the other end of the street who had begun to bother them. I was caught in the middle of a rock-throwing party, trying desperately to think of ways to distract them or redirect them. I tried thoughts with them like "I think you have shown them enough by now to make it known they can't push you around," but no reasoning helped and the war continued. Finally, it was over. "We won!" was the battle cry.

The next day I returned to the group but found a cool acceptance. I was neither hailed nor related to except by forced "hi's." I tried conversation but to no avail. The boys who were outside were not really playing with each other; other boys were inside looking out the window. I knew this unsettlement between them and me had something to do with yesterday's war and with our growing close to each other.

I kept hanging around, sitting on the stoop, not letting them reject me although I was feeling rejected. A block party was scheduled by a community group for the evening. I stayed around to be at it. When I got food, I deliberately went to several of the boys and offered them some of my food. They began coming near me again and cautiously conversing. One boy ventured to ask me, "Would you beat up a kid?" I said, "Me! Why would I want to do that? I might not like what a kid does, but beat him, never!" As the evening went on, I sat on the curb and four of the boys came over and ate with me. At last it came out. Robert said, "We thought you were real mad at us yesterday because we were throwing rocks. We thought you didn't like us anymore and weren't coming back." I commented that that was the way he felt, like I was through with them. Did the others feel this way too? They said they did and then talked more about people who get mad at them and become their enemies. I said, "I sure am glad you brought this up, that you were able to say these things to me. I'm pleased that you could tell me what was on your mind and how you felt." I then said that "I was not mad at you yesterday, but I was feeling something when the rock throwing was going on. I felt afraid, not angry. Afraid that someone might get hurt and I didn't want any of you to get hurt because I like you. You were right! I was feeling something but it was not what you thought. It pleased me so much that we could sit here and get to understand each other better."

We went over to the stoop and talked for another hour. The thoughts and feelings that emerged now were of a tender variety epitomized by Willy who commented at a certain point, "Wouldn't it be great if we could all live together in one big house?" I said that was a beautiful thought, but at least we could be real close friends who would care about each other.

"To live together in one big house." That reminded me of the psalmist who wrote, "How good it is and how noble for people to live together in unity." And so I drifted into reverie. Unity House, that's what the house would be called if we had one. But everyone here had a house, so why a house? But everyone did not have a home. That's why some of the boys traipsed into the neighborhood each day from their own homeless tenements to find a family among the stoopside group. And my reverie went on. Perhaps instead of a big house for children, a kind of "family" could be created, a community of people who could learn to care for each other. But the thought came to me, How would I do such a thing? Who would supervise me? There had to be someone somewhere who would guide me in such a venture. Perhaps there were courses, experts, consultants. And how would I justify such an idea to the mental health center? My function there was to be a clinician, not a trail blazer.

So, I struggled with the vision I was conceiving that perhaps a neighborhood community of children could be developed in which the needs of children could be met by other children and teenagers who lived on the same street, collectively acting in the capacities of symbolic mothers and fathers and brothers and sisters to each other. The thought haunted me but I was not ready to release that vision into a reality. Part of me was still clinging to institutional thinking: looking for a place already prepared for me and which offered supervision and a clear framework within which to function officially. The realization of my vision involved separation from dependency on the thinking and approval of my mentors and launching out, breaking into full scale belief in my own insights and creative leanings.

What finally released the vision into reality was my friendship with a little boy named Ray. During that summer, Ray sat in the schoolyard each morning, playing by himself with his toy cars. We smiled but he kept his distance. Then one day he came over to me and asked, "Will you be here forever?" And the question stumped me. How could I answer it? And then I smiled, looked him in the eye, and said with conviction, "Yes! You can be sure of that!" It was the clearest yes I had ever said. I knew then that my yes to Ray was really a decision to accept full responsibility for my vision of creating a caring community of children and teenagers right where I was.

Having formed friendships with a number of individual children and their small peer groupings, it was now necessary to begin to connect these separate parts into a unified whole. Making a healing community meant bringing together the Santos' and the Angels with the Eddies and the Martins and the Joeys of the neighborhood. The "niggers" who played ball on one end of the street needed to know that the brown-skinned Puerto Ricans who played ball on the other end of the street played the same game. And the Luis' and the Angels who lived on the same street needed to discover their availabilities to each other. How better to do this than through the language of childhood: play!

Together with Vera, an art therapist recruited from the mental health center and with the help of some Eddies and Willies, we set up the "clinic of the street." Art materials, games, and play equipment, begged and borrowed from a variety of sources, were stored in my automobile which became a mobile clinic that rolled in and out of Fox Street, the central point of my wanderings. Play enabled us to build ties between individual children and groups of children on the same and adjoining streets through bonding and empathic skills. Through play we were able to help groups of children in conflict with each other to resolve their anger through problem-solving skills. Through the trust engendered in play we were able to attend to the personal crises of individual children as they detailed their disrupted family lives. The children reacted to our studied interventions with amazing responsiveness.

The first summer ended -- a glorious time! During the school year that followed, I maintained my relationships with the community of children on Fox Street by meeting with them in their schools. I suggested they bring me into their schools and let me meet their teachers. And so I was introduced to the principal, the guidance counselors, and the teachers by some of the older children. In this way I gained entry to their schools as a friend and not as a professional seeking referrals.

Maintaining these bonds served three purposes: to reinforce the children's bonding with me as a "helping friend"; to use their relationship with me as a way of bonding others together with us in building a healing community; and to select and build up a cadre of older boys and girls who would start meeting with me regularly to learn how to take care of the children on their street and each other. During this time I realized that I was using myself as direct clinician to my young friends and as consultant to their educational caretakers who themselves, like me, retired to our different communities at the end of each day. Taking the traditional position of the doctor/patient relationship on the patient's own turf was one step nearer the mark of influencing children and their systems. It was a vast improvement on sitting in a clinic office where children did not come, but it was still removed from empowering a community to heal its own members. Thus, I began to address the task of shaping up that constituency of community helpers who were to become the bedrock of care for community children in the Unitas system, namely, the community teenagers.

It is this third purpose described above -- the selecting and training of a cadre of older boys and girls for the role of surrogate parents -- that enabled the "clinic of the street" to go beyond clinician- based therapy and become a healing community of children and teenagers who took care of each other. This "social mobilization of the neighborhood teenagers into a motivated and therapeutically trained cadre of symbolic parents"[1] was the gateway through which a neighborhood healing community came into being. Part II of this manual describes in detail the story of the first and subsequent groups of teenagers who accepted the challenge to become surrogate parents for needy youngsters in their own community.

As I developed this cadre of teenage helpers, they worked with me in developing the operation of Unitas as a healing community. Maintaining my own strong bonds of help with the children and teenagers and cultivating the helping capacities of the teenagers to come to bear on the other children resulted in a three-pronged system of healing in the evolving Unitas Therapeutic Community:

1.   Direct healing relationships between myself and the children and teenagers.

2.   Direct healing relationships between the teenagers and a specific child or a small group of children.

3.   Direct healing relationships among the teenagers themselves as they met with me to learn this skill.

This system of healing became integrative and interdependent. As the children became dependent on the teenagers, the teenagers looked for guid-

[1]Farber, Anne and Lloyd H. Rogler. Unitas: Hispanic and Black Children in a Healing Community. Bronx, New York; Hispanic Research Center, Fordham University, 1981 (Monograph No. 6), p. 128.

ance from me; as they looked to me, I looked to them to maintain their helping relationships with the children on their street. The building of a healing community became a collaborative venture: the children needed the teenagers, the teenagers needed me, and I needed the teenagers as the cornerstones in the building of an autonomous healing community. After a period of time, the teenagers were able to need me less as they became not merely helpers to the children but guides and teachers for each other in maintaining "their" therapeutic community.

By the spring of 1974 I became aware that the children, teenagers, and I were ready for the next phase of development of our healing community. This would involve the convocation of all the separate groups of children and teen helpers from the different streets. And so it happened that on one Thursday afternoon, 30 children and teenagers met for the first "family circle" around a stoop on Fox Street. This is what I might have said:

> As I told you when I met with you during the week, the reason we are meeting like this is to talk together and get to know each other. How many are from Beck Street? Fox? Kelly? Longwood? Elsewhere? ... How many of you go to PS 39, 133, Monroe, Gompers, other schools? ... Who's a good ball player? A musician? Good at making things? Good in school at reading and writing? A good cook? A scientist? What else do some of you do well? ...

> Look, we will make little schools here on the street right now. Each school will have a specialty. You will be in the school you like best. Over there on that stoop is the school for ball players and other athletes. That stoop over there is for music lovers. That one there is for crafts, for those who like to build and make things. Over there is for those who like cooking and making things in the house. Would you like any other schools? I want you to go to the stoop you like best. When you are there tell each other what you do and give some examples. Do that now for ten minutes. I will let you know when to come back.

After ten minutes, I reconvened the group.

> Who can share some things you talked about in your little schools? ... We are going to meet this way each week before we play. This will be the beginning of becoming a make-believe family right here in the neighborhood, a family made up of little groups from around the different streets. This big make-believe family we will call an extended family. Do you know what that means? ... How many of you have family in Puerto Rico? Down South? In Manhattan? Wherever you have relatives living but not in your house, they are the extension of your family, they are called your extended family. You don't all live together in the same house, but you are connected with each other through bonds of friendship or acquaintance. The purpose of our meeting each week will be to get to know each other like brothers and sisters in a big family. Do you think you can remember what I'm saying? ... Good, because next time we will have a lot of children who are not here now and they will have to know what this is all about. Do you think you can tell them in your own words? ...

Well, that's just fine. I'm very pleased you have come here today. We are beginning something today that will be a big help to you in your friendship with me and with each other. Now, let's just play.

During the following week, I visited the whole network of "little families" from all the streets, inviting them to bring their friends and instructing them where and how to meet with me. Each week, with reminders going out through the teenagers, the number of children attending the weekly meetings increased. The meetings, eventually attended by 150 to 200 youngsters, needed a highly visible and rule-oriented structure to maintain their purpose. And so, a ritual evolved -- the ceremony of the circle -- which defined the purpose of the group, described its structure, clarified the operating rules, and provided the forum for therapeutic interchange.

The ceremony of the circle, or family circle, served two purposes. First, it was the therapeutic medium through which cohesiveness among the neighborhood children and teenagers was fostered and interpersonal problems were resolved. Second, it was the vehicle through which the symbolic family structure was clearly established and reinforced. A typical family circle meeting is described in the appendix of this manual.

And so Unitas evolved, this therapeutic community of the street, consisting of teenagers from each street serving as symbolic mothers or fathers to groups of needy children from the same street. The family circle, the therapeutic community meeting, united all separate "street families" into one large extended symbolic family.

It is not my intention in this manual to elaborate each detail of the evolving therapeutic community of Unitas. This has been described accurately and sequentially in the original Farber and Rogler monograph. I have intended to introduce the reader to the crucial beginnings of Unitas from trailblazing the streets of the South Bronx to saying, "Yes, I would be here forever," to little Ray and to the use I made of clinical skills to relate to the needs of individual children and youths wherever they were: in streets, alleys, school yards, rooftops and eventually their schools and home settings as well.

The doggedly hard work of the next few years consisted essentially in reinforcing the bonds of the teenagers with me and with each other. The commitment of the teenagers to the children was directly related to my commitment to them as a mentor, friend, symbolic parent, and advocate. After a while they were available in a substantive way to each other. But I cannot emphasize enough to the reader that the need for a central, older, respected symbolic parent, represented in this case by myself, was, and remains, the *sine qua non* for Unitas' achievement in building and maintaining a therapeutic community in the neighborhood.

I cannot say that frustrations, disappointments and setbacks did not produce profound discouragement in me at times almost to the point of giving up. In the summer of 1975 I experienced an almost total washout of motivation to continue as a result of a growing undermining of authority, trust, and cooperation when the neighborhood teenagers at that time, including some of those most related to me, established factions among the children, lashed out against each other, produced work stoppages, and took to drugs. It culminated in an upheaval described by a college student who wrote:

> At the family circle, Anna wasn't feeling well and was sitting in the back on the stool for woodworking - above everyone else. Doc asked her quickly if her being there was something for the group to discuss or perhaps she could talk to him after. She yelled, "No, Doc, I tried to talk to you before, but you said wait until the group, so I waited, and now you say wait? Man, I'm sick and I'm not waiting." Now why did Doc jump on her like that? A lot of the older boys were standing around the circle. Something smelled fishy. The boys started to back Anna. Then Angélo made himself the center of attention to tell Doc that the counselors were afraid of him and he was unreasonable, etc.
>
> Miriam brought up the issue of Danny trying to drown Jose at the pool. Things started to get excited. Danny started cursing out Jose and James. James told Danny that he would drown him if he bothered Jose once more. Amando said to James that he would mess him up if he touched Danny. "He's my man! You have to mess with me if you mess with him!" James was fuming. More curses and threats.
>
> Angelo brought up the issue of Rick and his car and Rick yelling at Anna to get off. Rick's car had mysteriously gotten two low tires on the right side. This is an event that had been happening quite often lately. Angelo got really uptight about it and started to use Rick as a punching bag. He cursed Rick out with Danny and a few others joined in. Danny was cursing, raging, turning purple, and screaming about respect for a person, "If you don't want people to sit on your car don't bring it on the fuckin' block!"
>
> Doc saw Danny getting out of control and went to him to calm him down. He walked out of the circle holding Danny. As Doc left, so left the power of speech. Johnny walked over to Rick and punched him in his chest, walking away. Kids ran, yelling, and Doc turned around in time to see Amando choking Rick. When Doc got there Amando let Rick go.
>
> The circle was in chaos - people standing - nervous - what would happen? - Unitas - the power of the people failing in front of our eyes.
>
> Doc raised his voice, and with his hands he brought the family together. His hands were shaking. "We have just seen something very distressing. Let's stay together," he said. Very few kids stayed around. Frightened, they ran home and their mothers would not let them out. Windows were filled with people. Neighbors came out onto the street. Everyone was on edge.

The fury I felt and sat with for days after this immobilized me. The pivotal question was: Is the vision of creating a healing community of children and teenagers in a neighborhood a fantasy reflective of my own needs rather than an innovative and objective approach for healing dysfunctioning children? The vision seemed objectively sound. I had founded my practice on sound theoretical thinking, I had seen things work, I had seen children's spirits lifted from depression or acting-out to acceptable adjustment. But why then were things falling apart?

The soul-searching and discouragement I struggled with were perhaps no different from similar struggles people in close relationships experience when faith in the relationship is seriously shaken. The question then becomes: In spite of faith shaken, is there still enough love and belief in the relationship that not only can reinstate it, but even make it stronger the second time around? If not, the persons must separate. The crisis energized my belief that the forces for healing were stronger than the forces of decay. And so I rose against discouragement, renewed my determination that the positive relationships within Unitas would offset the negative, and that I could find answers to the present conflict by stepping back and observing carefully what was occurring before me.

My theoretical understanding of the broad network of relationships within the Unitas community now shifted and I saw that I had been stressing more of a one-to-one bonding between teenagers and children according to a very psychoanalytical frame of reference. Although the street circle was group-focused up to this point, it still breathed the theme of strong dyadic bonding between individual teenagers and children in their care. I now broadened my perception of what I understood to be going on within this network of relationships. Studying sociological ideas of organizational structures, particularly therapeutic community as practiced in contemporary mental hospitals and children's residential institutions, and calling upon systems theory in general and family systems in particular, enabled me to have a far wider perspective of the many facets of the network I had brought together for healing purposes. From these broader theories I was able to extract specific techniques to deal with the conflicts and needs expressed within the Unitas community than were possible through perceiving my community from a narrow psychoanalytical perspective alone.

And Unitas not only survived but flourished in such a way that when I had to make a decision a year later as to whether to adapt Unitas to the newly formed policies of the Community Mental Health Center, which became primarily a Medicaid Clinic, by reverting to the ineffective clinic-based approach of the early years, or to close the enterprise, I chose neither, but brought Unitas to its next step of growth, the step of autonomy. It happened this way:

In 1975, the administration of the Mental Health Center ordered that all outreach programs cease. I was ordered to remain in the center; my private office and the space created for the teenagers were "sealed" and I was told that to leave the center would result in docking of my salary. I was to remain in the clinic building and see children through Medicaid arrangements. I complied to what the letter of the law required, but used compensatory time, lunch time, and overtime to keep a skeletal form of Unitas alive, meeting with the teenagers at the local library and maintaining community meetings of all the neighborhood children in the local parochial school which eventually became Unitas' home base.

During the period of April to October 1976, to determine the accuracy of my impression that children were not responding to the services of the

Community Mental Health Center -- an impression which seven years before had resulted in the creation of Unitas as an alternative system of psychological care -- I conducted a small statistical study on the responsiveness of the clinic in treating children of the area. The study showed that in the outpatient unit that Unitas functioned from, among four clinicians employed to treat children, the mean intake was 1.8 children per clinician per month. This was even more dramatic a finding than I expected, especially coupled with the fact that in 1974, the Albert Einstein College of Medicine, the center's parent body, had compiled its own study of the psychological needs of children served by the mental health centers and hospitals under its jurisdiction and found that the Lincoln Mental Health Center catchment area contained the largest children's population and the most serious social/psychological needs. It seemed incredible that such a catchment area would be so untouched by its essential source of community psychiatric help.

I saw clearly what I needed to do, namely, to take the necessary steps to create an autonomous organization that would function independently of a parent body. And so I organized a Board of Directors, consisting primarily of South Bronx community leaders who had been involved in Unitas over the years and older Unitas participants. Unitas became incorporated with the New York State Board of Social Welfare as a charitable organization with tax exempt status. Financial assistance was sought from and granted by the Greater New York Fund and the New York Community Trust. I severed all ties with the Mental Health Center at the end of June 1977 and became the director of the "Unitas Therapeutic Community, Inc.," organizationally and financially independent of major institutional restraints.

That was 18 years ago. Unitas today continues to function strongly in its neighborhood through the belief and support of many people. It not only continues to maintain its symbolic parenting work among children but has expanded to include direct clinical services to children and families who respond to this more traditional form of care, in addition to the innovative alternate system described above for youngsters unresponsive to conservative approaches. Introduction of social work interns from Fordham University's Graduate School of Social Services, and an extensive system of undergraduate volunteers from its Bronx campus, have expanded Unitas' service delivery system, providing a substantial increase in helping power at virtually no cost. This observation itself is an interesting phenomenon in its own right in this day of budgetary cutbacks in social service and health organizations where the battle cry is "we can't help if we do not have money."

In collaboration with the Graduate School of Social Services Unitas has been able to arrange that the University be the conduit for its funding in order to take advantage of and participate in the administrative resources and technologies of the University. While the formal administrative structure of Unitas has joined hands with the administrative structure of the University, Unitas' informal connections with Fordham go back 18 years when the Hispanic Research Center, spearheaded by Dr. Lloyd Rogler, expressed great interest in studying Unitas as an example of a treatment approach depicting cultural sensitivity to Hispanic and Black populations of youth. From this interest, the Center published its three research mono-graphs attesting to the success and potential replicability of Unitas' method-ology in reaching minority populations of hard-to-reach youth.

Financial support has come through the New York City Department of Youth Services, The New York State Office of Alcohol and Substance Abuse Services, The United Way, and a variety of corporations and founda-tions. Were funding to cease or be drastically reduced Unitas would still continue its mission, since it remains today as a living community of people who, as children, experienced and internalized a way of life that they pass on voluntarily as a legacy to a new generation of children in their neighbor-hood. The legacy is that people everywhere have the capacity to be to each other as mothers and fathers and brothers and sisters in symbolic form wherever they are. And it is through the mediating influence of such corrective symbolic family structures that dysfunctional family experiences can be offset and social support offered.

PART II
NEIGHBORHOOD TEENAGERS AS
SYMBOLIC PARENTS

This section describes the process by which a neighborhood's teenagers accepted the challenge to become symbolic parents for needy youngsters who lived on their very street through the creation of a neighborhood therapeutic community. I believe the effectiveness of this process is due primarily to the inculcation of Unitas' ideology into its young people from the organization's inception, reinforced unswervingly and transmitted with utmost conviction to this very day.

Part III will explicate this ideology in terms of four basic postulates. Briefly, these postulates express the belief that all human beings have an innate desire and ability to be helpful and healing toward others. Exercising these abilities fulfills a deep existential need. To organize a system around this philosophy and utilize psychological and sociological constructs to operationalize this belief was where it all started, became maintained and is sustained to this day. The process of training the neighborhood teenagers into a cadre of symbolic parents profoundly interested in the welfare of children in their neighborhoods and in the worthiness of the Unitas undertaking could never have taken root or be maintained without the motivation derived from the ideology transmitted from myself as the self-appointed leader to the teenagers who worked with me.

Building this neighborhood teenage caretaker system can be best understood by considering four major components of its process:

1. The Leader

2. Neighborhood Teenagers

   a) Original Core Group
   b) Subsequent Core Group
   c) Non-Core Group
   d) Peripheral Teenagers

3. Motivation

   a) Why they came
   b) Why they wanted to work with children
   c) Why they stayed

4. Training

1. The Leader

Obviously, a leader's personality and way of thinking are vital to the success of any venture. Introspection and social hunger were and always have been my most deeply felt inner experiences. The valuation of ideology to satisfy my introspective questions and friendships to satisfy my social hunger were the chief expressions of this inner experience. As such, these expressions of ideology and friendship eventually found their culmination in the creation of Unitas, which is rooted in a clearly defined spiritual ideology and in a celebration of the love of friendship.

Thus, Unitas' effectiveness cannot be divorced from these values that I, as originator, implanted in the minds and hearts of the original core group of teenagers, who through the years, passed on these values to subsequent groups of children who grew up in Unitas and became its cadre of teenage leaders in due time.

I have no objective study of myself to offer that would specifically pinpoint those qualities of leadership in me that made a neighborhood of teenagers respond to my "call" to them. My ability to call neighborhood teenagers to form a working alliance with me and, as such, form a core group, came from their conviction of my beliefs, the deep caring they felt from me toward them personally, and my ability to "inspire" their basic altruism.

Freud described the process of group formation as residing in the leader's ability to form strong bonds between himself and each group member and then linking the group members together through their common bond with him. I believe in this formulation at the beginning of group formation, especially when a leader is communicating an ideology -- whether that ideology is rooted in psychotherapeutic, educational, or religious beliefs. When there is sufficient bondedness between individuals and an original leader, it then is the time to help the group members find strong bonds of interest and commonalities with each other.

In the beginnings of Unitas, I formed strong, separate bonds of adult friendship with a small core group of young men, eventually reinforcing their personal friendships with each other separately and together with me. This core group recruited other teenagers in the neighborhood to join them in working together with children. From these generally recruited others, the core group always selected a small number of additional key teenagers to add to the central core group.

What I have described above contains a basic principle, a norm for the effective building of the foundation of any humanitarian or religious system, namely, that the critical problem in the creation of any effective healing community is the choosing of the leader and the formation of the group; that is, those who will be closest to the leader.

It is through the leader and his core group that the ideology and the practices emanating from this ideology will impact upon the system's constituency. If the leader or core group includes the incompetent or those who imperfectly understand the values of the setting, trouble is inevitable.

2. Neighborhood Teenagers

a. Original Core Group

These beginning years focused first on building a core group of male leaders in recognition of aspects of Hispanic culture which strongly opposed bringing together intimate coed interconnections, since "inevitably" it was believed, sexual tensions would lead to acting out. Thus in the beginning of Unitas I looked at the interactions in front of me as I set up the "clinic of the street" and carefully selected four young men to work closely with me in building the network. These were Johnny, Jerry, Eric, and Papo. They became the links through which the neighborhood children as a whole were bonded to Unitas. These young men were responsive adolescents who demonstrated a leadership potential, a "social hunger," from the start when the clinic of the street took up residence outside their tenement windows. Johnny was assertive and outgoing. I saw that children gravitated about him. One day after I had met him, he came running out of his house and with a certain hurt said, "Doc, I didn't know you were here, why didn't you call me?" I challenged him by asserting my own command and inviting his own responsibility. I said to him that he knew what time I would be here and that I had no reason to call him. I told him that I wanted him to work with me helping the neighborhood children each day. Would he join me in this? And so he did for the next seven years. Then there was Jerry, friendly, warm and articulate. I met Jerry on a nearby street surrounded by young teens who looked to him to settle strifes between them. Or perhaps he looked for strifes to settle whether called to do so or not. For Jerry was a peacemaker. And so I hung around Jerry for a few days and then told him that I wanted him to join me on Fox Street and help children. Jerry, in 1981, 12 years later, remembered the event: "You picked the teenagers from Fox but I was living on Kelly. You told me you would make an exception with me because I had my head together to be able to work with you. I felt really good when you said that... like different from everyone else... I felt love." And Jerry stayed six years. Then there was Eric, shy at first but strong, cool and collected. Eric was introspective, but gentle and impressive. He was respected, though he tended to be distant. Eric was the oldest of six children, therefore, he had a lot of experience in being responsible for children. I saw this in how he related to children in the neighborhood. It was as though his role in life was to be a caretaker. I invited Eric to draw on his neighborhood stoop all summer and help other children draw. He responded. And Eric stayed for 12 years. There was Papo, a silent youth, stubborn, distant, and a mystic. His silent strength and kindness were only vaguely concealed behind his gruff facade. I invited him also to be a healing force in the lives of children on his street. For Papo, the invitation to work with me and his eventual desire to become a true symbolic father became the wedge to opening his communication with the world and changing the lives of children. And Papo stayed for 20 years.

I had a personal response to these young men and they to me. I nurtured these four relationships. They in turn nurtured other key teenagers in due time so that a core group of loyal believers and practitioners passed on the ideology of Unitas uninterrupted. With Johnny, Jerry, Eric, and Papo and a few others who became this original core group, I spent a great deal of time relating to their personal needs and problems, being their advocate at home and in school, setting up a pleasurable context for them at the mental health center, including feeding them, setting up a wood and art workshop and connecting them with clinic staff who were marvelous in the attention they heaped on these teenagers. The thrill of receiving such recognition and the opportunity to talk over very personal concerns for hours at a time without being officially prescribed, being driven home after clinic hours and talking more in the privacy of my automobile about dreams or despairs, being taken camping from time to time... all these "parenting gestures" made these young men bond fiercely with me and then with each other. Because of this relationship we were able to carry out the work of Unitas as though we were one. In retrospect, in 1981, Eric said:

> Twelve years ago I helped you with the kids strictly for our friendship, without which I would not have done it. If we had lost our friendship I would not have continued. But then after a while I began to see what I was doing as helpful to the kids and beneficial to myself. There came the point when you were busy and not available to me when I came over, but by that time the spaces between times we were together were not as critical. We could pick up where we last left off. There was that time you had me work with the kids at the mental health center from fall to spring. I felt by myself a lot there. You weren't over there. You had me working with you two and a half years before I even got paid. I did it because of our friendship.

From the bondedness these young men had with me, they eventually became bonded with each other. Individual relationships between each boy and myself were maintained, but lessened in quantity because of their growing availability to each other. Papo articulated this cohesiveness eloquently:

> When I came over to the clinic I saw Eric and Johnny helping kids. I looked at Eric and thought, "Who's that bookworm?" I saw other guys from Fox Street there, Tony, Danny, Elvin, and Angel. They were throwing a ball around. I saw Mr. Sherman from P.S. 39... I thought to myself, "This is like a school, it's not for crazy people after all." I got to meet Eric; he was building some crazy invention and he was into photography. We began walking home together and having fun. Then Eric said, "Come over to my house." Soon, there was a group of us guys who spent all this time with you, Doc, who now went home together, and all we talked about were the kids... the hard times, frustrations, ways of improving Unitas. Your concepts, Doc, were in each of us. The reason these concepts of Unitas are in the new core is because they got those ideas from us original guys. I didn't understand you at first, but then from the others I understood and said, "Oh, now I see what he is saying... to be human, to love and reach out and not be afraid." These guys here made it possible for me to do this.

From this original core group and the development of bonds with each other, over the years other teenagers became core group members, having been brought in by the original core members or having traits of responsiveness and leadership that made them "naturals" for Unitas.

b) Subsequent Core Group

Eric brought his brother Raymond and his sisters Angela and Rachel. Papo brought James who was a classmate; he also brought his brothers Miguel and Robert; Miguel in turn brought Cheo who in turn brought his classmates, Eric the younger, Sam, and Ileana. The genealogy goes on as each teenager convinced his or her friends about the marvels of friendship on Fox Street.

This was a transitional time. I was able to stand back now and let the nurturance, ideological transmission, and child-care know-how of symbolic parenting be channelled to other teenagers through the original core group. In particular, there was James, a muscular karate expert with a tender touch, who at age 15 was introduced into Unitas by Papo. James' whole world revolved around karate. He was shy, angry and preoccupied with being competent. Subsequently, as a social work student, James recalled his early years in Unitas:

> I felt inadequate, that I couldn't do things, that I was ugly, insecure about myself personally. Then I got into this group and began to feel "I'm okay." So many things you said to me, Doc, kept me going in life. Your availability, anything you said to me had a great deal of importance to me. But equally the guys and I were concerned about each other too. We saw from each other's face if something happened. It is the same with the kids we work with. I know what it feels like to be alone and what it feels like to be accepted and responded to by a group of caring guys. My best work is with the kids I take care of here in Unitas, giving them the caring and acceptance the way I got it with these guys here in our group and from you.

> I had no father to help me in growing up, and neither did Eric or Papo and a lot of the other guys. We fathered each other here in growing up. You see, Doc, the others had you at the beginning and that helped them. The fact that they had you in their life before I came here, that helped me because they were able to give me a lot of what you gave them. I attribute the way I have become to those guys.

Cheo, age 19, an architectural student at City College, recalled:

> I remember looking down from my window at you and thinking, "This man is crazy," but then one day you smiled at me and I felt good. I thought that maybe one day I'll know what it is about you that makes these kids care about you. One day Miguel brought me over to meet you and I played ball with him and some kids. I began watching Eric and Papo dealing with the kids and it fascinated me... they seemed so mature. That kept me coming. I thought, "I want to be like them." I asked them where they learned these ways of dealing with the children. They said in the training lessons with you. That reinforced my belief in you because I saw them and wanted to be like them. These people began showing a lot of love and caring for me. Eric let me in on his "masterful plans" about his inventions and other important things in his life. All this interest he showed in me helped me keep on coming. It was also the feeling that if anything happened to me he would be right with me, that's what made it worthwhile. And you, too, Doc, letting me into your life and understanding me and helping me with my struggles. You were an understanding father to me. That, too, kept me coming. There was a reaching out if anything was wrong. It was like a big family to me. I remember Eric always saying, "What you have had done for you that made you feel good, do for the children the

same way."

These feelings of being loved, cared about, accepted, and belonging were deeply experienced by the core members in their relationships with each other. It was the reason they came, remained, and invested themselves in the lives of children.

Cheo brought Eric the younger and Sam. Eric, age 19 and a student at City College, recalled:

> I'd been hearing about Unitas from Cheo and Sam. They liked it and talked about it so much. When I first came I was on the outside looking in... I wasn't sure I'd like it. I thought a lot of things were silly, but I was fascinated by the organization of everything going on, particularly the circle, a situation that could be very disjointed and confusing, but actually was not. I made friendships and learned from Doc and the other older teenagers how to really help children. The friendships are what really bonded me. They were real friendships in the sense of you could talk with somebody about a problem without being worried about gossip behind your back. This is a place where if you want to talk with somebody, they'll always be there. That above everything else is Unitas to me and what kept me coming. Sometimes, when I'm feeling real down I come because I know there'll be people here who'll be in a better mood and will care enough to ask me, "Is there anything the matter?" Not, "Aw, he's in a shitty mood, forget him!"

Sam, age 19, an architectural student at City College, reiterated the theme of friendship that sustained him in Unitas as a devoted core teenager. He was intrigued by Cheo's description of the place where teenagers became like mothers and fathers to neighborhood children. Sam also remembers the admiration he experienced for the older teenagers, particularly James and Eric the elder. He formed strong bonds of friendship with Raymond who at age 16 had been in Unitas since he was four. Sam experienced the same kind of caring from Raymond and the other core teenagers who taught him the ways of Unitas. He remembers how, through his strong friendship with Cheo, he was led to understand how pleasurable it was to have a strong bond with a child who needs you, that it goes both ways. Through this closeness with Raymond and Cheo, and under Cheo's tutelage, Sam reached out and made these bonds with the children. Sam says:

> I kept coming and keep coming now because of the friendships I have here. In Unitas it has always been said, like a commandment, "friendship is everything." If the friendships weren't there, I would stop coming. It is also important to me that I am considered part of the core group... that makes me feel I am believed in and taken seriously.

While the above recollections of some of the original and second generation core members reflect almost verbatim themes, their core co-peers, whose recollections are not transcribed here, are equally consistent about how the sense of caring, friendship and belonging profoundly touched them enabling them to be sustained as symbolic parents for years.

The original and subsequent core group represented the hub from which the program's ideology and healing interventions emanated. These young men and women, first through their strong ties of love to me and then, as the group grew to include others, through their ties of love to each other, were the magnets and influences through which neighborhood teenagers in general responded to Unitas' invitation to become surrogate parents to neighborhood children. What is striking in this arrangement was the observation that the reason, over the years, that at least 200 other teenagers in general responded to the invitation to be their "little brothers' keeper" was essentially the same as that of the core group: the friendship and caring they found in each other. While all were invited to join this work, only the strongest and most competent advocates became the core group at any one time.

c) Non-Core Group of Teenagers

Non-core group teenagers were those whose degree of investment in Unitas was loyal and generous but who never became the assertive and spoken leader advocates that the core group consisted of. The core group members were always around, almost 24 hours a day; the non-core members mostly when programming was actually in operation. Both core and non-core teenagers were effective lights in children's lives. They differed significantly from their more personally needy peers whose effectiveness with children was low level and remained such.

The personalities of the non-core teenagers, their needs, the reasons for their coming into Unitas, the reasons for their working with children and the reasons for their staying in Unitas are strikingly similar to those of the core teenagers. More than any other difference between them, it was shyness in demonstrating assertive leadership that distinguished them from their more outgoing peers who were core members.

d) Peripheral teenagers

Peripheral teenagers were those whose intentions were good but whose ability, potential, and predictability to give corrective emotional parenting to needy children were moderately to severely limited. These particularly needy teenagers were given the same sense of belonging and care in their own right by the other teenagers, but their responsibility with the children was tailored to their limited potential, with, however, the expectation that through their own continued exposure to personal caring from the group, they might grow emotionally to become capable, caring symbolic parents. Unfortunately, many of these teenagers did not stay long enough to grow in that direction.

3. Motivation

Since the non-core teens represented the bulk of the teenagers who eventually became the "cadre of symbolic parents" and probably would be the bulk of young people responding to any program's efforts doing similar work as Unitas, I want to describe these young people in such a way that understanding why they came, what they need, and what motivates them, a program wishing to replicate a similar undertaking can know what conditions must be present. With these conditions understood and operationalized, the basic altruism and goodness of youth can be elicited.

In seeking an answer to the question "Why do these teenagers give their time, energy, and love to their neighborhood children?", I did in-depth interviews with a cross-sample of original and subsequent core and non-core teenagers. These interviews lasted anywhere from two to six hours each, were taped, and then transcribed into written form. A massive collection of data resulted, which I then subjected to analysis. The following section of this chapter explicates this material from the teenagers' point of reference.

It should come as no surprise that to the last responder the answer to these questions revolved around the love, caring, friendship, and sense of belonging that teenagers give and get from each other. But this did not happen by chance. As already stated, the program worked because it inculcated the values of friendship among the teens, deliberately reinforcing and rewarding the expression of these values. In analyzing those responses in which caring was most profoundly experienced by the teens, a classification schema demonstrated that caring responses fell into six categories:

1. Experiencing acceptance and a sense of being wanted
2. Experiencing love
3. Experiencing a sense of belonging
4. Experiencing encouragement
5. Experiencing the giving and receiving of help
6. Experiencing a joy in learning

Reflection on these categories immediately suggests that therapeutic forces were indeed at work, similar to those suggested in studies of group therapy. Actually the teenager system was a therapeutic community in its own right, with teenagers evoking and having evoked in them those healing responses that made the difference between community as a merely socially understood construct and therapeutic community, where people received deep experiential fulfillment along psychological and spiritual lines. In order to clarify what these young people meant by the "caring" that touched their lives so much, and in order to make explicit what kinds of responses a system would need to provide in order to replicate a similar community or network with healing characteristics, I want to share the thoughts of these youth.

1. Experiencing Acceptance

Wilfredo, age 16, came sporadically to Unitas as a child. It was when Sherman, a teacher, made him feel really wanted as a person that turned the tide.

> Sherman remembered me when I came back after the summer. The first chance he got he came and said, "I see you're back." He put his arm around me and said, "Won't you come to my table later?" What made the difference was like he was saying I want to be with you. It made me feel I was wanted, not like "see

you around later." So I kept on coming to his table and he said, "You're growing up to be a teenager, so I want you to help me here so we'll be more together." I thought, "Wow!" to be working here, what a privilege." Sherman was the guy who made me want to keep coming. When I was 13 James' kids needed help, so I went over to them and James said, "I see you know these guys and you know how to treat them." James would always greet me and tell me to help certain kids. He had confidence in me. I felt comfortable here. You stay here because there's a strong bond that you feel with your friends here. It's like a brotherhood. Here everybody is a friend who knows you and your problems.

Sam, age 19, recalls how much it meant to him when Eileen used to greet him each week when he came to the circle. She would reach out her arms and smile to him and say:

...''I missed you last week, how are you? You look good." She would move over and make a space for me to sit near her and keep talking to me. I wanted people to treat me like this all the time, especially in our meetings. I made a close friendship with Raymond and later on with Miguel. They accepted me and wanted my friendship. That made me really feel accepted. I remember you, Doc, telling me everything I needed to know to get the summer job and how you considered me a core group member. All that really made me feel wanted.

2. Experiencing Love

Acceptance and feeling wanted are preconditions of love. Love itself reconfirms wantedness. David, age 16, an only child raised by a conscientious mother, knew Unitas over the years as he passively observed the program from the street. He remembers when Wilson, age 24, reached out to him and

...showed me kindness. He put his hand on my shoulders and hugged me at the end of the circle. Like he really cared. We used to go to the back fire escape and just talk. We were sitting real close together... like he had his arms around me ... we'd talk about school, where I live, my family, things like that, and we'd make jokes and laugh together. I was five years old when my father divorced my mother and I needed a father, so Wilson filled that need ... that made a real big difference ... that's what really made me start coming. In Unitas we have a lot of caring. That's what makes me come ... the way we all care about each other. I really like that.

Cheo recalls what was done for him in Unitas, itemizing a list of caring behaviors that older workers must demonstrate to new teens especially:

Besides one person's love, they need other people's caring, too. Greeting them, smiling, shaking hands, going to them, hugging, passing time with them on the street, eating with them, playing basketball or whatever they are about ... Show clear cut expressions of caring: "I love you;" "I miss you;" even, "I'm angry at you." For me this has been important in feeling cared about.

Miguel, age 19, who wants to stay in Unitas until he is 40, recalled a time when he was discouraged, tired and wanted to leave Unitas but decided to stay because of all the attention he got from the controversy:

> I loved it all. Maybe that's why I did it, I'm not sure. But I decided that since the summer was almost over, that I would stay. So I made a commitment, "Let me finish it off." So I stayed. And there was all these cheers. "Yeah! he stayed," things like that. The people showing how much they cared that I stayed. If the feeling of being cared for is gone, that you're really liked, I wouldn't want to stay.

3. Experiencing Belonging

A sense of belonging is the consequence of feeling accepted and loved by a caring group. It would come as no surprise that this curative dynamic should be reiterated by the teens with almost monotonous repetition. Wilfred, who felt the acceptance and caring from James and other teens, said:

> Here we are like brothers, you know. We don't fight, cause with a friend you might have a fight, but you really don't have a fight. You stay here because there's a strong bond that you feel with your friends here. It's like a brotherhood.

Jerry, the peacemaker from Kelly Street, recalled that at age 14, he experienced Unitas as unique in his life.

> Unitas was different. Like the circle... it was an atmosphere, a whole bunch of people ... a whole block of kids. I wanted to be in that group, be part of it, like a family and I wanted to help in that family, be somebody to one of those little kids. It gave me a sense of belonging, too. If there was a problem to deal with, everyone would listen rather than turn away. When Eric would say something, everyone would pay attention, and you, too. In other words, everyone paid attention to each other.

4. Experiencing Encouragement

Acceptance, love, and the sense of belonging were reinforced through the encouragement and confidence each person felt from each other. Papo remembers words I said to him that renewed his belief in his interpersonal ability:

> I remember building my own relationship with people ... that's what you told me. So I did that with Sister Ann, the principal. You used to say, "You have the power to make things happen that you want." That was significant to me and I always remembered it.

Vicky, age 16, but age 12 when she started coming to Unitas, and who used to hide in the bathroom rather than sit on the floor in that "crazy circle," was encouraged to get used to the Unitas experience by Papo who reached out to her, brought her into his symbolic family, explained its purpose and convinced her of her value:

> I found Papo a very kind person who wanted to help and let
> people understand ... it was mainly him that influenced me.
> He told me he needed me and really wanted me to be
> there. He told me he wanted me to help while I was there ...
> giving me responsibility, taking care of people, and that my
> being there really made a difference.

Eric the younger also repeats this theme of finding self confidence reaffirmed by the faith put in him to help out in taking care of children:

> The thing that stands out in my mind most was when Doc came
> over to me in the middle of a circle meeting and picked up a kid
> who was acting out and put him in my lap, telling me to take care
> of him. It shocked me. A lot of things ran through my mind be-
> cause I wasn't sure I was ready to deal directly with one of the
> children yet. But after I thought about it for a while, I felt that
> maybe I was ready and I felt that by Doc doing that, that maybe
> he felt that I was kind of ready, too. So maybe it was time to start
> working better with the kids to try to build the relationship to a
> better plateau. I was able then to deal after that with the circle
> and everything. It kind of brought me to a level where I thought,
> "Hey, I think I can really deal with it. I don't think it'll be that much
> of a problem, and I enjoy being here."

5. Experiencing the Giving and Receiving of Help

It is obvious that, given an atmosphere of security, friendliness and acceptance, the openness that people would feel in being received by others
would evoke a "therapeutic availability" of one to another. The awareness of
such availability and the culture value placed on such interchange in Unitas
appear to play a large part in the teenagers' craving both to give help to a
fellow and receive it back in need.

For Eric the younger to be able to have a place to come to when
"you're feeling down and shitty", knowing that people will come to you without
asking, take you aside and listen to you, was a unique and moving
experience for him.

Orlando recalls his special relationship with Miguel saying:

> What Miguel would do when you had a problem ... he'd take you
> to a corner or a quiet spot and talk it over with you ... that stood
> out in my mind. When I became a symbolic father, this little kid
> had a real problem and I did the same thing.

Raymond, age 17, but 4 at the time of his entry into Unitas, remembers
years ago when Unitas first started how he had a special relationship to Papo
his symbolic father. He worshiped Papo and knew that Papo liked him.
Raymond found a confidant in Papo to whom he would turn to talk about the
little problems of childhood.

> Papo used to say to me, "Why don't you come next to me?" or
> he'd buy me ice cream and things. We used to talk together
> about my brothers and that I didn't have a bike. We decided to

build a bike for me and it took us a week to do it. After we solved that we used to ride a lot together. I remember talking to him about how people used to like hitting me to show they liked me. He told me to tell them that I knew they liked me but to please not hit me because it hurts. He told me I had to explain that to them. So I did and they stopped hitting me. That made me want to talk more and more to Papo and spend more time with him. When I was little I don't remember having any big problems, but I just liked to spend time with him. But if there were any big prob-. lems in my life, I would have told him. Right now, when I have certain problems, I go to some of my special friends in Unitas. Papo is still one of them, so if I have a problem, I still go to him.

6. Experiencing Joy in Learning

The common work of "parenting" children brings these young people together. It is almost the excuse to be together for their own interpersonal experiences. Cheo said, "We grew more together because we were doing the common work of caring for the kids ... it was like building a house." In the "building" of this house, a craving for technical know-how in understanding how to be effective caretakers of children was a continued theme. Experiencing the weekly training sessions where methods of responding to children with psychological know-how was provided for them intensively with skills they could use immediately was a source of joy to the core teenagers. They also voiced a clear disapproval of many of the younger teens whose generosity in wanting to work with the children was not equal to their own quest for know-how. Miguel recalled how tough it was to get into Unitas as a symbolic parent when he first came because of the training, the

> philosophy and all the theories and that stuff ... there's so much stuff there, so much knowledge. A lot of times the younger teens they don't really adhere to it ... they don't listen to it ... there was a definite lack in approach with kids because of the lack of this training.

Jerry remembers that his response to the learning provided in the training sessions was directly related to the dedication he had and his motivation to stick with it.

> If I didn't have the learning to go with helping kids, knowing my-self, I would not have had the same kind of dedication, it wouldn't matter to me because then it would only have been a job. I would think at night, practice in my house something I had learned, and it was like something new every day and that kept me going ... it taught me things about kids and helped me in my private life, too.

David and Orlando spoke of the training sessions as existing on two levels: a level that provided training in direct dealing with kids and a level that built solidarity among the teenagers as a cohesive group. "The training sessions are very important to me," says David:

> In training sessions we had some of the symbolic mothers and fathers tell about a problem with a kid and and we would deal

with it. In the sessions we really get to know each other, to be friendly ... if we're not friends, it won't work out. I made good relationships with everybody. The training sessions provide you with better wave lengths.

Orlando clinches the argument:

If we're not together here we're not together with the kids. If we don't learn from the training sessions and just come from home to the street, it would be chaos because we wouldn't know how to take care of each other and keep control of the kids. In training sessions we learn how to care for specific kids and if we still can't figure it out we can put it into role play. Besides, the training sessions give me another goal, to get to really know new people.

The meaning of these experiences which provide the reasons why the teenagers maintain their commitment to the work of symbolic parenting would not be complete without making the connection between these experiences and the bearing they have on their actual work with the children.

The reason why the teenagers extend themselves to children in need, thereby transcending themselves, appears rooted in the rightness of giving to others what they themselves have received. Not to do that would seem wrong to them. Thus the thrust of a natural ethic seemingly impels social altruism. Orlando described the meaning that Cheo and Miguel had for him:

When Miguel asked me why I wanted to be a Unitas father, I said to him that I wanted to help kids like he did for me. When you help kids ... feeling or reaching into someone's heart and really helping, it's only right to move toward that person and make things right ... so that that person can have a smile on their face, since you have a smile on your face ... that makes things right.

Wilfredo's response to the question "Why should working with these children matter to you?" reaffirmed the basic of law of love:

It was probably the way I was treated here that made me want to treat someone like that, too. I experienced a lot here and to one who never got that, you are a brother to him.

Wilfredo remembered how James and Eric treated him as a child such as deliberately losing at a game so he could win, talking gently to him and sitting him in their laps and massaging his back: "I felt like they did that for me and so it is what I do with a kid."

Vicky, remembering the kindness she experienced from people in Unitas and how she was "lured" by such kindness, describes the same methods: "It is what I do with my young teenagers, I lure them, call them not because I need help but because I want them to be with me, like they did to me. I say 'Your being here will make a difference.' like Papo said to me. I would tell them that because it's true. And I say 'C'mon, you know you're my number one,' and it's true cause I have a lot of number ones."

Raymond saw a direct connection between what Papo did for him and knowing himself how to take care of his own symbolic children.

Now that I have my own kids, when they do something I usually think about what I've seen Papo and the other workers do. I remember the good things Papo did for me, so when I deal with my kids today I guess I'm wiser than other people because I have this knowledge. There was one of my kids, Pito, I was real mad at him one day. I had to do something, I had to get away. I had several flashbacks. One flashback was I remember when I was a kid I saw one of the workers get mad at a little kid because he wanted his attention all the time. He yelled at him, cursed at him, threatened him. When I pictured that in my mind, that was not the best thing to do. That's why at that point I kind of shut myself off from everyone else. I didn't say nothing. And when I shut myself off from everyone else I was trying to figure out what to do. Another flashback was to not hit him but to yell at him to let him know that I'm mad at him. But I did not trust myself to yell at him in a constructive way. The third one I remember was Papo got mad at this little kid and wanted to hit him. But he got very quiet and he just left the woodwork and told me to take care of everything. That's when I was a little boy and stuck around Papo. Papo just went off by himself and was kind of isolated till he could control himself again. So I said, "All right let me try that." So I went up to the top of the fire escape and stayed there until I was ready to come back and deal with Pito without getting mad.

The identification process between symbolic parent and child as played out in Unitas can be understood clearly from the above data. This process reflects the primary mode of learning parenting behaviors that we all absorb unconsciously within our family experience. Such a process, reflected also in Unitas, suggests the validity of the corrective symbolic parenting experience as well.

4. Training

Recognizing the importance of the identification process at work, enabling the teenagers to know through imitation how to exercise loving parenthood, in no way underestimated the value that was placed on formal systematized training. It is in regular and systematically organized training sessions that a more precise psychological sophistication is brought to the parenting endeavor.

Training sessions are conducted with three goals in mind. First, training provides a sound psychological base for developing skills by communicating knowledge about interpersonal processes. Teaching a wide array of interpersonal skills to effect behavioral change is a useful and well-established training method. The training modules in the fourth section of this book are aimed at that goal and constitute a major part of the training I give the Unitas teenagers.

Second, training sessions provide a forum for settling individual and group dissensions thereby reinforcing group unity and solidarity and providing the teenagers with the opportunity to resolve divisions among themselves. Such a forum of mutual help for personal problems which affects their functioning as "good parents," enables them to become an integrated caring group in their own right. Creating such healing among themselves provides a healing climate and a therapeutic community for the children. It was seen as essential that a sense of solidarity and good interpersonal feelings should exist in the caretaker group in order to be helpful to the children whose lives needed uniform healing responses. A staff that was at variance with itself would foster greater brokenness. Thus, the importance of developing caretaker solidarity.

Third, training allows the teenagers to touch base with their own historical experiences in order to foster feelings of kinship with the children. Since walking in the shoes of another seems a good way to understand those shoes, equal emphasis is given in the training sessions to helping the teenagers discover the similarities between their own past experiences and those of the children. Touching base with these similarities enables them to know what to say, what to think, how to compassionately understand the many moods of childhood. So the question is always raised when there is a discussion of any child, "When you were feeling that mood at any time in your life, what was it that you understood about yourself and wanted someone to say or do for you?."

The following excerpt reflects this last component where each teenager is asked to consider the similarity between a child, Jose, who has acted out in a trip to the swimming pool, and their own historical experiences related to loneliness and attention seeking.

> Maria says she is very upset at the behavior of Jose; yesterday he created a lot of disturbance on the trip to the Central Park pool. At the train station he wanted to jump on the tracks to get a ball. James had to hold him physically. James felt he should have been alone with Jose but the group gave Jose an undivided audience in trying to get him to stop. I defined two problems from what they were saying: "what was Jose doing and why was he doing it?; and what was the group doing and why were they doing it? But first let's hear more about Jose."

> Joseph related to the group that Jose's father shot someone in the building in which he and his wife are superintendents, although his wife does all the work. The father is now in jail. It seems that some people were having a party and they wouldn't turn down the music after 11 PM. They were drunk and rowdy. So, Joseph says, he thinks Jose needs his father but doesn't have him now. He runs away from his mother. The only time he gets attention is when he does something he shouldn't. Several members of the group decided that Jose is a very special case and should get all the attention he needs even if he acts bad. "He's acting bad because he wants a lot of attention, so let's give it to him," voiced many. "Well," I said, "it looks like we're onto some understanding about Jose's desperate need for attention which everyone agrees to. We also see how he got to you to give it to him in the train station. We don't know yet whether perhaps this bypasses the real

thing he is looking for. The only way we can understand that is to get more into ourselves by asking the question: "what is it that I would want if I were in Jose's shoes?"

I directed their thoughts inward, asking all to try to feel things in their own life that they think Jose might be experiencing: loneliness, hurt, anger, fear, depression.

Maria remembered that when her parents used to live together they would always be fighting. She had to take care of her three younger sisters. She said she used to eat food to feel better and got to be 200 pounds. She knows now that she was acting out her pain by trying to eat it away. She would have liked her family to be together and happy.

Ramon talked about how he longs for his father's love more than his mother's but can't have his father because he lives in Santo Domingo.

Margie was visibly affected by these revelations. I asked her to share her feelings. At first she didn't want to, but then she got into how she loves her mother and father but doesn't care as much about her father. This is a conflict for her. There is also a lot of trouble with her nine brothers and sisters. She expressed how she hates to go into the house where there is a lot of chaos and fighting. She cried soft tears of hopelessness. Ramon spoke up again about how he could relate to Margie's feelings about her father. In his case he feels the same way about his mother.

There was a long silence.

Wally talked of the time she was feeling so unwanted that she ran away to Miriam's house for three days. She felt that maybe she would be more attended to there than at her own house. Miriam said that she was so well taken care of there that Miriam was getting angry about it. Miriam went on to say that when she was four months pregnant she did not know how to tell her mother so she stayed on the street for three days without eating. A neighbor told her mother why she ran away and her mother went looking for her. After a truce was worked out with her mother and she eventually gave birth, the mother went back to hitting her and favoring her sister Elizabeth. Now Elizabeth runs away a lot and then gets everything she wants when she comes home.

Ramon also ran away, as did Rolando. Rolando talked of his anger because the work at home always falls to him. Although he has two older sisters, his mother always makes him go to the store. She would never let the sisters out of the house. He told his mother that his sisters would run away. He was right.

Silence.

"Then you really have been in some way in Jose's shoes," I said softly. "So what is it you and he really want?" Most agreed that they wanted a loving friendship with an understanding parent who could help them just feel wanted. In their desperation, they either over-ate, ran away, cried, drifted, or just swallowed their anger.

I reflected back to them that their thoughts and sharing here were terrific. They had come to a real understanding of Jose by knowing him through themselves. "Jose, too, wants a loving friendship with someone like a parent who will help him feel wanted. Without this, he has his own form of protest—running wild—as you have your forms that you shared so lovingly with each other this morning. It is for this reason that James has been linked up with Jose to take care of him as a symbolic parent."

"Maria, just as you needed to feel the understanding of your parents and not food, Jose needs the same kind of understanding you wanted; Miriam, just as you, too, needed an understanding mother and not a yelling one, Jose needs quiet, loving attention, not group scolding; Ramon, just as you long for your father, so does Jose; Margie, just as you are in conflict over your feelings toward your father, so is Jose. He feels in some way left out of his father's life, as you do."

"Jose needs James. The job of all of us here is to help each other. Help James when he needs the encouragement to stick with Jose. Parents, real or symbolic, need a lot of encouragement. Miriam can tell us more about that another time." Miriam bursts out, "I'll need 10 hours to do that."

As a result of the introspection each group member engaged in, locating in themselves dispositions and needs not so different from Jose's, they were now able to understand Jose's desperate need for compassion and positive attention from James as caregiving symbolic parent, with their support, by experiencing the parallel needs in their own lives.

In concluding this chapter on teenagers as symbolic parents for neighborhood children, it is obvious that the capacity for young people to move caringly into the lives of children is directly related to the caring they themselves have received in their own lives or within the Unitas system. As they were dealt with, they dealt; as they were loved, they loved. This thought comes as no surprise. It is human observation. However, love, when informed with wisdom from ideology and social science, is provided with an exquisite completeness. The next chapter will elaborate on the ideological, psychological, and sociological roots of Unitas as a healing enterprise.

PART III

THEORETICAL UNDERPINNINGS:

IDEOLOGY AND SCIENCE

Unitas is rooted in ideological, psychological, and sociological theories derived from the works of a number of scholars. While I cannot give full appreciation in this chapter to the perspectives and inspiration these individuals gave to me through their writings, I do wish broadly, at least, to indicate how their thinking influenced the evolution of Unitas as a healing community and how I used treatment approaches derived from their theories to effect therapeutic change among the Unitas children. In the healing profession I am indebted to people whom I have never actually met, but whose influence on me has been profound.

From the spiritual and existential perspectives reflected in the ancient Christian Gospels, Buddhist and Sufi parables, and multicultural folklore to more modern applications of enlightenment as articulated by DeMello, Nouwen, Berry, and Hahn, and existential writers as Frankl; to the analytic and post-analytic perspectives of Freud, Winnicott, Erickson, Kohut, Bettelheim, Adler, and Jung; to the humanistic psychologies of Rogers, Carkhuff, Truax, Axline, Ginnot, Gordon; to the group and systems practitioners as Redl, Moreno, Minuchin, Haley, Satir, Attneave, Speck, Jones; and to innumerate mentors whose names are unremembered—I have attempted to design a system of therapeutic care with ideological, psychological, and sociological holism.

1. Ideology

Ideology is a word I use to simply describe a certain way of perceiving or explaining reality. How does one make sense of oneself and the world? Ideology asks and attempts to answer the questions that people have always asked: Who am I in this world? How is life to be lived? Do I have a purpose? What is my relationship to be to my fellowman and the rest of the cosmos? How does one determine the rightness and wrongness of things?

Faith, Hope, Love and Purpose: These Four

My own Christian upbringing obviously played a significant part in my world view. My Christian journey has centered on developing in myself, and by analogy in Unitas, the dispositions of faith, hope, love and purpose. For what could be considered more a Christian ideology than living by faith, hope, love and for a purpose beyond oneself in this world? Such an ideology is not restricted, however, to Christianity. These are also the dispositions taught by major religious traditions other than Christianity.

a) Faith and Hope

It was Jerome Frank who, reviewing much of the literature on healing, concluded that regardless of any specific theory, the essential curative elements in healing resided in faith and hope, and explained that it was the belief or hope that a person had in a power that can heal, human or spiritual, that set healing energies in motion. For purposes of healing, Frank said, the matter of objective reality is insignificant; it is the belief in a certain way that influences us. So as one person can inspire another to perceive reality differently, reality changes for that person, whether or not it actually is that way. In fact, psychotherapy appears to do just that: to help a person break through crippling perceptions of reality or distortions and view the same reality differently. However, the ability of a person, for example, a therapist, to influence such a change of perception would depend, according to Frank, both on the therapist's own belief in the perspective of reality he offers and on the confidence which he is able to inspire in his patient to see reality similarly. These abilities of the therapist in turn evoke faith and hope in the patient. The more strongly the therapist believes in and persuasively conveys his ideology to the patient, the more strongly the healing forces of faith and hope are stirred up in that patient. So, strengthening a belief in an ideology and conveying this to other persons with the confident expectation that they too will believe in it are the basic common elements in all psychotherapies, according to Frank.

These thoughts from Frank had a profound meaning for me because they so accurately described a perception and conviction I had, derived from my religious experience, that people were meant to live in loving cooperation and mutual helpfulness with each other in partnership with a Higher Power. In fact, this perception of life influenced me far beyond even that of my scientific training and analytic experience. It was the power of this belief that enabled me to set out confidently to build a neighborhood of children and teenagers to become a family for each other and through which troubled psyches could be healed. This belief was, and remains, for me the very foundation of Unitas, the reason for its survival and success as a healing community.

b) Love

I was also aware that the belief I had that this loving community could be created needed to be communicated to the children and teenagers with a conviction that was contagious, for through the confidence that I could inspire in my young friends their faith and hope in me and the "reality" I was proposing to them would be awakened. The communication of my belief and the invitation to partake of it with me were to be done through love. From the writings of Carl Rogers and his followers I came to understand how to communicate love in a disciplined way so that the building of this "reality" I was proposing to my community of children and teenagers would evoke a belief in the same reality and the confidence that they had the powers to accomplish this. The Rogerians spoke of loving relationships as containing three essential ingredients: accurate empathy, respect, and authenticity, which when communicated from one person to another, would have a profound effect on that person in terms of healing for the troubled and reaffirmation for all. Such love, for Rogers, was the heart of psychotherapy. And so, when I took to the streets to invite Eric, Johnny, Papo and Jerry to work with me in starting to build the Unitas community and when I first met with the stoopside group who traipsed in from other streets to satisfy their social hunger, it was the empathic understanding, respect, and genuineness I communicated to them that enabled their faith and hope in themselves to be awakened. The belief that they could build a caring community among themselves and their little street brothers and sisters followed upon that.

What particularly impressed me about the Rogerian philosophy and method of healing which I used to "operationalize" love was its universality. Rogers was speaking of a loving disposition that all people need to receive from others to achieve harmonious relationships. Thus this thinking has had far-reaching effects not only in psychological treatment, but also in humanistic education and a diversity of human relationships training programs throughout the world. The universality of Rogers' approach to people in general, including those in therapy, had particular appeal to me since I was building a community composed of both normal and maladjusted children. Here was a man who spoke of the curative element of love to heal the broken and strengthen the unbroken, and implicitly asking for a belief in the power of love to do this.

c) Purpose

The question has been asked me repeatedly: "Why have you stayed for 28 years in a poverty-stricken community in the South Bronx whose social/psychological characteristics are so staggeringly notorious that they rate among the most problematic in New York City?" The question is no different than that asked of any people: Why do they stay faithful in a relationship, or loyal to their country, or work in underdeveloped countries, or raise a severely handicapped child? The answer usually has to do with love and purpose.

My own personal answer is that working in an abandoned section of the city with people who could be numbered among the most neglected fills for me a deep need to be wanted, useful, and significant. To contribute to the welfare of others satisfies for me a sense of ethical rightness. In this, I was touched and affirmed by the "social interest" concept of Adler who said,

> ... every human being strives for significance, but people
> make mistakes if they do not see that their whole signifi-
> cance must consist in their contribution to the lives of
> others.[1]

The extent to which purpose energized my belief in my vision with such fire as to stick with Unitas through all the setbacks was all-pervasive. It meant living for a purpose beyond myself. It was Victor Frankl who taught me

---

[1] Ansbacher H. and Ansbacher R. *The Individual Psychology of Alfred Adler*, New York: Harper and Row, 1956, p. 156.

how to transcend my immediate frustrations through defining a purposeful goal to aim at. Frankl learned how to survive the atrocities of Auschwitz, and help his fellow sufferers to do so too, by keeping alive in himself and others the meaning of their lives to the people outside who loved them and awaited their return. As Frankl said, "he who has a 'why' to live for, can bear any 'how'."

When Bruno Bettelheim studied the socialization processes in an Israeli Kibbutz, he was impressed with the cohesiveness of the collectivity in carrying out its work and childrearing tasks, and he concluded that it was purpose that gave these people the psychic energy to maintain their way of life against great odds.

> I am convinced that communal life can flourish only if it exists for an aim outside itself. Community is viable if it is the outgrowth of a deep involvement in a purpose which is other than, or above, that of being a community.[2]

I did not conceive of Unitas as a community of children and teenagers who would just be friends with each other as in community center, but a community of teenagers who would be bonded with children and with each other for the purpose of healing psychic brokenness. Their willingness to do this as well as their belief in their power to do this would be transmitted to them through my own belief in their capacity to do it. Although they too would meet with frustrations and setbacks with the children and with each other, they would need to remember and believe in the purpose of this community: to bring healing love to troubled children and to each other. And so the purpose of the community is always stated at the beginning of all meetings and training sessions: "We meet together to talk about better ways of understanding and helping each other."

For me, creating and maintaining a loving community of children and teenagers who cared for each other had a deep natural and spiritual meaning. I found natural meaning in the sense of being able to create a more loving world. I found spiritual meaning in the sense I had in finding God in this community of love, for I remembered the hymn I sang as a child:

> "Ubi caritas est ..."
> "Where love is, there is God ....",

And so an ideology rooted in faith, hope, love, and purpose that I had developed in response to the needs of my own life became the basis for the creation of Unitas. The faith and hope I had in the capacity of people to be healers to each other; the love I believed I had that, when given to them, they

[2]Bettelheim, Bruno. *A Home for the Heart*, New York: Alfred Knopf, 1974, p. 307.

could transmit to others; and the spiritual vision of creating a more loving place in some small part of the world, formed the unshakable foundation of Unitas, without which, I am truly convinced, Unitas could never have survived.

Unitas' emphasis on treatment methods, derived from psychological and sociological theories described in the following pages, must be understood and filtered through this ideology. It is my belief that these latter methods are effective in proportion to the strength of one's belief in an ideology.

Ideological Postulates of Unitas

The ideological base through which faith, hope, love, and purpose are expressed in Unitas are articulated through four postulates.

1. Nature has designed that people live together in community and provide for each other's needs. This postulate expresses a faith in the basic notion that communal existence follows nature's design and that through cooperation with this interconnectedness human needs will best be served.

2. People want naturally to live in community and provide for each other's needs. This postulate expresses the "innate predisposition" to live among others and to contribute to their welfare which Adler speaks of, and which reflects the degree and quality of mental health.

3. People innately have the powers to provide for the healing needs of others. This postulate expresses the belief that powers to effect psychological healing are innate in all people, but perhaps have lain dormant through disuse, non-discovery of their presence, the cultivation of an ethic of competition or rugged individualism rather than social feeling, or due to the cult of psychiatry which has been responsible for creating a fictive healing caste.

4. When people exercise their healing powers toward each other they provide a purpose for themselves, namely, becoming a loving community of human beings in a working relationship with clearly or vaguely defined spiritual powers that transcend both themselves and the community. This postulate expresses the belief that human beings yearn for a sense of purpose. A sense of purpose can be conceived of in a natural sense such as in a social or political cause, or in a supernatural sense such as in God.

2. Psychological Theory

Although Unitas has always functioned in a community context, in its early years my approach to helping troubled children was on a one-to-one basis, one teenager to one child. This was due to the heavy emphasis in my own training on psychoanalytic theory which stressed the "intrapsychic" nature of maladjustment. For this reason I linked specific needy children with specific teenagers according to this particular psychological frame of reference, which I operated with at the time. Later on, when my understanding broadened to include the interpersonal nature of maladjustment, I reconciled the intrapsychic and interpersonal points of view by looking at each child through Erik Erikson's stages of psychosocial growth to discover where he or she was on a developmental timetable.

Erikson's stages of growth, elaborated in his monograph *Identity and Life Cycle,* are so well known they need not be repeated here. But summarily, he delineated eight phases in the life cycle, each of which indicates a specific psychological need and social task to be mastered at that stage. Very early needs, for example, are manifested through infantile and dependent behavior. As the developmental cycle advances, one observes needs that are more commonly related to the quest for autonomy, independence, socialization, intimacy with someone outside the family, commitments to career and partnership, parenting one's own offspring, communal involvement, and the development of a sense of integrity and wisdom in old age.

The need of any developmental phase is best satisfied on a one-to-one basis, with children expressing early infantile behavior, or on a small group basis such as with children expressing a need to find their place among same sex peers. Children whose early needs are unmet may not be able to concentrate on school tasks since the energy to be expended there may still be locked up in the attempt to satisfy the earlier need.

All children in Unitas are assessed in terms of the stage of development in which they are currently functioning. If age appropriate, we provide opportunities for them to experience the tasks of that stage more fully, through encouragement by the teenager with whom they are bonded. Where children's behavior is judged age inappropriate, we locate where that stage of development might be and provide for its lack through the kind of relationship that was needed then but not available. We look for that relationship to be available now within the therapeutic community, either on an exclusive one-to-one basis or in a small group.

> Raphael was a 13-year-old boy living in the Unitas neighborhood who had been referred to child guidance clinics for three years. He demonstrated a "conduct disturbance" through fighting, seeking constant attention, roaming school halls, continually interrupting classmates and lessons. He lived with his mother and a younger brother and sister. He had two older brothers, both drifters. Raphael's father lived in the neighborhood, but remained emotionally distant from Raphael. He suffered chronic mental illness all of his life, having spent much time in a variety of mental

institutions. Raphael's mother was ineffectual in disciplining her sons. She had married young, and she was severely depressed. In his quest for a nurturing father, Raphael sought out male teachers and older male companions for friendship, but was not able to form a consistent tie with any male figure. However, when encouraged by a man, his behavior improved. The clinic diagnosis was behavior disorder of childhood: unsocialized aggresive reaction. The treatment plan recommended a big brother for Raphael to provide fatherly nurturance and a model for male identity. Result: Big Brothers rejected the application of Raphael's mother because "there is an older brother in the family who should act as a father for Raphael." Outcome: Raphael is still seeking the nurturing father and becoming more and more antisocial.

As we observed this boy in Unitas and heard him described by school, mother, and friends, we understood his developmental level. His constant movement, inability to socialize with peers, sibling rivalry, intrusiveness, school disinterest and subsequent failure, constant bid for attention from a man and lack of negotiating skills appropriate for his age were seen as indications of his arrest in an early developmental stage. We therefore linked Raphael on a one-to-one basis with Juan, a responsible 17-year-old adolescent who lived on the same street and who could therefore be in Raphael's life 24 hours a day.

Juan's task was to relate to Raphael as a father would to a 6 year old and through this relationship help him develop gross and fine motor coordination through games and building models, help him with school work, teach him how to negotiate conflicts with peers and how to get along with and feel comfortable with his own sex. Juan was carefully supervised and supported in this parental role through the weekly "teen circle" of Unitas, provided for all teenagers working with neighborhood children. In this linkup with Raphael, Juan became the significant provider, the "parent person" to help Raphael work through a developmental sticking point, while concomitantly encouraging him to get on with the business of finding success in age appropriate developmental tasks in school and neighborhood relationships.

Using the life cycle model as a diagnostic schema to understand the psychological needs of the children in Unitas provided an acceptable and sound theory for practice. Seeing the children within their own living context, that is, their neighborhood street and natural relationships, provided a wealth of observable data to assess their developmental stage, data which was not accessible in the formal clinic structure. In training sessions with teenagers, I brought them this developmental theory so they could understand why they needed to interact with a 12 year old as though he might be 6 or 7. The larger task however was to teach the teenagers an approach to talking with their street brothers and sisters in ways that really did meet their developmental needs on both emotional and cognitive levels. For this purpose I turned again to the thinking of Rogers and Adler. Rogers, because of the stress he put on emotional growth through empathic experience; Adler because of the stress he placed on the power of self-understanding and encouragement. Unitas children were sorely in need of a parental type relationship where an acceptance of their feelings on any developmental level and a friendly encouragement to understand and change their behavior needed to be conveyed. These two men both in their theories and in their therapeutic techniques offered such an approach, for derived from their theories were methods of communication that built self-esteem, gave hope, conveyed love, promoted self-understanding, and elicited cooperation and responsibility.

I have already commented on Roger's influence on me in the section on ideology. I stated there it was through Roger and his followers that I came to understand what the essential components of a healing relationship were, namely, empathy, respect and authenticity, and how I expressed this healing relationship to my early teenagers to influence their lives. The teenagers, too, needed to learn how to do something similar in relationship to the children I put in their care. And so they needed to be steeped in what I considered the main component of Rogerian practice: accurate empathy, the capacity to understand deeply what another person feels, and to convey this understanding back in a loving manner. To this end training sessions put a heavy emphasis on providing an empathic experience for the teenagers and helping them practice similar responses to children at different developmental stages through role playing.

The relationship between Jose, a 17-year-old adolescent, and Mark, age 11, describes such a healing interaction.

> Mark was an angry 11-year-old child living with his grandmother who ruled him with an iron hand. He was born out of wedlock to a young mother who became involved with Mark's father, an older man, in order to break away from her own overbearing mother, now Mark's caretaker. Mark's father abandoned his mother before Mark was born. His mother then returned to live with her mother, leaving Mark's care to the grandmother while she went to work. Gradually Mark's mother moved out and boarded elsewhere where she could live her life more freely. She left Mark entirely to the care of the grandmother who took care of Mark as a "religious obligation" at the direction of her minister.
>
> Whenever Mark would come to Unitas he would start trouble everywhere he went. He broke up activities, started

fights and got people furious at him. People "cooperated" with his strategy to get kicked out. Training the teenagers in empathic communication enabled them to start seeing the world from Mark's point of view: a place where he was not wanted, had no sense of belonging, and expecting rejection wherever he went. How could he feel other than discouragement and anger?

One day it was observed that Mark went from one activity to another on the street successfully getting other children to fight him and chase him away. When he got to the wood-work activity it started again. The children attacked him as he attacked them and blow came to blow. Jose, a teen-age symbolic father had a keen insight into what Mark was doing and feeling, having had a similar experience in his own past. As Mark expressed his revenge, born of a lifelong feeling of non-acceptance, Jose quickly went to him and gently said: "Wherever you go, it seems they don't want you." Mark hesitated, but said nothing. Jose continued: "That struck you, didn't it, what I said...it seems that's been a feeling you've had for a long time. I under-stand." Mark was immobilized and just stood there. Jose continued: "I'm sorry, I did not mean to embarrass you...you have a lot of feelings about what I said, don't you? Maybe we can talk about that another time, more pri-vate... But for now I would like you to stay and help me here." Mark worked cooperatively, almost slave-like, with Jose for the rest of the day.

The love conveyed by Jose to Mark during the time Mark was naturally "in the act of being himself" had a pronounced effect on Mark. Empathic com-munication enabled Mark to respond to Jose's love. It was the wedge through which Mark began to feel a welcome from the world. And it happened through Jose's real understanding of what this boy was feeling and the understanding he needed. From this dialogue, a healing relationship was established and developed as Mark struggled to maintain his old view of the world and adjust to the new one offered him through Jose. In addition to Jose's providing Mark with the experience of a new kind of relationship, Jose also offered Mark some cognitive understanding about the purpose his behavior served. Jose was able to do this because of his interest in Adler's concept of purpose in children's behavior, taught at the teenage training circle.

Adler's influence on me actually came later in the development of Unit-as. It coincided with my own training at the Adler Institute. In fact, Adler's so-cial and interpersonal orientation to life, its challenges and it problems were to have a strong impact on the eventual "systems" approach I took in designing therapeutic strategies within Unitas. However, at this early stage of

Unitas' evolution, still being more analytically persuaded, I applied Adler's thinking mostly in one-to-one situations. Adler's thinking reflected a cognitive point of view about behavioral problems and their remediation. It sought to help people understand the purpose that their behavior served and then through this insight, help them, through encouragement, to find more positive and socially useful methods for achieving their goals. The genius of Rogers provided me with a clearcut method for teaching the teenagers how to provide a corrective emotional experience to their children through empathic communication. But believing that "love is not enough," I also sought to help these teenagers help their children to understand the purpose in their aggressive, withdrawn or atypical behaviors. In this way, I integrated and operationalized an experiential and cognitive theory, in keeping with my belief in the dual nature of man as a rational and emotional creation, with developmental needs in both components of the duality.

One of Adler's foremost followers was Rudolph Dreikurs. Dreikurs taught at the Adler Institute in Chicago at the same time I studied at the Institute in New York, and through an inter-institute arrangement I was able to attend several of his lectures and demonstrations before his death and study his works. In this way, I came to apply his teachings first in the psychotherapy of children, then in training teachers to understand purpose in children's behavior, and finally to the training of the neighborhood teenagers in their dealings with the children in their care. Children's behavior, as explicated by Dreikurs, has one main goal: to achieve recognition from others. To achieve this sense of recognition, children will demonstrate any of four types of behavior: attention getting, power getting, revenge, and the appearance of being helpless.

It is not my purpose here to elaborate either on Dreikurs' or Adler's theories of personality or methods of treatment. I refer the reader to the excellent works of both clinicians suggested at the end of this manual. It is my aim here, however, to emphasize that determining the purpose behavior serves in a child's life and offering such understanding to him in a friendly manner, disclosing his goals to him, enables a child to begin to make cognitive, conscious sense out of his own confusing and not so conscious behavior. Such a clarification, together with encouragement to try alternative but positive forms of behavior to achieve the same goals, can have a powerful influence on a child's life, stimulating his social adjustment now and for the future. Dreikurs himself states:

> "We must keep in mind that a child who disturbs and does
> not work or behave well does not know the reasons for his
> inadequate behavior. It would be a mistake to assume that
> he does not want to do better; he cannot help himself as he
> is not aware of the purposes he is pursuing. This is why
> telling the child to behave better is futile, he already knows
> that he should. But telling him the purpose behind his be-

havior can be extremely helpful to him... His reaction is quite different when he is made aware of what he wants: to get attention, to show his superiority, to be the boss, to demonstrate his power, to get special service or consideration, to get even, or to punish others... After the goal is established, future discussions may be devoted to other possibilities for obtaining a place in the group.[3]

In the interaction between Jose and Mark described above, Jose's empathy toward Mark touched him profoundly. Mark sought out Jose incessantly after this. This had good and bad effects. On the one hand, Jose had won Mark's heart through the genuinely empathic disposition and attitude he conveyed toward him. Mark would do anything for Jose. This made it possible for Jose to be able to influence Mark's thinking and behavior more than anyone else. He felt Jose's love and allowed himself to be vulnerable to it. It also put Jose; on the other hand, in a very difficult position, for Mark began making more and more demands on Jose, encrouching on his time, energies and other relationships. He wanted Jose exclusively for himself.

In supervision with Jose, he recounted his experiences with Mark during a recent week:

Jose: I can't deal with him any more... Monday I came to see all the kids and I told Mark I would see him later. Then it was time to go so I patted Mark on the head and told him I'd see him tomorrow. He then climbed on the top of Sam's car and wouldn't come down. We drove off with him there and I was real mad at his not listening to me. When we got to Sam's house, he jumped off and into the car when I opened the door and then stayed in there. Sam and I threatened and pleaded with him but he stayed there sulking. We walked away and then he came out and ran home. The next day I was talking in the school with Eileen and I told Mark I'd see him in a little while. When I was with her inside Mark came banging on the door. I came and said, "What do you want?" He said, "Is Eileen inside?" I said we were here talking and we'd be out in a little while. After ten minutes he comes again and started banging on the door. I went to him again and said, "Mark, cut that out!" A few minutes after that he came back with a big rock and started throwing it at the doors. I went to him and said, "Mark stop throwing rocks at the doors" He said, "No!" Then Eileen came out. She told him we would see him later but he should wait outside until we came to him. He said nothing to her but in a few minutes he started again. Eileen left the school and went over to the Plaza. I came out after that and looked for her asking Mark and the others where she was. They said, "in the library." So I went in there. Then another boy, Rene, comes and says, "are you coming out to the

[3]Adler, Alfred. *Psychology in the Classroom,* New York: Harper and Row, 1968, p.54.

Plaza?" I said "who wants to know?" "Mark," he says. I said, "tell Mark if he wants to talk to me to come see me." Then Mark comes in and just walked back and forth for ten minutes then he left. Then ten minutes later he comes again and does the same thing. I said, "Mark if you want to talk with me sit down." He walked away. Then he comes back and takes big heavy books and begins dropping them on the floor. Then he comes back and just sits across from me and Eileen. I said, "Mark you just have to stop doing those things." Then he starts making noises. I said, "I just hate rude people.'. He had a fit after I said this and left in a rage. I don't know why I said "I hate" because I care for him a lot. I got real upset again then at what I said. Then he comes back and throws a pair of sneakers I had given him, on the floor in front of me and stomped them. At that point, I really had to control myself and said, "put the sneakers back on." He does and then ties the laces together and trips over them as he walks. I tell him to tie them right and then do it for him. Eileen and I left the library then and she went home. Then I spent three hours with Mark. He told me he hadn't eaten yesterday or today and was never going to eat again. That got me so I said "come on let's go eat." We did and now he was more friendly, polite and a pleasure to be with. He asked me about Eileen and told me about things he used to do with his father, places they would go, things they used to do.

Doc: And when you got home yourself, how did you feel?

Jose: Mark had pushed me to an emotional point where I had not been before. He's been pushing me to these emotional points this last week to such an extent that I really don't want to deal with him anymore.

Doc: O.K., Jose, Let's try to make some sense of all this, because it does make sense. You say you have never been pushed to those emotional points before. But maybe in a personal way you have. If you can think of a time or times in your own life when you have really been pushed to those points, it might help you understand what was making Mark feel and do as he did. Have you ever been pushed to points of desperation or jealousy or love...that can you know how a human being can be brought to the panic that Mark was brought to?

      Jose then recounted an experience he had with a special friend, Luis, two years his senior, who had been very close with him even to the point of pledging friendship "forever." When Luis graduated from the school where they both attended, Luis assured Jose that, though they would not see each other every day as they had before, since he would now be in college, they would always be close and would see each other always on weekends.

Besides this he would talk by phone to Jose during the week. As it happened Luis never called, was never home when Jose called, did not return calls, and was not available on weekends, since he was now dating a girl he had met in college and was spending most of his time with her.

Jose: I began to think of ways of getting even with Luis -- I was so mad -- like saying bad things about him to others, slashing the tires of his car during the night, or breaking the windows, or never talking to him again.

Doc: You were feeling revenge because of his neglect of you, feeling abandoned was probably more like it. And so feeling abandoned by Luis, what would you have liked him to have done to make up to you, to reassure you?

Jose: I would have liked him to come and tell me what was going on... to spend time with me that I could depend on. I thought his not see-ing me meant that he didn't care for me anymore. Each time his mother told me he was at school or with his girlfriend, I felt hurt and then furious. It was during those times that I thought of revenge.

Doc: So you didn't know where you stood with him. Suppose Luis had told you again that he was your friend and you felt good about this. Then one day you see him at the corner with a lot of friends and you run to be with him because he said that you could count on his being your friend. And then he treats you like all the others there, with no specialness of any kind. And when it was time to go he just left, just hopped the bus when you weren't looking. What would you feel?

Jose: I'd resent it. I'd hate him again. I know what you're getting at, that my feeling about Luis is like Mark's feeling toward me.

Doc: Good! I just want to make sure you understand that what Mark is doing makes sense. It just isn't happening because of craziness. His behavior makes him constantly seek reassurance that he is loved. Probably with that reassurance, something calming happens, as with you too, it would have had if Luis had contacted you and reassured you that what he originally said still stood.

Jose: It makes sense what you say. But I don't know if anything can re-ally change Mark. He wants this attention and reassurance every day, all the time, and I cannot do that.

Doc: Well maybe yes and maybe no. The question seems to be why he keeps doing these things that make you furious while at the same time he loves you because you are like a father to him, he told you that. Listen, Jose, what you have developed with Mark over time is tremendous. You have taken him into your heart, even into your home, have fed and taken care of him. You have a chance to come to terms with the kind of thing that goes into a loving relationship which you have already experienced with Luis and which has many similarities with Mark. Do you have any idea why his behavior is becoming badder and badder? There is something that he doesn't know that his behavior is accomplishing for him.

Jose: What's that?

Doc: Well, he knows this is making you angry, even furious. And it gets worse. The night at Sam's car, he made you angry at him and when you cooled down you reasoned with him. Then the next day he continued to make you mad at him, even furious, by throwing rocks. You would think that logically he would have been reassured from the night before that you did care for him. Well, the reason he is doing what he is doing is to get your attention on a regular basis, to get your attention in a way that he can depend on. He has found out that the badder he becomes, the more you will attend to him. When he is good and waits around for you as you ask, there are no dividends. So he has found out that acting up is a sure-fire way of getting you to recognize him. He is an attention seeking child who will resort even to revenge in order for you to recoginze him. That should not sound foreign to you, after all that's how you felt when Luis stopped recognizing you. There are two things that will be extremely helpful for you and for him.

First is that you talk to him in a friendly way about the purpose of his behavior, saying something such as "Mark, could it be that the reason you do these things that upset me is to get back at me for not paying attention to you the way you would really like, in ways that you could really depend on?" Then wait to see his reaction, then go on. "I've been thinking about this a lot and it now makes sense to me why you have been misbehaving. I guess I have put you off a lot telling you to wait all the time. I wouldn't be surprised if you began to think that meant I didn't care for you anymore. Well, I do care for you a great deal and just so that won't confuse you anymore, I want to work out a plan for both of us to be together that you can depend on." You can then ask him for some ideas on this... brainstorm with him and work out a specific time, days and hours, when he can depend on you spending time with him. That will take the place of saying, "I'll see you later," which he learned he could not depend on.

The second thing that will be helpful follows from your disclosing his behavior's purpose to him. Make sure you actually do set aside the time you agree to give him and stick to it. Both the attention you give him, together with its predictability, should eliminate the behavior that has "pushed you to the limits" with him.

And so, Jose did meet with Mark and said, almost verbatim, what I had suggested. A plan to see Mark exclusively two times during the week at a specific hour was agreed upon. Jose wrote the plan down and gave it to Mark. During these times, they walked, talked, ate, and played ball together. It was also understood that Jose would be around at other times during the week, and that Mark could be part of that, too. That was not to be their exclusive time together, however, although Mark might want it that way.

During those in-between times, Mark tried his maneuvers to get Jose's exclusive attention, but now Jose did not become anxious about it or give Mark undue attention. Before Jose became aware of the purpose in Mark's behavior, if Mark took his keys and ran off with them, Jose would chase after him for an hour to get them back and give Mark dramatic attention afterward. After Jose understood the goal of Mark's behavior and talked with him about it, when Mark took his keys again, Jose merely said, "Just don't lose them," and continued his conversation with the other children. With no attention given him on the basis of this kind of misbehavior, Mark relied more and more on acceptable behavior to get Jose's approval.

As a result of Jose's relaxation and clear-cut plan with Mark, as well as Mark's awareness of the purpose behind his attention-getting behavior, Mark's panic and hyperactivity subsided and he began to enjoy both the exclusive attention Jose gave him and the attention he gave him daily in contexts including other children.

3. Sociological Theory

In Part I of this manual, I described a period of distrust, polarization, competition, and antisocial actions on the part of the teenagers which exploded in a major street disruption in the summer of 1975. This event, the most frustrating of many lesser but similar ones throughout the years, challenged me to look more carefully at the social context of my community. Up to that point, as already described, my design for Unitas as a healing community followed an analytic model and capitalized on dyadic bondings between children and teenagers within this social context, but now I sought an alternative way of perceiving my community of children and teenagers. I turned first to what, for me, as a clinician, was the nearest application of sociological thought within mental health practice: the therapeutic community as it operated in contemporary mental hospitals, and subsequently in family system theory.

a) Therapeutic Community

From the writings of Maxwell Jones, I became aware of my community of children and teenagers as having a structure and interconnectedness that was greater than a mere collection of dyadic bondings between individual teenagers and individual children. Jones' work made sense of the concept that the whole is greater than the sum of its parts. I saw that I could understand Unitas as an organizational structure with a unique kind of life and interactional processes. I found great compatibility, even affirmation, with the primary assumption underlying the practice of therapeutic community. This assumption was ideological and its primary tenet was similar to the one that Unitas assumed as well, namely, that all people possess natural healing abilities some more, some less, as with talents, and that these abilities could be brought to bear on other persons. Jones tied together and made explicit for me how reasonable it was, yet clinically correct, to cultivate peoples' natural healing abilities to bear on each other, especially when they are already joined in natural relationships. Although I had been cultivating the teenagers' natural healing skills, I had arranged these bondings with particular children for them instead of seeing who was best related to whom in natural ways and building on this natural phenomenon.

Thus, I saw that Unitas would become a therapeutic community when, in addition to maintaining needed one-to-one and small group bondings, these separate bondings would also come to bear influentially on others, rather than be separate entities merely existing in the same social context. This meant that therapeutic leverage was to be found in constant observation of who was seen at any one time to be having a positive and helpful influence on who and zeroing in on those people to cultivate that influence. In this way, a community of people as a whole would be available to each other for healing purposes in addition to their more special one-to-one or small group ties.

It became increasingly clearer to me that therapeutic community was an age-old method for influencing behavior, which most teachers and scout leaders are probably aware of. What newness it presented in clinical circles was due to its specific application to a patient population. Psychiatry had actually rendered its patient population powerless by attributing healing powers primarily, if not exclusively, to its own practitioners. Jones brought back balance into the psychiatric arena by attributing healing charisma to all members of the healing community -- staff as well as patients. Of course, when people come together naturally as in friendships, children on a street, students in a classroom, relatives in a family, or religious groups, certain helpful interactions "happen naturally." They happen "naturally" because of the bonds that already exist. People move toward or away from each other in the process of forming their natural groupings. Chemistry, attractiveness, common interests, mannerisms, culture, language, common origins, personality traits, attitudes, values -- these are some of the attractions that pull or bond people together naturally. In a therapeutic community, such natural "pulls" and influences of people on each other would be the fertile soil from which helping, healing, and learning would be cultivated. The leader of such a group looks for helping interactions, then reinforces them. He does not have to create them, they are there if he observes what is in front of him. For example, a teacher has a collection of 30 students. She can teach them in such a way that they learn from her and from their books. She can deal with discipline by establishing clear-cut rules, which, if broken will bring punishment to the offender. On the other hand, a teacher may design both learning and the handling of discipline in her classroom by cultivating the influence of the students to bear on each other. When some students do not grasp a concept, those who do can become the helpers of those who do not; in turn, the receivers can become the givers to others who can learn something from them. Likewise, discipline and rules for living together can be a joint venture between teachers and students. The influence of students' natural friendships can be a joint venture between teachers and students. The influence of students' natural friendships can be cultivated to control misbehavior. Conflicts within the class can be resolved if the teacher activates the students' thinking to come to bear on each other.

As I began to utilize therapeutic community concepts within Unitas as a system, I also taught teachers, in my consultation work with them, how to set up a therapeutic community within their own classrooms.

> Mike was a behavior problem in class. The teacher observed that Mike took direction from Ray in basketball each day without any of the oppositional behavior she observed from him in class. She arranged for Ray to help Mike with his classwork. She seated them next to each other so that as "neighbors" they could help one another. Ray was then available to help Mike in ways that Mike could accept. The teacher had actually organized a small therapeutic community for Ray and Mike.

> Maria was a shy child. She had no brothers or sisters. Nancy was a classmate, gentle but popular. She came from a large family of which she was the oldest. The teacher arranged it so Nancy and Maria would sit near each other. The teacher saw that Maria needed the "motherly" qualities that Nancy had fostered in relationship to her own siblings at home. Taking advantage of this reciprocal role disposition of the two girls, the teacher fostered a nurturing relationship between them. The teacher also nurtured Nancy in small ways through kind words, smiles, empathy, and encouragement. Thus, the teacher extended herself naturally to Nancy, seeing her need to receive, as a child too, the nurturance she gave to another child in a maternal way. The teacher had organized a small therapeutic community for Nancy and Maria, using herself as the healing catalyst.

> Tom, Robert, Hector, Ben, and Mark were a troublesome quintet. Mark was the oldest and most repected. The teacher recognized the influence he had on the others and cultivated a special relationship with him in order to help

him use his positive influence on his friends. The teacher had organized a small therapeutic community for these boys, using his own relationship skills to influence Mark's relationship skills to influence his peers.

Both as an organizational concept and as a treatment method, therapeutic community aims to help a group of people to help each other by drawing on their strengths and the positive influences that they can have on each other.

It is not the intent of this manual to further elaborate the concept of therapeutic community. It will be sufficient to briefly mention that Unitas took the therapeutic community theory and techniques as explicated by Jones and adapted them for use with children and adolescents in the South Bronx.

Farber and Rogler's observation of the adaptation of Jones' principles to Unitas' operation is summarized here:

1. The therapeutic setting should closely resemble the patients' natural environment. Unitas operates in its clients' true natural milieu. As such, it goes beyond a mere treatment approach as practiced in a hospital by its inclusion of normal as well as disturbed children in its constituency, thus embracing prevention as well as treatment in its practice.

2. The therapeutic setting should provide clear-cut boundaries and structure within which participation in administration and therapeutic decision making is encouraged. Unitas does this by "flattening" the hierarchy between "staff" and "patient" and substituting a culturally acceptable "family" type hierarchy with decision making powers progressively assumed as one demonstrates responsibility within the hierarchy.

3. In a therapeutic community, all persons are expected to be active agents in their own treatment and that of others. In Unitas, all are viewed as dependent on and responsible for their neighbors as well as themselves. This is effected through fostering the influence of natural relationships on each other.

4. A therapeutic community should foster open and direct communication between staff and patients, fostering social insight. In Unitas, this goal is explicated regularly and treatment techniques are aimed at encouraging such communication.

5. In a therapeutic community encouragement is given to participation in formal as well as informal group activities for therapeutic purposes. In Unitas, equal value is placed on formally organized meetings such as treatment, interest, and training groups, as well as informal meetings in which encouragement is given to teenagers and children to meet together in their homes, streets, and schools. In Unitas unstructured free time is set aside for recreational interactions.

6. In a therapeutic community the whole community takes part in regular meetings as a matter of therapeutic technique. In Unitas this weekly therapeutic community meeting or "extended family council" is the fulcrum around which the organization's ideology, structure, and goals are tightly maintained and reinforced.[4]

The development of Unitas' potential to become a healing milieu for its members through the application of the principles of therapeutic community as explicated above created a mutually supportive network of relationships among the children and teenagers from which nurturance, belonging, comfort, order and discipline were given and taken. It was amazing how analogous this structure was to a well-functioning family. Thus, cashing in on the value attributed to family life among Unitas' Hispanic and Black constituency, I began to speak of this therapeutic community of children and teenagers as a "symbolic family" instead of a "therapeutic community."

b) Family Systems

Thinking in family terms, I now sought further refinement of therapeutic community theory in family therapy theory and practice. Both therapeutic communities and families are social systems. The therapeutic community can be large; so are extended families; or it can be small as is a nuclear family. Therefore, there must be similarities of organizational structure and interactional processes in both. Perhaps, too, family therapy theory had its own insights which were unfamiliar to therapeutic community theorists, and since I now conceptualized Unitas as a "symbolic family" such insights might profitably be applied in Unitas.

I began reading the family therapy literature, particularly the works of Salvador Minuchin and Jay Haley for an understanding of family systems theory as applied to treatment of the nuclear family; and the works of Speck and Attneave for an understanding of family systems theory as applied to the networking and mobilization of the extended family. As I conceptualized Unitas as "one big symbolic extended family made up of smaller symbolic nuclear families," the literature I referred to seemed made to order for Unitas. At the same time that I undertook these readings, I joined the Family Studies Institute of the Bronx Psychiatric Center for more academic study and supervised practice. I found that, indeed, there were great similarities between family and therapeutic community structures as we practiced them in Unitas and the interactional processes that flowed from these structures.

In addition to seeing the significant influence, as understood through therapeutic community theory, family systems theory delineated that influence more pointedly. I looked more carefully at my 15 to 20 small symbolic families composed of children and teenagers and conceptualized the structure of each family group in terms of the subsystems in each one. I ar-

---

[4]Farber, A. and Rogler, L. *Unitas: Hispanic and Black Children in a Healing Community,* Bronx, New York: Fordham University, Hispanic Research Center, 1981, pp. 26-30.

ranged those subsystems hierarchically, in keeping with family systems theory, so that in each group there were teenagers who constituted a support group among themselves, teenagers who functioned as symbolic parents, and children of different age levels. Within this hierarchical structure, I established clear-cut rules for family functioning:

1. Teenagers as a group needed to develop strong friendships among themselves, be available to each other in times of need, and be guides and caretakers for each other. Strong, personal healing bonds among themselves as a caring group were a *sine qua non* for effective functioning as symbolic parents. Programs were set up to promote and reinforce this cohesiveness.

2. Teenagers as symbolic parents needed to support each other in nurturing and disciplining the children. Training sessions were aimed at achieving this goal through their focus on parenting skills and mutual support activities.

3. Children as symbolic siblings needed to learn how to take care of each other and learn appropriate behaviors and responsibility. They learn to do this through the mediation of their symbolic parents or aunts and uncles who learned through the parenting training sessions how to develop these capacities in their children.

Outlining these subsystems and their functions was always helpful in maintaining in my own mind, and in the minds of the Unitas members, that we were indeed in the business of replicating family life as it is understood to exist in the Black and Hispanic cultures. Our focus was on offering a corrective family experience, albeit symbolically.

When the children in the neighborhood were in trouble or in need they would be told to go to their symbolic parent. If symbolic parents did not know how to help, they were to seek out one of the other teenagers in their family with whom they shared "executive power." Both would then deal with the child. If that were unsuccessful, they were to discuss the problem with other teenagers and children in their little family. Only when that procedure failed were they to consult me. If my "consultative advice" did not help, I would ask them to bring the problem to the larger family circle for input from the whole family of children and teenagers. In this way, the whole network of children, the extended symbolic family, was conceptualized as an additional subsystem or a symbolic kinship network whose function was to provide extra support, satisfaction, and control to all the individual family subsystems. As such, its function was to express opinions and insights into the larger family problems or the incalcitrant problems of any one member whose smaller family was unable to touch him. Crisis situations were, particularly, the objects of intervention on the part of the larger family circle.

Calling together the extended family for problem solving is referred to as social network intervention by Speck and Attneave. They say:

> In social network intervention, we assemble together all members of a kinship system, all friends and neighbors of the family and, in fact, everyone who is of significance to the nuclear family that offers the presenting problem. These meetings are held in the home. Gathering the network group together in one place at one time provides great therapeutic potential. The assembly of the tribe in a crisis situation probably originated with prehistoric man. Tribal meetings for healing purposes are well known in many widely varying cultures. Social network intervention organizes this group force in a systematic way.[5]

With the added symbolic kinship network, Unitas, too, became for its "kin" a full system of family influence including provisions for small dyadic intimacies, small group belonging, and tribal assembly. In this arrangement, Unitas built a structure for neighborhood children that hierarchically recreated nuclear and extended family life in symbolic form.

Thus, Unitas evolved from a simple outreach program utilizing relationship therapy between individual children and neighborhood teenagers, to a therapeutic community where the helping influence of everyone's relationship on each other was cultivated, to a final stage where corrective emotional experiences were provided to children in a surrogate family life.

Summary

In this chapter, I have tried to describe the rationale that underpins Unitas as a healing enterprise. The rationale is rooted in ideological beliefs, as well as in psychological and sociological science. Ideologically, Unitas adheres to a belief system that stresses the curative forces of faith, hope, love, and purpose. It is within the framework of these beliefs that Unitas filters its psychological and sociological practice.

Psychologically, Unitas draws upon clinical notions of growth as theorized by Erikson, Rogers, and Adler. According to Erikson, people grow through psychosocial phases from birth to old age. Dysfunctional behavior is understood as an interruption of a phase of growth as conceptualized in a developmental timetable. Reinstating growth is accomplished by providing a child with the type of parenting needed during a previous phase, but unavailable then, through surrogate parenting in the present. Parenting experiences are provided on both experiential and cognitive levels and are derived from the therapeutic methods of Rogers and Adler.

[5]Speck, R. and Attneave, C.: "Social Network Intervention," in Sager, C. and Kaplan, H. (eds.): *Progress in Group and Family Therapy*, New York: Brunner/Mazel, 1972, p. 416.

Sociologically, Unitas draws upon organizational notions of therapeutic community and family systems and the interactional processes that flow from them, adapting these processes to its own large and small group contexts.

Unitas' psychological and sociological practice is adapted to its unique structure built as a symbolic family with hierarchical lines and reciprocal role relationships and derived from the model of actual nuclear and extended family life. Within this structure a corrective reenactment of family living is cultivated deliberately and symbolically. In this reenactment, it is theorized that psychological deficits experienced by children in their real but ineffective family life can be healed through the corrective emotional experiences of therapeutically designed surrogate family life. Such surrogate families, built and located on the child's own street, provide relationships, support, nurturance, and the discipline essential to psychological health and ordinarily found in healthy intact family life.

The following section of this book presents a training format composed of modules to be used by leaders to impart some basic knowledge and skills to helpers of children everywhere. Its contents and methods express my own understanding of healing processes on individual, group, and communal levels, which I have developed and used for training the Unitas teenagers.

They are not restricted, however, to a teenage population of caretakers but are applicable to helpers of children from a wide range of social systems whose goals may be psychotherapeutic, educational, or religious. It is my hope that both the content as well as the training format will be useful and healing to trainer and trainee alike.

PART IV
BUILDING HEALING COMMUNITIES
FOR CHILDREN: A TRAINING CURRICULUM

Index

AN INTRODUCTION FOR THE LEADER

In this training program it is essential that the climate created for learning contain the ingredients of a healing community for the trainees. During the course of this training, the participants will be struggling together, and alone, to learn interpersonal healing skills. They will resist some, learn others, and cope with stirred up memories of their own childhood. The more each member of the group feels accepted, secure, and unthreatened, the greater the chances are that the learning will be integrated and applied confidently to his/her own particular situation. People feel at ease, unthreatened, and cooperative when they interact and get to know others around them in positive ways. Such an interaction offsets fears of the unknown, raises self-esteem, lowers defensiveness, and invites active participation. It begins the process of bonding, a necessary ingredient in education as well as in therapy.

It is vital, therefore, that from the beginning of this training venture the leader display the dispositions and tactics that he wants his students to learn. In this way, he will not only provide a climate in which learning is most likely to take place but he will also be modelling in practice the very skills he intends to teach. Thus, the leader must create from the start a healing community among the participants in which acceptance, belonging, trust, and security can be felt and from which growth in learning can follow.

Objectives of the Training Curriculum

The training modules which follow form part of the training that is given to teenagers in the Unitas program. The overall goal of this training curriculum is to enable helpers of children to learn interpersonal skills which will encourage children to become effective, happy, and cooperative. This goal comprises the following objectives:

1. To learn skills to raise children's self-esteem and feelings of competency.

2. To learn the skills of communicating effectively with children.

3. To learn skills to help children resolve conflicts and solve problems.

4. To learn skills for effectively leading children in small task or counseling groups, as well as in larger therapeutic community groups.

The Participants: Who Are They?

Although the Unitas community was built around the concept that neighborhood teenagers could be recruited to serve as therapeutic caretakers to needy neighborhood children, a process described in Parts I, II, and III of this manual, the training curriculum to follow is not restricted to an adolescent population. The Unitas program made use of highly motivated teenagers in helping children; however, the interpersonal skills they were taught over the years were not tailored specifically for an adolescent population. It just happened that they were Unitas' responsive neighborhood audience. The skills taught in the curriculum are applicable to all caretakers of children, professional and paraprofessional alike.

The training curriculum is but one part of any clinically oriented program. An equally important role is played by those workers recruited to partake of the training. Every profession has its criteria for selecting suitable candidates. My decision for determining the suitability of any particular teenager to work with children in Unitas was based on the following:

1. The teenager had to have a responsible commitment to already existing expectations of school and family. I required two letters of reference from school personnel and a personal meeting with the teenager's family.

2. The teenager had to be willing to work voluntarily with children over a period of four months for two hours each week in the overall Unitas program so that he could be observed by myself and other teens. This enabled the observers to judge his suitability for this kind of work and enabled the teenager to know first-hand whether he liked the work sufficiently to stick with it.

3. The teenager had to be willing to attend training sessions for two hours each week for four months in order to determine his ability to learn mental health concepts, to participate helpfully, and to bond with other like-minded teenagers.

I found that I lost many teenagers by following such exacting guidelines, but I also found that the guidelines brought me some of the best teens around who were challenged by such criteria. I was never at a loss for want of recruits.

While school and agencies hiring professional and paraprofessional workers may not be able to use the criteria I suggest in precisely the same way, I do urge that the spirit of the criteria be maintained in order to bring the most enthusiastic, dedicated, and empathic individuals to bear on childrens' lives. Look for excellence and that is what you will get; accept mediocrity and that too is what you will get. Assuming that you want to develop an educational program to teach interpersonal skills to caretakers of children, build your criteria around the following: enthusiasm, responsibleness, commitment, an empathic disposition, and an ability to be helpful to others.

The Leader: Who Is He/She?

The intent of this training manual is to serve as an educational tool for trainers to be used in conjunction with supervision, whether that supervision occurs within Unitas in the South Bronx or on the work site of any organization interested in replicating the Unitas program or parts of it. A leader wishing to build and replicate a similar type of healing community as Unitas is strongly advised to seek out this supervised training experience before attempting to train others in a method of service delivery that one has only read from a book. A do-it-yourself approach is not the intention of this manual.

In the absence of supervised training as described above, the manual could be used in the following way. A leader functioning as the trainer for this curriculum should be versed in individual and group clinical practice at least on a graduate student level. I have designed each module in such a way that the more inexperienced leader can depend on reading the modules verbatim to his trainees. This is the reason I have elaborated each session in great detail. The more experienced clinical educator can read over the material and then integrate it for presentation in his own way.

Environment

The trainer should consider a setting for training the participants which is quiet and comfortable, free of interruptions or distractions. This may seem elementary and simplistic, but in the South Bronx where I have trained hundreds of teens and agency staffs over the years, the street and hallway noise, ringing telephones, summer heat, and even physical hunger and thirst due to a frenetic schedule have rendered training sessions unbearable and, therefore, unlearnable. So I ask you to consider moving to a secluded section of a building where you will enjoy a quiet, uninterrupted environment, such as in a church annex or library. In this way your environment will be conducive to the training you intend.

Suggestions for Conducting the Training Sessions

Training sessions are divided into major subjects, called modules. Modules, in turn, are divided into one or more sessions, depending on the amount of material to be covered. Thus, "Module 1: Development of Self-Regard" is a major theme that will be covered over four training sessions. The following suggestions are offered to guide the leader in the use of the modules, session by session.

1. *Time allotment:* The training sessions were designed to be conducted over a six-to eight-month school-year period, with three hours allotted for each session. Because it is difficult to determine how much time a particular audience will need to cover the material of a particular session, it is suggested that the leader be flexible in running each session and not feel that he "needs" to finish the entire content of any one session during that session itself. Sessions that flow evenly and whose content is covered quickly may include the beginnings of the following session. In turn, sessions that need to be covered more slowly may take two sessions instead of one, as arranged in the manual. The leader must use common sense so that the material exists for the trainees and not the trainees for the material.

2. *Format of each session:* Each session follows a clearly designed plan composed of a statement of objectives and materials needed, a lecture, a practice exercise called an activity, and a summary. In conducting each session, keep in mind the following instructions:

   A. All areas that are boxed in are private instructions to the leader. They tell you what to do or what is to happen next.

   B. All areas that are indented and in smaller type are activities to be carried out by the trainees to learn how to integrate the content of the lecture with practice.

C. Except for the boxed-in areas, the entire content of each session, lecture and activities alike, may be read verbatim to the trainees or read by you beforehand and taught in your own way.

3. *Intermissions:* A break should be planned at the mid-point of each session when it seems that the group has arrived at a certain point of success in the session.

4. *Sequence of sessions:* The ultimate aim of the training curriculum is to teach trainees to build a healing community for children. The objectives in each session teach the skills needed to achieve this. The fifth and final module of the training curriculum integrates the healing skills taught in all previous modules and applies them to conducting the therapeutic community meeting. Because the skill building of each session is sequential, unless a particular audience is already skilled in techniques described in a prior module, do not skip sessions. Follow them sequentially. They were designed to follow each other and to culminate in the module on therapeutic community.

ORIENTATION SESSION

Objectives:

1. To develop a healing climate and group bondedness among the participants in the training program through:
   - Welcoming
   - Introductions
   - Sharing experiences and interests

2. To establish clearly the structure for the training program:
   - Practical concerns
   - Administrative concerns
   - Training format

3. To state the purpose of the training program.

4. To make a statement of the participants' expectations.

Materials:

1. Pencils and pads for all.

2. Newsprint and markers for leader.

3. Identification or registration forms for participants.

Welcome, Introductions, and Sharing

I want to welcome all of you to our community (agency, family, school, etc.). I am pleased to see such a large group as well as your own personal response in being here. My name is _____.

Say two or three personal things about yourself that this particular group can identify with. For example, talk about your professional background if this is a professional group; about your children if this is a parents group; about children you work with if this is a child-care group. Tell also about your interest in leading this group.

I would like us to get to know each other a little bit now.

- Activity 1: Introductions

I want each of you to introduce yourself to the people on your left and right in your own way: ask their names where they are from, and how they happen to be here. You can then talk about whatever else you usually talk about in getting to know someone. Do that now.

Pause for 5 minutes

Now take whoever you are talking with right now and join another couple on the other side of the room and get to know each other as a four-some. But this time your partner is to introduce you to the new couple and vice versa. Make sure everyone in your foursome knows each other's name, where each is from and how they happen to be here. Then find out something you have in common with someone in your group and talk about your common interest for the remaining time. If you do not discover a common interest, listen in on someone else in the group as they talk about their's.

> Pause for 10 minutes

Please assemble again as a large group. You can stay where you are or come back to your original place. Pause Sometimes people feel good about getting to know other people the way we did and sometimes they feel pressured or shy. What were your feelings about what we did?

> Pause for 5 minutes for responses from trainees. Then continue to inform trainees about the structure of the program.

Structure of Training Program

This training program teaches specific skills for helping children become effective, happy, and cooperative. But before we actually begin to get into our work together, I want to mention some useful facts:

> **Describe:**
>
> 1. Length of sessions (e.g., two-hour sessions with a 10 minute break).
>
> 2. Time of sessions (e.g., 9 to 11 a.m. on Tuesday and Thursday).
>
> 3. Location of restrooms.
>
> 4. Format of training sessions (procedure for discussing administrative matters, making announcements, etc. before or after the training sessions themselves).

As for the training sessions themselves there are two points I want to stress:

1. The entire course is designed so each session builds on the previous session.

2. The method I use is non-traditional but highly effective in learning skills. During the sessions I will review the previous session and then give a short talk on the specific skills you will be learning during the present session. We will then practice these skills through activities that are fun, personal, and practical. Such activities will include role playing, script reading, and sharing experiences in small and large groups. I will explain each activity

in detail. If directions are not always clear, please interrupt me and request further explanation. I would like to encourage you to actively participate in these activities which are carefully planned to make sure you learn the skill under consideration. Obviously, the more you enter into the spirit of the activities and risk yourself a bit, the greater will be your reward in learning the skill.

Statement of Purpose

As stated before, the training program teaches specific skills for helping children become effective, happy, and cooperative. In this training program you will learn how to:

1. Build children's self-esteem and feelings of competence.

2. Understand and communicate more effectively with children.

3. Learn skills of problem solving and conflict resolution.

4. Learn leadership methods for effective communication and conflict resolution in: (a) family groups, (b) small extra-familial groups, (c) larger community groups, and (d) your own particular context with children.

That was quite a handful to say, no less to learn. Each of you comes here with varying degrees of knowledge about and experience with children. The purpose of your being here is to learn more in order to be more helpful to children. In addition to the goals I have stated, you may have your own goals or expectations in coming to this training program.

Activity 2: Trainee Expectations

I would like you to think of three specific concerns or questions you have related to dealing with children that you would like to consider as goals for yourself here. Write them down, if you want, on the pads provided. Take a few minutes to do that now.

```
Pause for 5 minutes
```

We are going to practice an activity now on sharing concerns in small groups. Divide into threesomes beginning on my right. Count off 1-2-3, 1-2-3 around the group. Introduce yourselves again, if needed, and elect a recorder to jot down your concerns as you share them with each other. There will be 10 minutes to do this.

```
After 8 minutes announce that there are 2 minutes left, then announce
that time is up.
```

Please assemble as a whole group again. Which recorder can begin to share his group's goals with us?

List all goals stated by trainees on newsprint or blackboard. You will find that there are many similarities, all of which can be broken down into three categories: Communication (C), Behavior (B), and Theory or the "Why" (W) of behavior. You will now explain this to your trainees. Examples of each category could be:

- I want to know how to "make" my child listen to me. (C)
- I want to know what to do when a child disobeys. (B)
- I want to know why children take drugs. (W)

There are many expectations and similarities that you share in common. In fact, it seems that they can be divided into three major categories: how to develop better communication (C), how to deal more effectively with behavior (B), and how to understand why children behave in a certain way (W). Let's go over the whole list and see which category each of your goals fits into.

Go over each expectation or goal you have written and invite responses to each one, marking a C,B, or W next to the expectation, according to the consensus of the participants. You can then either transfer the stated expectations directly onto the newsprint at this time in the order illustrated below or rearrange these expectations into their specific categories on newsprint before the next session with the trainees.

The format would be something like this:

Communication (C)	Behavior (B)	Why (W)

This visual aid can be posted in the training room for the duration of the training in order to aid the trainees to keep their goals in mind. The chart can also be referred to by the leader as he moves into these particular areas during each session.

We will begin to deal with the concerns you have expressed.

Activity 3: Eliciting Trainees' Ideas

1. What are some ways of developing better communication with children?

   Elicit thoughts from trainees on this

2. What are some ways of dealing more effectively with behavior?

3. How can we begin to understand why children behave as they do?

These are some of the things we are going to be learning in the training here so that by the time you finish the program you will have gained some skills that will help you become effective helpers and healers of children.

As a preparation for next time, I want to leave you with the thought that there are certain experiences in a family that children need as they grow up. These experiences make the difference between their being happy or unhappy. Happy children have had these experiences; unhappy children have not. In the next session, we are going to learn about those experiences and how to begin to provide them for children if they are not getting enough of them at home.

MODULE I: DEVELOPMENT OF SELF-REGARD

SESSION 1: Expressions of Caring in Family Relationships

Objectives:

1. To teach the concept that we are deeply affected by experiences in our own family.

2. To develop an awareness of experiences of feeling loved by specific people in one's own family through group exercises and sharing.

3. To develop a list of "caring words" and "caring actions" to use with children as means to communicate love.

Materials:

1. Newsprint and markers. Newsprint in following format:

Caring Words	Caring Actions

Belonging to a Family

The last time we met we talked about your expectations in this training program. We put them down on paper and divided them into three categories as we have listed here. Today we will discuss ways of communicating more effectively with children and their behavior and attempt to understand some reasons why children feel or act as they do. Today we want to begin to fulfill some of your expectations. So we will begin with the most basic of all psychological facts: all of us are deeply affected by our place in our own family.

Everyone is born into a family and is raised by a family: one's own natural or nuclear group, a foster or adoptive family, or a communal family such as a kibbutz collective. Whatever form one's family takes, everyone develops a sense of who he is and how worthwhile, lovable, and competent he is from the way he is treated in a family. Basically, a family has to provide a person with three kinds of experiences in order for that person to grow up healthy:

1. The experience of a deeply felt one-to-one caring relationship with at least one family member. This experience makes a child capable of loving himself and loving others.

2. The experience of belonging to a family as a caring group. This experience makes a child capable of working together cooperatively with others in friendships, partnerships, and support net-

works to fulfill his own needs as well as the needs of others.

3. The experience of connecting with and being responsible to a wider social order outside the immediate family group. This experience teaches a child how to get along cooperatively in the world at large.

We are going to concentrate for a couple of sessions on the first of these experiences, the one-to-one relationship which gives a child a sense of worthwhileness and lovability, and develops in him that same feeling toward others. Children need to experience themselves as worthwhile and lovable in order to treat themselves well and to treat others well. To become loving human beings, people must be treated as loving human beings. When children do not receive loving care, they begin to feel unwanted and express this feeling through destructive or abnormal behavior. When totally neglected, some infants will die. Some people act out their feelings of being unwanted in the form of antisocial aggression or by living in their own fantasy worlds.

The purpose of such behavior is compensatory. It is an attempt to create feelings of love to replace the pain of emptiness. Families, therefore, need to provide the experience of feeling loved and of being worthwhile to each member in some way.

In the following activity, pause for responses after each question and designate specific locations for groups to assemble.

Activity 1: Sibling Position and Feeling Cared For

How many people here are oldest children in their own families? How many are youngest children? How many are sandwiched in between? How many are only children? How many have been in foster or adoptive families? I would like to ask you now to meet together in small family groups according to whether you are oldest, youngest, in between, only, or foster or adoptive children. Oldest, meet over there. Foster and adoptive, over there. If you are a very small group or have no "siblings" here, you can join whichever family group you wish. When you have done this, I will tell you what you will be doing together.

Pause for groupings to take place, then go on.

Step I:

What I want you to do is to discover some common experiences you have had through being in similar roles in your families. I want you to talk together about what it was like or is like in your family to be the oldest, youngest, middle, only, foster or adoptive child. Consider what you like and do not like about this position; and if you could change positions with someone else, who would that person be? Someone in each group should serve as a moderator to allow time for each person to express himself while the others listen. Do that now.

Allow 10 to 15 minutes for this activity, saying toward the end, "Take 2 minutes more to finish up," then continue.

Step II:

Staying where you are, I want you to think about a person or persons in your family who most helped you feel that you were worthwhile, that you really mattered to them. I would like you to name this person or persons to yourself and consider what they did or said to you that made you feel cared about. If you cannot think of anyone in your family who fits this description, think of someone whom you would like to have had in your family who would have made you feel you mattered and what you would have liked that person to have done with you or said to you to make you feel cared about. Keep your focus on specific things the person said and did toward you that made you feel you were a very special person to them. Think about this for a few minutes ... Now talk to each other about this.

Pause for 10 to 15 minutes for this activity, saying toward the end, "Take 2 more minutes to finish up," then continue.

Step III:

Please reassemble now in the larger circle. Who can share their thoughts and memories about this person you have talked about in your group who made you feel really cared about? What did they say? What did they do?

The newsprint prepared beforehand with the columns labeled "Caring Words" and "Caring Actions" should now be posted. The memories of caring words and actions which the trainees have come in touch with in themselves should now be written into the appropriate column of the newsprint. An illustrated list of typical responses from children is itemized on the last page of this session. This list is just an example and should not be used for class. Trainees should develop their own list. After all sharing is done, continue.

Are there any other caring statements or actions that have not been mentioned which somebody would like to add here? What we have here is a beginning vocabulary of caring words and caring actions for use with children. If they made you feel worthwhile about yourself, they will have the same loving effect on your children, but you have to mean them.

As you can see, we are deeply affected by our positions in our families and by those who care for us within those families. Caring can be equally expressed by words or by actions. We are going to explore and practice each of these forms of caring behaviors in depth over the next couple of sessions. In our next session, we are going to focus on learning effective words for use with children for the purpose of helping them feel worthwhile and cared about.

Specifically, we will learn how to praise and encourage children in ways that affirm their sense of worth. As we close this session today, I would like to remind and urge you to practice and use the concepts learned in these sessions in your interactions with children during the hours between our sessions together.

Illustration of Typical Caring Words and Caring Actions

CARING WORDS	CARING ACTIONS
- I love you	
- I am fond of you	
- I care for you	- Hugging
- I am sorry	
- You are very special	- Piggybacking
- You are the heart of my life	
- You're "neat"	- Massaging
- You're fun to be with	
- You're my best friend	- Throwing kisses
- I want to talk with you	
- Your hair looks nice	- Sending notes
- You're cute	
- I like you a lot	- Sharing candy
- You're wonderful	
- I like you as if you were my sister (or brother)	- Smiling
- I wish you were my son (or daughter)	-Waving with a smile
- I know you are going to become someone important some day	- Nodding in recognition
- You are brave	- Telephoning
- It's nice being with you	
- I never had a friend like you	- Writing letters
- You are a champion	
- You share things with me	- Offering food (especially ice cream and candy)
- You're great!	
- I will always be your friend and be with you	- Giving gifts (especially if related to a person's hobby)
- I need you	
- If you ever feel alone, come to me	- Extending occasional treats (especially to the movies or eating out)
- I am glad you were with me when I needed you the most	
- I like you the most	
- I wish I could be with you all the time	- Playing together
- I've missed you a lot	
	- Introducing you to a friend of theirs

MODULE I: DEVELOPMENT OF SELF-REGARD

SESSION 2: Expressions of Praise, Recognition, and Encouragement

Objectives:

1. To teach the importance of words of praise, recognition, and encouragement in developing self-regard in children.

2. To develop an awareness of personal experiences of praise, recognition, and encouragement in creating a positive self-concept.

3. To develop lists of words of praise, recognition, and encouragement with children as means to enhance self-regard.

Materials:

1. Newsprint and markers. Newsprint prepared in following formats:

Praise

Recognition	Specific Behavior	Effect

Encouragement

Encouragement	
Recognition	Strength

Praise and Recognition

When we last met we discussed how our feelings about ourselves are closely connected with experiences we have had in growing up in our families. We talked about our positions in our families and what we liked or did not like about being in those positions. We thought about someone in our family who was special to us and remembered things that person said or did that made us feel deeply cared about. We shared those memories with our small family groups here and then with the entire group. From our sharing we developed a list of caring words and actions. Here it is.

> Gesture to the newsprint

The last time we met we agreed to begin to use these expressions with children to help them develop positive self-regard, just as these words and actions helped us. Did anyone have time to do this between then and now?

Pause for response. If some people did, ask them to share the situation, their words, their children's responses, and their own feelings. Thank these people for sharing. If no one responds, suggest using these expressions and actions again, since the value of this kind of training is not in knowing things in our heads, but in experiencing their application in our hearts.

Today we are going to deepen our understanding and use of verbal expressions of caring that build children's positive self-regard. We will learn how to constructively recognize children's strengths through praise and encouragement.

Everyone has their own idea of what praise is. Think of praise you have received sometime in your life.

Pause

Let's make a list of expressions of praise on the newsprint as we did before for expressions of caring words and actions.

Encourage trainees to think back to their childhood or more recent time in order to get in touch with praises they have received. Make a list on newsprint in this format:

Praise

There are two distinct kinds of praise in this list. Let's go over the list and see if you can distinguish between the two types.

Go over the list slowly, emphasizing the distinction between praise directed to the person such as "you are a good boy" and praise directed to behavior such as "it was kind of you to help Gary with his homework." Usually trainees pick up these distinctions quickly. If not, point out this difference to them by saying ...

There is praise that is directed to the personality and praise directed to a person's behavior. I would like to discourage you from using praise that is directed to the personality because that is like a moral judgment on a person. No one in their entirety is great, good, honest, a saint. Nor is anyone totally monstrous, evil, dishonest, a devil. We use these terms either when we are in love or when we despair, and in both conditions we are temporarily unbalanced in objectivity. Thus, statements directed to the person such as "you are good," or "you are bad," or "you are beautiful" are general statements which are not always true. They are phony praises. While this kind of praise makes the recipient feel good, it also may make snobs of people, satisfy a neurotic need for personal glory, feed vanity, and reinforce a false sense of values; namely, that we are good and worthwhile as long as we are winning the game, getting good report cards, preparing for entry into an Ivy League college, are nominated beauty queens or the most beautiful child of the year, remain the basketball champ, and so on. But what happens when beauty fades, the fists no longer pack a punch, the legs are crippled in an accident, others outscore us academically, and so on? If our sense of worth rides on this kind of praise, we sink when we no longer shine in that way.

More helpful is praise that develops positive self-regard and good feelings about ourselves that we know are honest and not phony. Praise that is helpful is praise that describes the actions someone did that were pleasing to you. Helpful praise has three parts:

Put up newsprint in this format:		
Recognition	Specific Behavior	Effect

A positive recognition is expressed about a specific behavior of a person with mention of the effect of that behavior on you or others. Let me give you some examples:

   a) Sam, age 10, helps a neighbor carry groceries. His mother says to him: "That was really thoughtful of you, Sam, to help Mrs. Jones with her packages. She sure looked relieved."

What were the words of recognition? (That was really thoughtful of you.) What was the specific behavior? (Carrying groceries). What was the effect? (She was relieved.)

Record these responses on newsprint in the following way:
Words of recognition: "That was really thoughtful of you"
Specific behavior: Carrying groceries
Effect: She (neighbor) was relieved

b) Vicky's mother has to work on the late afternoon shift. She gets home very late. Vicky gets up by herself to go to school in in the morning without being called. Mother says: "Vicky, I sure do appreciate how you get up by yourself so I can get the rest I need in the morning."

> Record on newsprint:
>
> Words of recognition: I sure do appreciate
>
> Specific behavior: Getting up by yourself
>
> Effect: Mother gets needed rest.

c) Raymond and Rachel fight over what television programs they watch each evening. Their brother, Eric, is attending college part-time and finds it very hard to study with all the noise. One night the children sit to watch television quietly. Later Eric says: "You kids were really helpful to me by watching TV quietly. I was able to get my homework done in half the time."

> Record on newsprint:
>
> Words of recognition: Really helpful to me
>
> Specific behavior: Watching television quietly
>
> Effect: Eric is able to finish his homework in half the time

Activity 1: How to Praise

How about trying your hand at this now? Think back again to the examples some of you gave in the praise list we made over here.

> Gesture to the original list on the newsprint

Let's go over some of these examples again. Who can take the statement written here and describe to us what situation brought praise?

> After someone describes his situation, take the class through a practice period similar to what you did with your own examples above. Add their responses to the list you have begun on the newsprint.

If you were the person praising:

--What words of praise would you give? Record

--What is the behavior you would be praising? Record

Encouragement

During the last few sessions, we have talked about words and actions that promote positive self-regard and help children feel good about themselves. Feeling good about themselves helps them to become good people. We have talked about caring words and actions and praise as powerful responses that communicate love.

There is another kind of communication closely connected with the others and which all of us need perhaps even more than praise or caring expressions. It is called encouragement. Everyone has their own idea about what encouragement is. Think of times in your life when people gave you encouragement... in the past, in your childhood, or more recently. Remember what people said to you or did that gave you encouragement.

| Pause for few minutes |

Let's make a list of these expressions of encouragement you remember receiving as we did for the expressions of caring and praise.

Make a list of responses on newsprint.

| Encouragement |

There are two kinds of encouragement illustrated in this list. Let's go over the expressions and see if you can distinguish the two types.

Go over the list slowly, emphasizing the distinction between "pep talk" or "sermonette types of encouragement such as "don't worry, everyone feels that way at times; just snap out of it and everything will be all right" and those responses that give recognition to an internal strength of a person such as "you have a real eye for color" or "to play the way you do must have taken a lot of discipline." Usually trainees pick out these distinctions easily. If not, point them out by saying...

There is a popular way of understanding encouragement as a kind of pep talk or sermon to overcome discouragement. This kind of encouragement is minimally helpful, since it tends to deny the other person's actual feelings, tries to talk him out of what he is experiencing and to convince him that everything will be all right. Actually, this kind of encouragement is more discouraging than encouraging.

Real encouragement is words or actions that recognize a person's internal strengths or values as well as the person's strivings to achieve. Praise centers on external accomplishments. Encouragement is not concerned with whether or not achievements ever occur, but with the abilities and values in a person by which these achievements take place or could take place. In real encouragement what we recognize or admire in a person is his internal capacity, talent, or strength for accomplishment. Real encouragement has two parts:

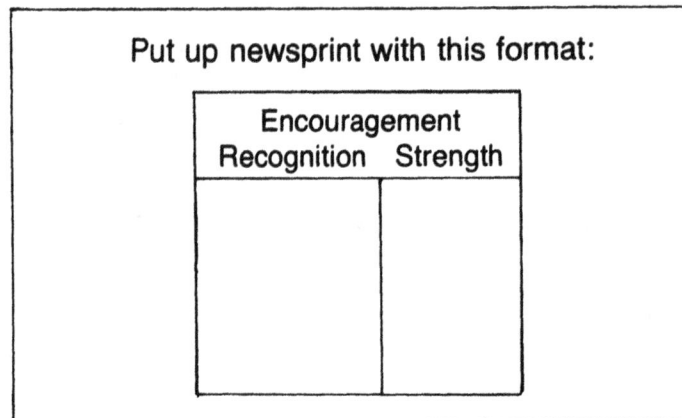

```
Put up newsprint with this format:

          Encouragement
    Recognition    Strength
```

The first part is a positive recognition of an action and the second is a statement of the internal strength or value which you imply brings about that action.

Let me give you some examples:

a) Edna, age 11, comes to her mother with a drawing she made. She asks her mother, "How do you like it?" Mother says, "That is a very attractive drawing. You really have an eye for color."

```
Record on newsprint:

Positive recognition: Attractive drawing

Strength observed: An eye for color
```

b) Carmen, age 15, has spent a great deal of time writing up a report for school. It has been a struggle but she has not given up on it. She shows the report to her father. He says, "That report is really well written. You sure know how to organize your thinking and stick with things."

> Record on newsprint:
>
> Positive recognition: A well-written report
>
> Strength observed: Organized thinking and perseverance

c) David, age 14, saw two of his peers assaulting each other in the school hallway. Although they were angry and stronger than he is, he broke up the fight. A friend later said to him, "I really admired the way you broke up that fight. I guess it wasn't easy. You could have gotten beaten up too. That took real courage."

> Record on newsprint:
>
> Positive recognition: Admiration
>
> Strength observed: Courage

Activity 2: How to Encourage

How about trying your hand at this now? Think back to situations in your own life that made someone say to you what we have recorded here. [Gesture to expressions of encouragement listed on newsprint] Let's go over some of these examples again. Who can take his statement written here and describe to us what the situation was that brought about this statement of encouragement?

> After someone describes his situation, take the class through an exercise similar to what you did in your examples above. Add the trainees' responses to the list you have begun on the newsprint.

If you were a person doing the encouraging:

-- What words of positive recognition would you use?

-- What is the strength observed or implied?

> Take several situations offered by the trainees and practice this exercise for about 15 minutes.

Those are really clear and touching responses. Many of you, perhaps all, have shown capacities to understand and respond to the hidden strengths of others.

Undoing Praise and Encouragement by

Negative Criticism

It is important to remember that words of praise and encouragement can produce the kinds of experiences described previously if they are not undone in the same breath by negative criticism. Remember Sam who helped Mrs. Jones carry the groceries? His mother said, "That was really thoughtful of you to help Mrs. Jones. She sure looked relieved." Supposing his mother added, "I don't know why you can't help me the same way. Someday you'll wish you had helped me more, but then it will be too late." What would Sam have felt? | Pause for responses | Yes, and discouraged.

Remember Vicky who got up by herself in the morning so her mother could sleep late. Her mother said, "I sure appreciate how you get up by yourself. That lets me get some needed sleep." Supposing her mother had added, "But you make so much noise in the kitchen and you put the radio on. I might as well be up myself for all the rest I can get." What would Vicky have felt? | Pause for responses | Yes and discouraged.

Remember Carmen who wrote that school report. Her father, said, "That report is well written. You sure know how to organize your thinking and stick with things." Supposing he had added, It's a shame you don't keep your room organized as well as your report." What would Carmen have felt? | Pause for responses | Yes, and discouraged.

Remember David who broke up a fight between two of his peers. A friend said to him, "I really admired the way you broke up that fight. I guess that wasn't easy. That took real courage." But suppose that another friend of his who was there had added," ... but..." What do you think he might have said?

> Lead students to express all the negative criticisms that accompany discouraging remarks in order to reinforce the concept of "undoing" what you are teaching here.

See how good we all are at saying discouraging things without even realizing it. So, when you encourage someone, say what is encouraging with no "buts." There are helpful ways to criticize and confront people when they do wrong. We will talk about this later on.

We have been talking about praise and encouragement. Praise focuses on external achievements and accomplishments. Encouragement calls forth a belief in oneself. When a person feels encouraged, he experiences an increase in self-confidence, is more willing to cooperate and try new things, is more able to believe he can change the world, and accepts responsibility for what he does. Encouraged people can throw off anxiety and depression as healthy people can throw off colds. Chronically lonely, unhappy, and complaining people are discouraged people.

Remember the two cardinal rules of encouragement:

1. Discover an internal strength, talent, or value that a person possesses and acknowledge it.

2. Focus only on the positive part of his actions or attitude. Ignore the negative part in a given action.

Activity 3: More Encouragement

Does anyone here have a situation with a child in which you would like to be encouraging but don't know where or how to start?

> After a trainee presents such a case, elicit thoughts from everyone on the principles of locating strengths and reinforcing positive responses. Develop the group's thinking on precise words to say that express praise or encouragement as explained in this training session.

Activity 4: And More Encouragement

> Ask the group to break into subgroups of five persons. In each subgroup, each person is to talk about something he can do well. The other members are to figure out the internal strengths it took for that person to develop his ability to do well what he describes. Thus, a person who writes well must have an array of not so obvious strengths to draw on. These could include:
>
> * Organizational abilities
> * A sense of order, logic, and structure
> * Imagination
> * A way with language
> * An ability to concentrate
> * A highly developed sensory awareness

As you listen to each other, give to each other the recognition of these implied abilities by which the person became good at what he describes.

> Reconvene the whole group and ask for sharing

Activity 5: And Still More Encouragement

> Give the following case to the class and have them present examples of words or actions they would use to give encouragement.

Robert, a sixth-grade student, had been involved in classroom disruptions for most of his years in school. He was suspended eight times during those years and was frequently found wandering in the halls or sitting in the principal's office. He is placed in your room by the principal who says that your only job will be to keep him contained. He suggests you use him to clean desks, sweep, pick up papers in the school yard. He will be leaving in two months anyway to go to junior high school. He will be their problem then. But right now we need to tolerate him and keep things cool.

So there he is in your class the next day. You have succeeded in getting him to help you clean out the book closet. A shelf is loose. He asks you for a screwdriver and fixes it. Another shelf is missing. He

asks you if you can get a piece of wood and a hammer and nails. You tell him you will see. He tells you that your closet is all messed up and nothing is where it is supposed to be. Besides it is dirty and needs painting. He says the closet is like the whole school, fit for pigs; it is dirty, smells, and nobody knows anything about keeping it fit. What will you do with this boy?

MODULE I: DEVELOPMENT OF SELF-REGARD

SESSION 3: Non-Verbal Communication: Body Language and the Written Word

Objective:

To teach non-verbal and non-vocal caring behaviors:
- Body language
- The written word

Materials:

1. Pads and pencils for participants.
2. Basket or box or man's hat.
3. Newsprint and markers. Newsprint prepared in following format:

Body Language as Caring	

Body and Language

Over the past few weeks we have been talking about methods of developing self-esteem in children. We have focused on words and actions that convey caring, praise, and encouragement. We made lists of such expressions which are taped on the wall over there. [Gesture to list] Caring expressions were derived from your own remembrances of words and actions that someone expressed to you as a child. Helpful praise gives recognition to a person for specific behavior and notes the effect of that behavior on others. This list here illustrates our work during the last session. [Gesture to list] Today we will continue to develop our repertoire of communication skills that build self-esteem in children. The methods I want to talk about today are non-verbal and non-vocal forms of showing caring. There are two kinds: body language and the written word.

There is a saying: "Actions speak louder than words." It doesn't mean that words do not matter; certainly, up to this point we have been emphasizing words as expressions of caring. But "putting one's actions where one's mouth is" is a way of reinforcing the caring kinds of communication contained in the words we use. Words and actions together can drive home the message of caring in ways words alone may not adequately convey. The reason that non-verbal communication is as important as verbal communication is because we are mind-body creatures: neither body alone as the animals, nor spirit alone as the angels. Our thoughts and feelings get communicated to others through the body, its brain, senses, and physical mannerisms. Sometimes our words will say one thing and our body another. The communication is then confusing or contradictory. A person may say "I love you" and say this with clenched teeth, a stern look, and a cold voice. The body gives a message of hostility while the words say love. It is important, therefore, to know how to use our bodies to confirm the caring expressions our words intend to convey.

Activity 1: How the Body Can Say "I Care"

I would like you to sit back and relax, close your eyes if you wish, and think about someone you felt or feel cares about you deeply. This can be a member of your family, a friend of either sex, an adult, a child, whoever fills the description. Picture this person together with you. You are feeling kind of low and need their comforting. Picture yourself with that person in a quiet place... maybe a place where you felt their comforting care in the past. I want you to think of some comforting or caring words they said to you... but even more than that begin to see their body expressions. Look at this person carefully. Look first at their face. How do their eyes look? What do they seem to be saying? Look at their mouth, notice whether it is smiling, pouting, still, or moving. Observe their face as a whole. Do wrinkles seem to be more pronounced? Where? Do the wrinkles express any feeling? Look at their hands, arms, legs, feet. What are they doing? Look carefully. How near or far is their body in relationship to yours? How does their voice sound when they speak. Stay with this person for a while, getting more in touch with the messages his or her body is conveying to you. What are your own responses to that person's body messages? What are you thinking? Why?

> Pause for this exercise for about 10 minutes

Come gradually out of your reverie. Five... four... three... two... one... and welcome back. The person with whom you've just spent time has taught you something. Could you share with the group the kinds of body language you observed in the person through whom caring was expressed?

> Make a list on the prepared newsprint of all the observed body language expressions of caring

Activity 2: Caring Actions and Words

I want you to look straight across the room at the person sitting opposite you. You are going to form a twosome with this person. Do that now. [Pause] I want you to look at the list of body expressions of caring we just made and also at the list over there of caring phrases. I want you to write down three caring phrases that you feel comfortable with and next to them write three body expressions of caring that you feel comfortable with to give to your partner. I will give you an example of what I mean.

> Demonstrate this task from the two lists

Take 5 minutes to put your caring phrases and caring actions together. Do that now. [Pause for 5 minutes] Now take turns and communicate these caring expressions and actions to your partner. I will come around and help you out.

> Do this for 5 to 10 minutes

Please come back to the whole group now. How did you feel about what you did? Was it easy, difficult, confusing, irritating, enjoyable?

> Allow 5 minutes for responses

Yes, I imagine it was all those things. Again, it is similar to learning a new language, but with practice, which we will do, it will become easy.

Activity 3: Written Words as Expressions of Caring

I would like you to sit back again and relax and think of something that you always wished someone would have said to you, or perhaps a person did, which made you feel good about yourself. Think about that for a few minutes and then write down the phrase on a piece of paper and fold it in half so no one can see it. Draw a stamp on the front of it as if you were going to mail it. Do not put any personal names in the message, although you may use endearing names if you wish.

> Allow 5 minutes for this exercise

Now please deposit your messages in this box that I will pass around.

> Shake box when it is returned in order to thoroughly mix the messages

I will pass the box around again. Please take a message from the box. It is yours. Read it, think about it, and feel it. If you get your own message back, put it back and take another. Do that now.

Allow 5 minutes for this. Then ask members to share their message with the group. Leader should respond with enthusiasm if that is the response of the responders. If there is an uncomfortable feeling from responders, leader should reflect that back in an accepting way. If time allows, repeat this exercise by collecting the papers again and reprocessing the experience.

Do you have any idea why we wrote out our caring messages, why we did not just say our messages as we did the other day? What is the purpose of writing instead of speaking?

Pause and wait for responses. Leader should acceptingly repeat and reflect back each response.

Yes, I agree with all that you have said. The fact is that the written word is one of the most powerful influences on people's thinking. Political writings have changed governments; the Bible has molded people's lives religiously, and poets have touched hearts in ways that orators have not. A letter of love can change your world. So you see, although you always knew this, today I merely wanted you to become more aware of how powerful notes and letters can be to express caring.

The written word as a vehicle through which caring is communicated is certainly equal to the physical or bodily ways through which caring is also communicated. Together, they represent powerful channels through which loving—as well as destructive—messages can be transmitted. Because they are not articulated vocally, they are non-verbal and non-vocal modes of communication.

MODULE I: DEVELOPMENT OF SELF-REGARD

SESSION 4: Non-Verbal Communication: Touch

Objective:

To teach about the power of touch in communicating caring.

Materials:

1. Pads and pencils.

2. Newsprint and markers. Newsprint prepared in following format:

Physical Caring	
Man	Woman

Touch as Communication

We have been talking about building self-esteem in children. As children feel, so they act. In feeling good about themselves, they will behave in good ways. We have developed lists of caring expressions; expressions of praise, recognition, and encouragement; and bodily expressions of caring.

Gesture to the various newsprints

We also spoke last time about the significance of the written word in developing self-esteem. Today we will continue to build our repertoire of caring skills. We are going to focus on the power and significance of touch in the communication of caring.

"Have you hugged your kid today?" How many of you have seen that phrase on bumper stickers on cars? The way we touch people with our words, eyes, posture, and mannerisms transmits powerful messages of acceptance or rejection. But probably the most powerful vehicle through which love and rejection are communicated to others is through physical touch.

By touching I mean the satisfying contact or feeling that is experienced from the warm skin of someone else. I am not speaking about the special kind of touching that is connected with sexuality. This can be most confusing since many people interpret a simple warm touch as a sexual advance. Touch is powerful and can lead to sexuality, but it does not have to. Sometimes the line between the two can be fine. But most people know in their hearts what a simple, warm, affectionate touch is as distinguished from a touch that brings on sexual reaction. Women who are good friends hold each other's hands and even kiss and embrace. Men in foreign countries also do this with their male friends. In our country, boys put their arms around each other in cama-raderie. Watch how men behave toward each other after a good play in football or after someone hits a home run. The athletes almost always show their affection and respect by patting, touching, or hugging. You will notice that this kind of touching is filled with feelings of affection and caring. But its distinguishing feature is that it does not go on to become a sexual advance or prelude to sexual involvement.

We know that humans are born with a skin hunger that is just as vital a need for survival as food is. And just as food is needed not only when we are infants, but all throughout life, likewise skin contact is needed also not only as infants when we are picked up and cuddled and held, but all throughout life as well. Let me tell you about some experiments with animals.

Animal psychologists have studied differences between groups of rats. One group was made up of baby rats separated from their mother and from each other. They were put into separate cages and deprived of touching, fondling, or licking. The other group was kept in close contact with their mother and each other where they were cuddled, handled, licked, and fondled. Over a period of time it was demonstrated that the first group became dull, confused, vicious and even violent. The second group became smarter, gentler, healthier. The same kind of experiments were duplicated by the thousands and extended to monkeys as well. The results were always the same.

There have also been innumerable studies of the effects of lack of touching on human babies in hospitals and institutions. The effects of such lack of physical touch resulted in behavior that was withdrawn or violent. Rocking and head banging were frequent. Many babies totally deprived of physical touch tend to just die. Now, that is dramatic. Many studies of children and adults deprived of warm, affectionate body touch show that such deprivation leads to depression, hyperactivity, drug abuse, and violence.

I hope I have convinced you of the power of touch to bring about both physical as well as psychological healing.

Activity 1: Touch as Caring

I would like you to sit back and relax and take a trip again into your own memory where I want you to discover two people in your life in the past or even now whom you have allowed to express their caring for you in some kind of physical non-sexual way. One person should be of the same sex and the other of the opposite sex. In either case, remember that I am talking about non-sexual physical expressions of caring. Do that now. Pretend that you are with that person and experiencing their affection for you in physical ways.

Get in touch with what part of their body they are using on what part of your body. For example, is their hand holding yours? Is their foot touching yours? Are they sitting right next to you so you feel the whole side of them next to the whole side of you? Get in touch with several kinds of touch they are giving you as expressions of their affection. Note also how it makes you feel.

Pause now for 4 or 5 minutes

Please start to come out of your reverie now. Five...four... three...two... and welcome back. How many of you wanted to stay there? I want you now to form foursomes with people near where you are seated. When you do that I will tell you what to do.

Pause.

I would like you to share with each other some of your memories of this man and woman who showed you his/her affection in physical ways. Would one of each group serve as recorder? The recorder is to take a piece of paper and divide it into two columns. One column is to be headed Man, and the other, Woman. Whatever anyone says pertaining to the expression of physical caring given by the man you thought of, or the woman, is to go into the appropriate column. Do not write up the memory itself, only the particular behavior that was experienced by each of you as caring. An example would be "holding hands," "hugging," "cuddling," etc. This may be very hard to do, might even feel embarrassing. It is okay to feel that way. Try to do this. There will be 10 minutes for this exercise.

Pause for 10 minutes. After 8 minutes tell the group to take 2 minutes more to finish up. During this time, leader should prepare newsprint on wall.

Physical Caring	
Man	Woman

We are going to make a list now of physical expressions of caring, again like a vocabulary. Could the recorders share the findings of each group?

Leader should go around and write all expressions down, expressing acceptance and warmth, even playfulness, to minimize the effects of anxiety which this exercise often elicits. Leader will become aware that there are many overlaps of expressions of caring that are common to men and women. There will also be some expressions that are sex-biased. This will provide for some discussion after the entire list is completed. As an introduction to considering the completed list now in full view of the group, the leader can say...

Well, what do you make of this list?

Wait for a response and take up the discussion according to what is said. Group members will probably point out the similarities between the two lists as well as some differences. Where sex bias appears, accept this unemotionally but question why this is so, stressing that cultures differ in the way they train people to think, but when you think about it logically, since what is acceptable in one culture is not in another and vice versa, it really does not seem that a man or woman could not express their physical expressions of caring completely in the same ways if they chose. Allow about 20 minutes for this part.

You have done beautifully in sharing your feelings and thoughts on a very difficult subject.

This may be a good time for a break, if desired

Activity 2: Shaking Hands

I would like you now to get back into the foursomes you were with before our break. Pause. There are two things I want you to do now: (1) shake hands with each other in a friendly way; don't rush; and (2) tell the person you have shaken hands with how their handshake felt to you. If the handshake felt friendly and warm, tell the person that; if the handshake felt nervous or shy, tell the person that too. Keep practicing shaking hands with the person until both of you agree that it feels like a mutually friendly exchange. Do this now with everyone in your foursome group and learn what your handshake communicates to people.

Take 10 minutes for this exercise

Activity 3: Speaking and Touching

Now I want you to look at the list of physical expressions of caring that we have here on the wall and find one that you feel most comfortable with. I want you to then look at each person in your group and find something positive to say to that person about him or herself that you observe now or have observed. It could be something like their smile, intelligence, clothing, ability to do something, shyness, friendliness, hair style, the way they walk, a contribution they made to this class, anything. Say this to the person while expressing yourself also through the touch behavior you have chosen. Do this now with each person in your foursome group.

Take 10 minutes for this exercise

Activity 4: Soothing Massage

Please get back now into the larger group. Pause I want the half of you on this side of the room to turn your chairs around with your backs to the others on the other side of the room. Now I want you to just relax with your elbows on your knees and your chin cupped in your hands, like this. Demonstrate The rest of you will go over and gently massage the neck and upper shoulders of someone over there. You are to take away the fatigue and tiredness from the person. Do this in a comforting, gentle, soothing, healing touch. Do this now for about 30 seconds. [Pause for this to be done] Now all of you move to another person and do the same. You are the givers, the others are takers. Takers, enjoy this healing touch. Note any differences you experience from the two touch messages you are receiving.

Now arrange for the group to reverse the process. The givers will now occupy the chairs of the receivers and the receivers will occupy the chairs of the original givers. The new givers are instructed to do the same that was done to them, following the above procedure.

You have done very well with this intimate exercise of developing your abilities to communicate caring through touch. Please come back to the whole group now with chairs in their original positions. How did you experience what you just did for each other? Could you share your reactions and feelings with each other.

The sharing will probably be multifaceted, including the good and caring elements as well as the denial of any feelings. There will probably also be references to the differences between the two touch messages the trainees have received. Accept and reflect each one's feelings about what they have experienced.

So, today we have added touch to our repertoire of non-verbal skills of communicating caring to others. In a world where touch is so commonly understood as equivalent to sexual expression, we have discussed the effects of a caring, non-sexual touch on the development and maintenance of emotional well-being. We have talked about the ill effects, even tragedies of children deprived of touch resulting in a wide spectrum of emotional disorders.

MODULE II: EMPATHIC COMMUNICATION

SESSION 1: Listening and Responding

Objective:

> To develop skills of empathic listening and responding to children's feelings.

Materials:

1. Newsprint and markers. Newsprint prepared in following format:

You are feeling...	about..	because...

Empathy

During our past weeks together we have considered a variety of methods by which children's self-esteem can be built. Caring expressions, praise, encouragement, body language, the written word and touch have been our main considerations for the building of such self-regard. While I would like you to keep on practicing these methods of caring with your children by continued application at home, we are going to move today into another important form of communicating caring. It is the language of empathy.

One of the most powerful ways of showing caring and building a close relationship with someone is by developing the ability to feel what they are feeling and letting them know this in an accepting way. What a difference it makes when we are feeling low if someone says, "You're feeling blue today, aren't you?" rather than "What's bugging you? Come on now, cheer up." When someone recognizes our feelings and lets us know they understand, we experience a sense of integrity, an affirmation of our self. The ability of a therapist to help a client seems to be highly related to his ability to be in touch with what his client feels and his ability to communicate this understanding to the client. The forces of healing that are needed when we feel "broken" can come from both friendship and therapy. Both relationships depend on a person's capacity to enter into and respond to another's feeling state. A person with such a capacity enables another to feel relieved, affirmed, and cared about, thus enabling the person to cope with even the most painful experiences.

I am going to spend time today helping you to develop your natural capacity to get more in touch with the feeling state of another person and then to teach you how to communicate this understanding back to him. The first part of this development is called empathic listening, and the second part is called empathic responding.

Empathic listening is the ability to perceive what another person is feeling through that person's actions and words. We understand or "hear" messages in two "languages": through the actions of the body and through the use of words. Let's take each of these "languages" separately. First, we have to know how to understand or "hear" the language of the body. We do this primarily by observing someone. You will recall that a few sessions ago we talked of non-verbal behavior. I asked you to think of a person who showed you he cared about you and to remember how he showed this through body language, such as facial expressions, mannerisms, and other actions. The body speaks messages without words in its own way. Our observation of the body's messages enables us to "hear" what a person is feeling. Here are some examples. For each situation, identify the person's feelings based on the body messages.

1. Jimmy comes in the house, slams the door, stomps to his room, slams the door to his room, and blasts the hi-fi set.

> Pause for responses, such as anger, fury, revenge, etc.

2. Mary does not finish supper, goes to her room, and cries softly.

> Pause for responses, such as sadness, depression, loneliness, etc.

3. Eddy can't sleep, jumps at little noises, and appears to be in a trance, preoccupied.

> Pause for responses, such as tension, anxiety, worry, etc.

Yes, you are right. Jimmy is obviously upset and angry. Mary is depressed or worried, and Eddy is upset, tense, and anxious. Let us now put words together with their body language.

1. Jimmy: "I'm not ever going back to that rotten school again!"

> Pause for feeling words. Comment on how the body language already told us the message without words.

2. Mary: "Cathy always played with me, but now she is always playing with that new girl who moved next door."

> Pause for feeling words. Comment that the body language already expressed the message without words.

3. Eddy: "I sure hope I pass those exams. The competition is stiff. I don't know what I'll do if I don't make it."

Terrific! See how your capacity to be in touch with what a person is feeling as shown through your "hearing" their body language and their words, both separately and together, is so natural. What is also natural is our ability to respond to feelings. However, it is precisely one's responding to another's feelings in an accepting way that may feel unnatural because our tendency, through conditioning, is to talk a person out of what he or she is feeling and offer reassurance that all will be well. At other times, we try to present possible solutions for their problems. What I would like to persuade you to do now is to develop your natural abilities to be in touch with another person's feeling state and attempt to communicate this understanding back to him or her.

Here is a formula for identifying a person's feelings and why he/she is feeling that way:

Post the prepared newsprint.

You are feeling...	about...	because...

"You are feeling (name feeling) about (name specific behavior) because (tell its effect on you)."

Let us look at the case of Jimmy, as an example. He did not want to "go back to that rotten school because they don't care." Using the formula, you would say:

"Jimmy, you are feeling angry about something that happened at school today because you felt neglected." Do you see what I mean?

Pause for questions and comments

Let us use the formula to identify the feelings of Mary and Eddy, whom we spoke about a few minutes ago. Let's make responses to them.

Activity 1: Empathic Listening

1. Mary says: "Cathy always played with me, but now she is always playing with that new girl who moved next door."

What is Mary feeling?

> Pause and record trainees' responses on newsprint ("left out")

About what?

> Pause and record on newsprint ("Cathy not playing with me")

Why?

> Pause and record trainees' responses on newsprint ("because you miss her friendship")

2. Eddy says: "I sure hope I pass those exams. The competition is stiff. I don't know what I will do if I don't make it."

What is Eddy feeling?

> Pause and record trainees' responses on newsprint ("feeling on edge")

About what?

> Pause and record on newsprint ("about not passing those exams")

Why?

> Pause and record trainees' responses on newsprint ("because your plans for the immediate future depend on that")

That's the idea. We will now continue to use the formula in a couple of activities to develop beginning skills in listening and responding with empathy. Remember the formula:

You feel _____ about _____ because _____.

Activity 2: More Empathic Listening and Responding

What I would like you to do now is to practice listening and responding with each other.

> Go around the room and designate each person as A or B

All A's will form twosomes with B's to their left. All the A's will be the speakers. For now, B's will be the listeners. A's, you will talk to B's about some situation that occurred at home within the last two days in which you had some feeling, any kind of feeling. You will do this for 2 minutes. Then, for 1 minute after this, B's will reflect back to you your understanding of what the feeling was that A conveyed and your understanding of the reason for it, using the formula: "You feel _____ about _____ because _____."

Then both of you will reverse roles and B will become the speaker and A will become the listener. I will announce when the minutes have passed, so you don't have to worry about that. Are there any questions? [Pause]

Now exchange partners with the twosomes to your left and repeat what you have already done using the same example of a situation at home or a different one, if you prefer. Again, I will announce when the minutes are up.

> Repeat procedure as above

Please assemble again in the large group. How did you find that experience?

> Pause now for about 10 minutes to process the reactions of the group members. For some, this experience may have been enjoyable. For others, it may have been embarrassing; for still others, it may have been frightening or inhibiting. During this period, when the group members express their reactions to this exercise, the leader should use the opportunity to reflect feelings that are communicated by the members on the spot, using the formula himself after each member speaks.

We talked today about empathic listening and responding. Learning what people feel from what they say and do, and responding to these feelings with empathy is a powerful means of helping others to feel loved and understood. It is a way to heal brokenness and build cooperative relationships among people. Learning empathic communication is similar to learning a new language. It takes root through the repetition of basic phrases. So we begin our language of empathy with a basic formula: "You feel _____ about _____ because _____." Practice this often wherever you are. It will soon begin to feel natural.

MODULE II: EMPATHIC COMMUNICATION

SESSION 2: Developing a Vocabulary of Feeling Words

Objectives:

1. To develop a repertoire of words to use in empathic communication.
2. To develop a list of body behaviors which express feeling states to aid in empathic communication.

Materials:

1. Newsprint and markers. Newsprint prepared in the following formats:

Vocabulary of Feelings				
Happy	Caring	Depression	Inadequacy	Fear

Vocabulary of Feelings				
Confused	Hurt	Angry	Lonely	Guilt

Vocabulary of Body Language		
Body Language	Specific Trait	Emotion Conveyed

Developing a Vocabulary of Feelings

Last time we talked of the importance of communicating with empathy to others in order to heal emotional brokenness and develop positive interpersonal relationships. Today we are going to expand our repertoire of words and phrases to use in that part of the formula we learned during the last session which began: "You feel _____."

In other words, we will develop a feeling and behavior vocabulary. Studies on effective counseling have shown that the more precise a counselor is in pinpointing the feeling a person is sharing with him in word or behavior, the better the chances are that the person will feel understood and make progress in therapy. Thus, if a person is furious and you tell him he feels "annoyed," he will not feel understood, although both these feeling states come under the category of anger.

We will start by developing a vocabulary of feeling words. All feelings can generally be categorized into ten classifications such as I have listed here on the newsprint.

> Post the prepared newsprint on vocabulary of feelings

There are many ways of describing each of these feeling states. Let's take each one and find different ways of expressing the same feeling.

> Elicit and write down all the feeling words trainees can think of to go under each classification

That's a fine list. Since this list will remain on the wall, please feel free to add more words as you think of them. That will further expand our vocabulary.

I want to shift now to developing a list of feeling behaviors, cues the body gives us through its own body language of its feeling messages. Body behaviors can generally be categorized into the classifications I have listed here on this newsprint.

> Post the prepared newsprint on vocabulary of body language. Elicit and write down the specific traits and emotions conveyed by the body language to go under each classification. If time does not allow for the development of the vocabulary, the leader can fill in the columns himself with some of the words or traits listed in Tables 1 and 2 and review these expressions with the group.

And so, we now have an increased understanding of body cues to look for in order to understand a person's state and an increased vocabulary of feeling words to use. We will now try to integrate the two.

Activity 1: Integrating Body and Verbal Cues in Empathic Communication

I want everyone to think of a situation involving a friend and yourself... a situation that had some feeling in it for you... Any feeling, happy, sad, fearful, whatever. As you think of this situation, you are going to share it with a partner. I want you to express your situation through two forms of body language from this list and through words. Take a minute or two to decide how your body will reinforce what your words say.

> Pause

Form the same A and B team you had before. A, tell B your particular situation in words and body language. B, observe A's body language while listening also to the feeling conveyed in words. Do this for 4 minutes. After this, for 1 minute, B is to put all his "data" together and say, "You feel_____ about _____ because _____." That's all. I will announce the minutes. Do that now.

| Pause for 5 minutes |

Time is up. B's, I want you now to talk with A's about the body language you observed from them that led you to say what you did. Check it out with A and see if you were correct. Do that now.

| Pause for 2 minutes |

Activity 2: More Integration of Body and Verbal Cues

We are going to shift roles now. Everything that A and B did will now be done in reverse. B's are now to be the speakers and A's the listeners. A, observe B's body language while listening also to the feeling conveyed in his words. Do this for 4 minutes. Then A will put his "data" together and say, "You feel _____ about _____ because _____." Again, I will announce the minutes. Do that now.

| Pause for 5 minutes |

Time is up. A's, I want you to talk with B about the body language you observed from him that led you to say what you did. Check it out with B and see if you were correct.
Do that now.

| Pause for 2 minutes |

That brings us to the end of today's session in which we developed lists of feeling words and body behaviors. I wonder if we could pull the main points of the session together in a summary form. Perhaps we could do this by your comments on any part of today's session that was particularly meaningful to you such as where you learned something new or made a new discovery.

| Accept what is said by each trainee while reflecting the feeling state and message expressed |

TABLE 1-A

VOCABULARY OF FEELINGS

HAPPY	CARING	DEPRESSED	INADEQUATE	FEARFUL
thrilled	tenderness	desolate	worthless	terrified
on cloud nine	toward	dejected	good for	frightened
ecstatic	affection for	hopeless	nothing	intimidated
overjoyed	captivated by	alienated	washed up	horrified
excited	attached to	depressed	powerless	desperate
elated	devoted to	gloomy	helpless	panicky
sensational	adoration	dismal	impotent	terror-
exhilarated	loving	bleak	crippled	stricken
fantastic	infatuated	in despair	inferior	stage fright
terrific	enamored	empty	emasculated	dread
	cherish		useless	vulnerable
on top of		barren		
the world	idolize	grieved	finished	paralyzed
turned on	worship	grief	like a	afraid
euphoric	affirmed	despair	failure	scared
enthusiastic	caring	grim	born loser	fearful
delighted	fond of	the pits	beaten	apprehensive
marvelous	regard	drained	trapped	jumpy
great	respectful	discarded	bungling	shaky
cheerful	admiration	futile	inadequate	threatened
light	concern for	distressed	whipped	distrustful
hearted	hold dear		defeated	risky
happy		upset	incompetent	
	prize	downcast		alarmed
serene	taken with	sorrowful	inept	butterflies
wonderful	turned on	demoralized	overwhelmed	awkward
up	trust	discouraged	ineffective	defensive
aglow	close	miserable	lacking	nervous
glowing	encouraged	pessimistic	deficient	anxious
in high	recognized	tearful	unable	unsure
spirits	touched	weepy	incapable	hesitant
jovial	welcomed	rotten	small	timid
riding high	included		insignificant	shy
mellow		awful		
bubbly	chosen	horrible	dumb	worried
	attended to	crummy	stupid	uneasy
cheerful	appreciated	troubled	deprived	bashful
content	provided for	torn	no good	embarrassed
radiant	protected	terrible	worthless	ill at ease
alive	accepted	blue	can't hack it	doubtful
fulfilled	warm toward	lost	can't cope	jittery
elevated	friendly	melancholy	like Casper	on edge
neat	like	unhappy	Milquetoast	uncomfortable
glad	positive		unfit	self-conscious
good	toward	down	unimportant	
		low		
		bad	incomplete	
satisfied		blah	no good	
gratified		disappointed	immobilized	
pleasant		sad		
pleased		glum	lacking	
fine			confidence	
peaceful			unsure of	
			yourself	
			uncertain	

TABLE 1-B

VOCABULARY OF FEELINGS

CONFUSED	HURT	ANGRY	LONELY	GUILT -SHAME
bewildered	crushed	furious	isolated	sick at heart
puzzled	destroyed	enraged	abandoned	unforgivable
baffled	ruined	seething	all alone	humiliated
perplexed	degraded	outraged	forsaken	disgraced
trapped	pain(ed)	infuriated	cut off	degraded
confounded	wounded	burned up	deserted	horrible
in a	devastated	pissed off	cast aside	mortified
dilemma	tortured	fighting	impersonal	exposed
befuddled	disgraced	mad	stranded	red-faced
in a	humiliated	nauseated		sinful
quandary		violent		
full of	at the		worlds apart	damned
questions	mercy of		lonely	haunted
	cast off	indignant	alienated	obsessed
confused	forsaken	hatred	estranged	deluged
mixed-up	rejected	bitter	remote	naked
disorganized	discarded	galled	alone	nailed
foggy	hurt	vengeful	apart from	ashamed
troubled	belittled	hateful	others	guilty
adrift	shot down	vicious	insulated	remorseful
lost	overlooked	resentful	from others	crummy
at loose ends	abused	irritated	ignored	
going around		hostile	useless	to blame
in circles	depreciated			lost face
disconcerted	criticized	annoyed	down in the	demeaned
	defamed	upset with	dumps	weighed down
frustrated	censured	agitated	out in the	sorrowful
flustered	discredited	mad	cold	heavy
in a bind	disparaged	aggravated	unwanted	discovered
ambivalent	laughed at	offended	walled out	burdened
disturbed	maligned	antagonistic	solitary	regretful
helpless	stabbed	exasperated	neglected	wrong
embroiled	shot	belligerent	"lost sheep"	
uncertain		mean	blue	embarrassed
unsure	mistreated		sad	at fault
bothered	ridiculed	vexed	left out	in error
	devalued	spiteful		responsible
uncomfortable	scorned	vindictive	excluded	for
undecided	mocked	uptight	lonesome	blew it
	scoffed at	disgusted	distant	goofed
	used	bugged	aloof	lament
	exploited	turned off		
	debased	put out		
	slammed	miffed		
		irked		
	slandered			
	impugned	perturbed		
	cheapened	ticked off		
	put down	teed off		
	neglected	chagrined		
	overlooked	cross		
	minimized	dismayed		
	let down	impatient		
	unappreciated			
	taken for			
	granted			

Adapted from: Hammond, D.C., Hepworth D. and Smith, V.: *Improving Therapeutic Communication. San Francisco: Jossey-Bass Publishers, 1977.*

TABLE 2

VOCABULARY OF BODY LANGUAGE

Body Language	Specific Traits	Possible Emotion conveyed
General physical appearance	alert unkempt sloppy	happy depressed
Emotional expression	furrowed brow rushed speech chain smoking sweaty hands blushing overpoliteness	anxiety, nervousness, worry fear, shyness
Tone of voice	loud soft slow fast mumbled	anger depression anxiety fear of disclosure
Gestures and mannerisms	twitching jumpy relaxed	nervous happy
Behavior	playful slamming banging passive hyper	happy angry dependency anxiety

MODULE II: EMPATHIC COMMUNICATION

SESSION 3: Continuation of Empathic Expression

Objective:
To practice skills of empathic listening and responding.
Materials:
Pads and pencils.

Need to Practice Empathic Communication

Expressions of caring, praise, encouragement, body language, touch, the written word, and most recently empathic communication are methods of raising children's self-regard that we have been learning and practicing together here. Today we will continue to talk about and experience more of the language of empathy.

The special kind of listening and responding called empathy that we learned about in the last session is one of the most effective kinds of communication there is to build closeness, caring, and responsibility into a relationship. Essentially, we focused on the observation that people's behavior, even their thinking, is influenced greatly by what they feel. When people feel understood and responded to empathically they experience a sense of relief, a sense of appreciation and dignity, a sense of affirmation. Positive relationships require empathic communication, especially relationships where love or healing is to grow such as in friendships and therapy.

You will recall that you spent a lot of time considering situations that you had some feeling about and sharing them with a partner. Your partner listened and then reflected back to you as precisely as he could what he perceived as your feeling about what you said both from your words and body language. He said: "You feel _____ about _____ because _____."

We developed a vocabulary of feelings both on a verbal and body language level in order to learn how to be more precise in understanding and responding to a person's situation. Just as the learning of a new language requires much practice before it becomes second nature, so also the language of empathy. To master this highly effective means of communicating caring and building closeness requires much practice. Practice it whenever you can. You can even let other people know what you are doing. Then check out your understanding with them to see if they agree that this is what they are feeling. Remember the process: Locate the feeling ("You feel _____"); attach the feeling to the specific event or behavior that gave rise to the feeling ("about _____"); and state the effect of the event or behavior on the person ("because _____").

Activity 1: Empathic Expression

In order to reinforce this learning, let's practice some more. You will form small groups.

> Leader goes around the group assigning each one a letter: A...B...C...D...E; A...B...C...D...E, etc.

All A's form a group; all B's form a group; all C's; all D's; all E's. Take a pencil and paper with you.

> Pause until groups are in place

I am going to read a situation to you about a boy whose watch was stolen in school. The purpose of this activity is to improve your skills in empathic communication. This exercise will be divided into two parts.

Part 1:

You are going to figure out something to say to the boy so he feels understood and not judged or criticized as he seemed to feel in school. In order to do this you have to figure out three things: his feeling; what specific event triggered the feeling; and finally, what effect losing his watch will have on him. So follow the steps as you listen to the incident and write down:

    a)   the boy's feeling
    b)   the event that set off his feeling
    c)   why he feels this way

Here is the boy's situation:

Jimmy received a watch for his birthday from his father. He had waited a long time for the watch and his father told him to take good care of it as it had taken a long time for him to earn the money to buy it. Jimmy needed the watch in order to leave school on time to get to a job he had after school. He wore the watch to school the next day. In gym, he took the watch off, put it into his pants pocket, and put the pants on the bleachers where everyone else put their clothing. He then got involved in a game of volleyball. It was a good game and his team won, so he felt pleased. When he put his pants back on, he discovered the watch was gone. He started cursing and shouting and when told by his teacher to be quiet, he got into a fight with him to such an extent that others had to break it up. He was sent to the dean who told him that the school would have none of his outbursts and that if he did not come to order he would be suspended. Jimmy stormed out of the office, left the school, and smashed a couple of windows on the way. He kept shouting that the school was dumb, the teachers even dumber, and no one cared anyway.

Take a few minutes to jot down Jimmy's feeling, the event which triggered his feeling, and the reason why he felt that way. When you have these three parts answered, you are ready to put your "data" into the formula. Do that now in writing.

Answer: You are feeling (furious) about (your watch being stolen) because (you waited so long to get one, it was a gift from your father, he will be disappointed in you, your work will suffer, it makes you disgusted with school).

I want you to share your completed formula with your group members. Go around so each one in your group hears each other. From your sharing, come to some agreement among yourselves about the best way to reflect back to Jimmy that you understand the way he feels about his situation. Take into account everyone's thinking in your group and compose a fuller and more precise response. One person in the group should write everything down. Take 5 minutes to do this. Pause Please stay in your groupings, but form a whole group again.

Put two chairs in the middle of the room

Part 2:

I need someone to play the part of Jimmy. Jimmy will sit here on this chair. He does not have to say anything. He is just going to hear what some of his friends who really understand him have to say to him. Could I have a volunteer to play Jimmy? Thank you. Jimmy, all these people here are your friends. They know what happened in the gym even though they were not there and do not know who stole your watch. Yet they know what it feels like, because many of them have had a similar thing happen to them. They want to talk to you.

Could the recorder of each group, you who know best what Jimmy's feelings are, come up one at a time and share with him what you and your friends in the group want to express to Jimmy?

Direct this process. The recorder of each group should occupy the second chair and speak to Jimmy based on what he has written down on his pad. Allow 10 minutes for this process.

Jimmy, please let us know how you feel now. Was there any particular message that you were given that helped more than another? Was there any particular person who said his message in a certain way that made you feel better understood? Allow a few minutes for this process. Thank you, Jimmy, and all you friends of Jimmy.

Activity 2: More Empathic Expression

I would like each of you to make a brief statement, about 1 minute apiece, about something that you have felt sometime during our session today. When one person speaks, the others are to listen. After a person makes his statement, the person to his right is to make a brief response back showing that he has understood his message by using our formula. Then that person will make a brief statement about something that he has felt during our time together. Then the person to his right will make a brief response back and then take his turn as the speaker. Do this around the group until everyone has been both a speaker and a responder. Take a minute to get your thoughts together for this. [Pause] I will begin. I am pleased about how you are responding to this training because it makes me feel successful as a teacher.

Direct this process around the group as explained. Compliment the group and then proceed to the summary:

What we have been doing together today is obvious: reinforcing our skills in empathic communication through practice. Again, I encourage you to practice these skills in your everyday life. You may find that everyday relationships will begin to improve.

MODULE II: EMPATHIC COMMUNICATION

SESSION 4:

- Empathic Self-Expression
- Who Owns the Problem?
- Roadblocks to Effective Communication

Objectives:

1. To develop skills of empathic self-expression in order to help children learn consideration for and cooperation with others.

2. To teach the concept that the person who feels the pain "owns the problem."

3. To teach common, but ineffective, methods of communication called roadblocks.

Materials:

1. Pads and pencils.

2. Newsprint prepared in following format:

Roadblock	Examples
Threat	"If you don't..." "No T.V. ..." "You must..."
Advice	"Why don't you..." "You should..." "If It were you..."
Reassurance	"Don't worry!.." "It's not so bad..."
Analysis	"Why? Who?" "What! When?" "Isn't it because?.."

Empathic Self-Expression

We have been talking a great deal about building closeness and caring into our relationships with others by "seeing the world through their eyes" or "walking in their shoes." We have done this by learning how to listen carefully to the feelings others express with their bodies and in their words, responding to these feelings and helping the other person to feel understood. We have learned that we can build a close relationship with another person through responding to their thoughts and feelings, but we can also promote closeness by showing our own thoughts and feelings to the other person. To achieve closeness it is necessary to be personal and authentic. Not knowing what another person feels or thinks can be perceived as distinterest in him or a wish to avoid closeness. It does not allow the other person to know where he stands with us. And it robs a relationship of the flow of real and authentic interpersonalness.

Parents and other caretakers may have strong feelings about certain behaviors elicited by children that need to be expressed in order for the child to learn how others feel and how he affects them. It is important to share ideas, values, expectations and standards with children as guidelines to them in forming their judgments and building closeness. How to do this so that closeness is fostered, and socially acceptable behavior is developed rather than a power struggle against us, is what I wish to talk about now.

We have talked about empathic listening and responding to others with the formula: "You feel _____ about _____ because _____." The skill needed to build closeness through sharing your own feelings is similar to empathic listening, but in reverse. Instead of listening for the other person's feelings, you express your own. Instead of, "You feel _____," you now say, "I feel _____." All feelings that one human being has are pretty much the feelings that all human beings have at some time or another. So, if Jimmy was angry when his watch was stolen because his father would be disappointed in him, you too can be angry about your coat being stolen because you saved a long time to buy it. Sharing your feeling about an event and your reasons for this feeling lets another person enter your private world, thus enabling him to "see the world through your eyes."

Activity 1: Empathic Self-Expression

We are going to share some feelings with each other now as a way of learning how to develop empathic self-expression. Look at the vocabulary list and find a feeling that best describes an emotion you had during the week about some situation. Take a minute or two to do that now. [Pause] Locate your feeling, indicate the event that brought the feeling on and, finally, state what effect it had on you. Use the formula: "I felt _____ about _____ because _____." Here is an example: "I feel annoyed about the loudspeaker coming on because I lose my train of thought." Also: "I was so pleased about coming home and finding supper already cooked because I was so tired." Now do the same thing and write it out. [Pause]

Direct the flow of responses clockwise after the first volunteer speaks. Make sure all statements are brief and kept to the formula focus.

Who Owns the Problem?

Strong negative feelings toward another can interfere with maintaining closeness. It is important to know how to deal with such feelings so that closeness is maintained and fostered. When you have strong negative feelings about someone else's behavior, that is a problem for you and your relationship with that person. When someone has strong feelings about your behavior, that is a problem for them and their relationship with you. Sometimes the problem belongs to both of you and your mutual relationship. So, whoever feels the pain owns the problem, even though each person may think the problem belongs to the other. Let's clarify this concept with some examples:

Activity 2: Who Owns the Problem?

1. Lynn was supposed to clean her room by the time her mother came home. Mother comes home. Room is not cleaned yet. Mother is furious. Whose problem is this?

   Ans: It is mother's problem, she has the pain, not Lynn.

2. Eric comes in the house, slams the door and goes to his room. Dad says hello as he passes. Eric does not respond. Dad shrugs his shoulders and keeps reading the paper. Who has the problem?

   Ans: Eric owns the problem, he has the pain, not Dad.

3. Raymond's best friend moved. He misses him and thinks about him all the time. He can't eat well and his sleeping is disturbed. Dad feels bad because this has been going on for some time now. He would like Raymond to feel better and be his old self. He tries talking to Raymond, but this does not help. Dad feels helpless. Who has the problem?

   Ans: Both have the problem because both have pain.

So, you begin to see the idea behind deciding who has the problem and therefore needs to express his concern.

Roadblocks to Effective Communication

It is important when we listen to a child's problem or express our own that we stick to the spirit of the formula "You feel _____ about _____ because _____" or "I feel _____ about _____ because _____." It is so easy to get sidetracked into responses that are called roadblocks. Roadblocks are responses that put people down or imply that they are not competent to think out a solution for themselves. There are four basic roadblocks: threatening, advising, reassuring, and analyzing.

> Post prepared newsprint with roadblocks and explain them with examples, then go on to the following exercise.

Activity 3: Roadblocking

Try your hand at roadblocking now. I will read some situations. You respond as the parent.

1. Edna asks her mother what she should wear to school today.

2. Sam leaves all his father's tools out after he finishes a project.

3. Mike comes in two hours later at night than the time agreed on.

4. Don asks his father for an advance on his allowance.

5. Ruth was minding her younger sister. Younger sister fell down the

stairs while in Ruth's charge. Mother comes home and discovers what happened.

6. Rick comes home drunk one night. His father, a very devout person sees him stagger to his room.

So, you can see from the responses what experts we are in roadblock responding. All that means is that we need more practice in both therapeutic listening and responding and in developing our capacity for therapeutic self-expression.

Activity 4: Return to Empathic Communication

To continue our work of developing our capacity to express our own feelings helpfully to others, let's take some further examples of problems that cause us pain and practice on them. Do not roadblock this time. Go back to the formula: "I feel _____ about _____ because _____ ."

1. Mario interrupts your conversation with someone.

2. Cynthia does not brush her teeth unless constantly reminded to do so.

3. Peter bullies his younger brothers and sisters.

4. Edward swears and curses constantly.

5. Gil keeps watching TV when he should be doing his homework.

6. Rachel is supposed to feed the dog, but neglects this unless nagged about her task.

7. Ben hogs the phone for hours each night.

From these cases, you can see how difficult it is to stick to expressing just our own feelings and not get into roadblocking.

Activity 5: Roadblocking vs. Empathic Communication

Sit back now and listen to this story. Mrs. Cruz, Jimmy's mother, received a call from the school that her son was suspended because of abusive talk and assault on a teacher. She was told that he could be reinstated only through her appearance at a District hearing made up of the principal, the superintendent of schools, the dean of boys, the guidance personnel, the teacher, and the security guard. She was further informed that the teacher would probably press charges. Imagine you are Mrs. Cruz. You hang up the phone and sit there for a long time with a lot of feelings about this call and Jimmy's situation. Jimmy comes in whistling and saying, "Hi, mom. When's supper?" He does not seem to be bothered too much by this incident, but you certainly are. Thus, you own the problem. You ask him to come sit down, you need to speak with him. You, as Mrs. Cruz, will talk with Jimmy. We will do this in three parts. Write down your responses:

Part 1:

First, communicate your feelings to Jimmy using at least three roadblocks in your self-expression. Do that now. ⟨ Pause ⟩

Part 2:

Now you will communicate with Jimmy using therapeutic self-expression. Again, remember that in doing this you have to figure out three things:

Your feeling, what situation brought on this feeling and, finally, what effect this situation will have on you. When you have these three parts answered, you are ready to put your "data" into the formula. Do that now.

> The answer should result in something similar to this: "I am feeling very upset, confused, angry, and embarrassed about your assault on a teacher and abusive talk because I care a great deal about your getting on in school and they will think that I am not raising you right and I could be sued. Tell me what happened."

With your completed formula I want you now to share this with five group members. Go around so each one in your group hears each other. From your sharing, come to some agreement among yourselves about the best way for Mrs. Cruz to express herself to Jimmy that will enable her to let her feelings be known to him about his situation and yet not put him down in the process of expressing herself. Take part of everyone's thinking in your group and compose a fuller and more precise response. One person in your group should serve as recorder and write it down. Take 5 minutes to do this. ⬚Pause⬚ Please stay in your groupings but form a whole group again now.

Part 3:

⬚ Put two chairs in the middle of the room ⬚

I need someone to be Jimmy. Jimmy will sit on this chair. He does not have to say anything. He is just going to listen to some responses from his mother.

All persons out here have taken the role of Mrs. Cruz. You have been rehearsing in your mind a variety of responses to give to Jimmy when he comes home. At first you went through a lot of roadblocking, but then you said to yourselves, "That won't really help, that will only add fuel to the fire. Let me get my head together and think through the most helpful way of communicating to my son so at least he does not feel attacked and put down by me."

We had smaller groups of you consider the best way to formulate therapeutic sefl-expression. Before we hear the therapeutic self-expressions, could we have one round of a person from each group taking the chair up here as Mrs. Cruz and really roadblock Jimmy? Who can begin? Just come to the chair, sit down and give it to him. Use body language as well. Then go back to the chair and the next person from the next grouping will come up and do the same, and so on around the circle. ⬚Pause for this process⬚

Now, in contrast, could one of you from each group again come up, take the chair and communicate the empathic self-expression your group has composed to Jimmy in such a way that through your words and body language you let him know your feelings clearly but in such a way that he does not feel put down? ⬚Pause for this process⬚

Activity 6: Concluding this Session with Empathic Self-Expression

Before we end for the day, I would like to make one more round around the room and ask each of you to make a brief statement, about a minute or so, about something that pleased you during the last few days, something you felt happy or joyful about, or something that made you feel hopeful such as good news about something personal. Again, just use the formula:

I felt _____ about _____ because _____.

MODULE II: EMPATHIC COMMUNICATION

SESSION 5: Developing Empathic Dialogue and a Mutual Problem-Solving Strategy

Objectives:

1. To integrate empathic listening/responding and empathic self-expression in a dialogue.

2. To teach a mutual problem-solving strategy through communication based on empathic listening/responding and empathic self-expression.

Materials:

1. Paper and pencils.

2. Copies of script on Dad and Nelson (see Activity 2)

Reinforcement of Empathic Expression

Whoever is troubled or pained by some situation owns the problem. That person feels "broken" or "torn" in some way. Brokenness is healed through a special kind of talking which we have described as empathic listening/responding and empathic self-expression. One person needs to express his feeling and another must be available to hear and respond to that person. Empathic listening and responding can be offered to a person in a situation where one person experiences the problem and it does not substantially affect another person. When this can reasonably be done, a listener can "be with" a speaker, hear his brokenness, respond empathically, and help him sort out his troubled feelings. If a listener shares the problem with the speaker they both will need to serve as listeners/responders to each other. We will talk about that arrangement later on. Now we will practice listener and speaker roles again to give us further experience.

Activity 1: Listener and Speaker Roles

I will give you several examples of problem situations. Take a paper and figure out three things in each example:

1. Who has the problem?

2. Type of response called for? (Empathic listening/responding or empathic self-expression)

3. What to say empathically? Use the formula "You feel _____ about _____ because _____" or "I feel _____ about _____, because _____."

After a few minutes on each example, which I will read to you, and after you have written all your responses, we will share some of your responses to reinforce our understanding of this language of empathy.

Read examples in Situation column only. The other columns are guides for you, the Trainer. Follow each situation asking the trainees the three basic questions listed above. Allow sufficient time between each question for the trainees to write down their responses.

Situation	Who Has Problem	Type of Response	Model Response
Edgar worked hard to get on baseball team. He was not accepted. He comes home, goes to his room without having supper.	Edgar	Empathic listening	"You're really feeling discouraged about not making the team because you worked hard to make it."
Angela and Ray are fighting over TV. Mother screams at them and tells them to go to their room.	Both: children and mother	Empathic listening and empathic self-expression	"It bothers me a lot when you fight that way because I take pride in my children's ability to solve problems peacefully." and "You are both really upset about wanting to watch two different programs at the same time because each of you have different interests."
Oscar says: "I can't do this homework. The teacher can't teach and no one likes him."	Oscar	Empathic listening	"The homework stumps you and you really feel lousy about the teacher because he doesn't seem to come across clearly."
Edwin says: "I can't learn in that classroom. The bars on the windows make me feel like I'm in jail."	Edwin	Empathic listening	"You feel very uncomfortable in class. You feel like a captive, walled in."
Mother is upset because Dalma eats in her room and leave dirty dishes and food scraps all over. She tells her mother it is her room, not mother's. She can keep it the way she wants.	Mother	Empathic self-expression	"It disturbs me a lot that you leave dirty dishes and food scraps around your room because that attracts the roaches."
Ada comes home two hours late from a party. Mother has been waiting up, alternating between being worried and being angry.	Mother	Empathic self-expression	"I was so worried when you didn't come home as planned because I thought something happened to you. I was also angry that you did not call because that made me think something really did happen to you."

David does not dry the dishes unless nagged to do so. Mother nags and feels exasperated.	Mother	Empathic self-expression	"I really feel let down that the dishes are never dried unless I nag because I count on you to do that."
Nestor is inconsistent about taking out the garbage. Dad uses sarcasm each night to prod him, but having to do this makes Dad more and more irritated.	Dad	Empathic self-expression	"I feel disappointed that I have to get after you so much about taking the garbage out because I would really like to know that I can depend on you . That would really make me feel good."
Joey has a habit of interrupting his mother's conversations with her friends. Mother is always correcting him, wondering when he will stop this kind of behavior.	Mother	Empathic self-expression	"I feel annoyed when you interrupt my conversations because I lose my train of thought with the person I am talking to."

> Invite the trainees to share their written responses to the three questions by reading over each case situation again.

Mutual Ownership of a Problem

Sometimes what would seem to be the problem person is not necessarily that person at all. It would seem that Nestor's not taking the garbage out is his problem, but since that does not bother him at all, but does bother Dad, it really becomes Dad's problem because he has the pain. Although we could say Nestor has a problem that he just doesn't recognize, that fact would not motivate him to work on it because he would not perceive having anything to work on.

There are situations in which two persons do have pain resulting from a conflict of interests. This can be a conflict between a parent and child; student and teacher; friend and friend; husband and wife, or employer and employee. In these cases, it is necessary not only to be aware of what the other person feels and respond to that, but also to express one's own needs in the process of working out a relationship problem. Problems that are the result of a conflict of interests can be worked out if both parties are willing to hear each other. The power of empathic listening/responding and sharing can have a powerful influence on bringing two people closer in their relationship and in helping them to settle a conflict of interests.

Activity 2: Two People with a Problem

Consider the following situation:

Nelson, age 8, is happy to see his father when he comes home from work. He has been waiting for him all day because his father said he would take him to the park to play ball with him. However, when Father comes home, he is exhausted. Nelson jumps all over him saying,

- 111 -

"Let's go, let's go!" Father grows annoyed and makes Nelson feel pushed aside. Nelson goes to the living room and kicks his younger brother. They scream and fight. Dad comes in and smacks Nelson. They both are angry, they both hurt and have a feeling of unfriendliness toward each other by this time.

Let's use our understanding of defining who has the problem and our empathic listening and empathic self-expression skills to come to bear on this mutual problem.

Part 1:

Write down your opinions:
1. Who has the problem, Nelson or Dad?
2. What is the problem?
3. Imagine you are Nelson. What do you feel? About what? For what reason? Put your thoughts into a sentence: "I feel _____ about _____ because _____."
4. Imagine you are Dad. What do you feel? About what? For what reason? Put your thoughts into a sentence: "I feel _____ about _____ because _____."

Two people in pain need to feel understood by each other. There is a way for them to work it out together using empathic skills. One of them will have to take the lead in this. This will probably be the person who most wants to solve the problem, keep the relationship going, and is the most mature. In order to see what Dad could do in this situation, let's get some of your responses to the questions you answered.

> Go through the above questions again, eliciting trainees' responses. Encourage them to clarify unclear points for each other. Get a consensus on the empathic statements arrived at through use of the formula.

Part 2:

Now that we are clear as to what both Nelson and Dad feel and about their reasons for feeling as they do, we can help Dad take the lead and have a talk with Nelson that will enable both of them to feel understood, be considerate of each other's needs, and work out a plan where their mutual needs will be met. I need two volunteers to play the parts of Dad and Nelson. [Pause for volunteers] The script Nelson and Dad will read from pulls together the spirit of your own responses.

> Give copies of the script to Dad and Nelson. You will read all items in the first column. Either Dad or Nelson will respond to you with the items listed in the second column.

SCRIPT

LEADER		DAD OR NELSON

LEADER

Dad, Nelson was so happy to see you when you came home. He couldn't wait for you to go to the park with him. When you didn't take him right away, he felt very disappointed. He felt so despondent when you ignored him that his feelings turned to anger. Let him know that you can understand his feelings.

→

Dad
You were disappointed and even angry at me when I didn't go with you to the park, because you had been looking forward to the two of us having fun there together.

Nelson, Dad has understood your feelings and let you know that. That is just how you really feel. You remember other situations like this one and feel Dad makes excuses and puts you off. Say these things to him.

→

Nelson
That's right. You never take me anywhere. All the other kids' fathers take them out, but you never do. You are always saying "later" or "I'm tired, we'll do it another time."

Dad, Nelson is really letting you in on his disappointment in you. It is because he values you so much. He is telling you he feels he can't count on you. Say this to him.

→

Dad
You feel you can't count on me to come through with what I say I will do with you. Is that it?

Nelson, Dad feels you are saying you can't count on him. Tell him now that sometimes you can count on him, but right now you don't understand why he isn't taking you to the park.

→

Nelson
Sometimes I can count on you, but why aren't we going to the park now like you promised?

Dad, Nelson is puzzled about your putting him off and not keeping your promise. Say this to him.

→

Dad
You feel puzzled about my not going to the park right now. Is that it?

Nelson, tell Dad, "That's it!"

→

Nelson
That's it!

Dad
I'm really proud of the way you have told me how you feel straight out. That kind of honesty is something I really go for. Nelson, I felt very tired when I came home and needed to rest because I worked very hard today. I knew if I rested I would feel good about going to the park later on.

Dad, Nelson has really expressed his feelings to you honestly. Let him know how much you value his honesty; how pleased you are that he can speak his mind to you this way. Then let him in on your feelings of being very tired when you come in from work and needing to get some rest.

→

Nelson
How am I supposed to know that you are so tired? You should tell me, otherwise I think you just don't want to go. How long will you have to rest? I want to go as soon as possible.

Nelson, Dad appreciated your honest communication with him and now is honestly communicating his feeling of tiredness to you. Tell him you did not know this because he did not say anything to you. Then let him know that you are still impatient about having to wait and wonder how long he will have to rest.

→

Dad, Nelson understands you

→

Dad
You felt I was putting you off because

better now that you have
expressed your feeling and
the reason for it. He is
still feeling impatient
about wanting to get to the
park soon. Tell him you
feel an hour will enable
you to rest enough before
going.

Nelson, Dad appreciates
your sharing your feelings
with him. He really
values this. Sounds also
like he is looking forward
to going with you to the
park and will really feel
up to it after he rests.
Tell him to hurry up resting
though.

I did not let you know that I was really
tired. Thanks again for letting me know
your thoughts. You really would like to
get going as soon as possible; you can
hardly wait and hope that my resting will
not take up too much time. I think an hour
will do it.

Nelson

OK. But no more than an hour. And,
to make the hour go fast, I'll watch
TV for a while.

Thank you, Nelson; thank you, Dad. Now you go off to the park together.

What did you feel about that dialogue between Nelson and his father? Wait for responses from trainees The father showed a lot of empathic listening and responding to Nelson. There was one part where the father expressed his own feelings directly. Do you remember where that was? Does anyone have any question about the dialogue as a whole? Now you have seen how a dialogue between two people can lead to mutually acceptable solutions to a conflict of interests if they are willing to listen to each other, express their feelings openly, and not put each other down.

Activity 3: Empathic Problem Solving

We are going to spend the rest of the session practicing in groups of two. Would you look directly across the room at whoever is sitting opposite you? Join together as a twosome. Pause Here is the situation you are going to consider:

You are a parent raising five children, aged 2 to 13, on a welfare budget. Your 13-year-old son, Miguel, wants a pair of Puma sneakers which cost $35. You can't afford this and you both feel bad. He, because all the other kids have name-brand sneakers and he feels different with a lesser brand. You, because you would like to be able to buy them for him, but your finances don't allow it; otherwise, your family needs, such as food and rent, will not be able to be provided for. Thus you both have the problem because you both feel the pain. He thinks you should get a job and get off welfare so that the family can have more money. But you have a two-year-old child and a five-year-old child and there are other reasons why getting a job is impractical for you. Talk together in such a way that you empathically listen and respond to your child's feelings and also empathically self-express your own feelings in such a way that your child is not put down. Remember to hear his feelings and let him know your own as well. Remember to state the reason why you feel the way you do. Again, refer to the formula.

> Allow about 10 minutes for this exercise. Go around and monitor the practice in such a way that the twosomes are accomplishing the purpose of the exercise to your satisfaction.

Please come back again to the whole group. That brings us to the end of this session. You are doing beautifully. Keep practicing at home and with each other between sessions.

In this session we have been clarifying "who owns the problem" and learning how to listen and respond empathically to the other person as well as express our own feelings in order to feel understood by the other person. In our next session we are going to apply these skills to a clearly formulated conflict resolution blueprint. There is a method for resolving conflict made up of six steps. It presupposes empathic skills have been learned. Since we have developed these skills to some degree now, we are ready to move on to learn effective conflict resolution.

MODULE III: CONFLICT RESOLUTION

SESSION I: Concepts of Conflict

Objectives:

1. To introduce the concept of conflict and conflict resolution.

2. To teach the distinction between "conflict of need" and "conflict of value."

3. To teach ways of articulating conflict without roadblocking.

Materials:

Newsprint prepared in following format:

Needs	Values

Conflict of Needs vs. Conflict of Values

For the past few sessions we have been focusing on a way of communicating with others that recognizes their feelings as well as our own in an attempt to build a closer relationship. We also began to use this "feeling" communication in a dialogue form to settle problems or conflicts between ourselves and others. Remember the dialogue between Nelson, who wanted to go to the park, and his father who was tired? We are going to focus on problem or conflict resolution for the next couple of sessions. As usual, we will be drawing on the communication skills we have been learning in past sessions.

Empathic listening and self-expression are powerful means of building the kind of closeness in a relationship that enhances a sense of another's loveability, worthwhileness, and responsible cooperation. Because of the positive emotions it stirs in a person, this type of communication facilitates problem solving when two or more people are in conflict. Conflict resolution is needed when people have different points of view that affect their lives together.

Today we will learn what conflict is and begin to understand different kinds of conflict. We will learn a problem-solving strategy that respects the other person's point of view as well as our own. In this way, self-respect, self-esteem, and a sense of confidence are maintained and reinforced in both parties. Conflict is defined by Webster as a mental struggle resulting from incompatible or opposing needs, drives, or wishes. Most conflicts between people fall into either of two categories: 1. *conflict of needs* and *conflict of values.*

Conflict of needs is present when one person's needs adversely affect another person's needs at the same time. So, if Nelson wants Dad to play with him and Dad is tired, there are two incompatible needs at stake and conflict results. If Mom needs quiet to talk on the phone and the children want to play the stereo loudly, there are incompatible needs at stake and conflict is the result. The important thing about conflict of needs is that the behavior of one person directly affects the behavior of the other person. This is different from the conflict we see where a person wants his preferences or beliefs to be accepted by another person, but whether the other person does or not, does not directly affect the well-being of the first person. In this case we have a conflict, not of needs, but of values.

Values are beliefs, opinions, personal tastes, or preferences. They are very personally ours. We may want others to adopt them also and we might even die for them, but whether or not others do adopt them in no way has a direct effect on our living out our own lives guided by what we believe. A parent might want his child to associate with certain friends, cut his hair, go to church, do homework, and may encourage such values, but whether or not the child adopts the parent's preferences in no way interferes with what a parent needs directly for himself. Although these different points of view between what a parent prefers and what a child prefers may elicit a parent's concern, or even anxiety, the child's behavior does not clash with or directly affect the needs of the parent as in the case where there is a definite conflict of needs.

Activity 1: Conflict of Needs vs. Conflict of Values

Let's try our hand now at figuring out the kinds of situations where a child's behavior interferes with something a parent needs and the kind of situation where a child's behavior represents a different point of view than the parent's but does not interfere with a parent's needs. We will make a needs list and a values list. I will start it off:

Put up newsprint and start the list as illustrated:

Needs	Values
Telephone	Homework
Use of bathroom	Friends
TV	Religious practice
Chores	Future plans
etc.	etc.

Explain how each item represents either a conflict of need or a conflict of value. Whenever there is a conflict, the question can be asked: "How does this conflict directly interfere with my need?" Two people may want to watch a different TV show at the same time; or use the bathroom at the same time. Both parties are affected by the need. Thus, a conflict of need arises. On the other hand, a child may not do his homework and I may become upset. But his doing or not doing his homework has no direct effect on my life then or in the future, although I may be concerned that the child do well in school. My concern, wish, or worry about his homework, friends, future plans, religious practice, or style of dress does not directly interfere with what I need myself as a separate person from the other. The trainees may need some time to process this distinction as you invite them to consider whether the conflicts they offer belong to either category. However, it will be well worth the time spent on this distinction since the skills of conflict resolution to be presented to them shortly are highly effective with conflicts of needs between people but less so with conflicts of values.

The reason why it is important to know whether we are dealing with a conflict of need or value in relationship to another person is because it is in the conflict of need category that problem-solving leading to negotiation and resolution is most possible. People are willing to cooperate, compromise, bargain, and accept a solution to a problem as long as they are convinced that some behavior on their part affects a need on our part. The stronger the argument in behalf of your own need, the more likely are the chances for a resolution of the conflict. With conflicts of values, one can state one's belief about something and even present arguments supporting it, but preferences alone do not directly affect other persons' lives. This fact, then, limits the possibility of changing behavior through the method we will be practicing. Because conflict resolution works best where the issue is one of need, our learning will focus on this area.

Let's take the list of conflict of needs on the newsprint. Imagine a conflict between yourself and your child on these items and how you might talk to your child in such a way that he sees how his behavior affects your needs. Here are some examples beginning at the top of the list:

Use of telephone: James, I know you like to use the phone a lot, but I need to have the telephone open between 9 and 5 so I can get business calls that I depend on in my work.

Nancy, I know how much you enjoy talking on the phone each night, but our telephone costs must come down because I can't pay the bill this month.

Use of bathroom: Jimmy, I know you like to shower between 7 and 8 a.m., but I need to use the bathroom at 7 and not later, or else I'll miss my bus to work at 8.

Use of TV: Paula, I would like to watch a special program tonight at 8. I know that is when you watch _____, but it is a program we have been assigned for homework and if I don't see it, I get a failure for the day.

I trust these distinctions are clear as we go on to discuss actual strategies for resolving such conflicts.

MODULE III: CONFLICT RESOLUTION

SESSION 2: Conflict Resolution Between Self and Another

Objectives:

1. To teach a specific and clearly defined method of conflict resolution in six steps.

2. To teach the application of conflict resolution to situations between self and another.

Materials:

1. Newsprint.

2. Conflict-resolution worksheets for all trainees (see last page of this session).

3. Carbon paper (one for every four Trainees).

A Strategy for Conflict Resolution

Last time we talked about the distinction between conflicts of need and conflicts of value. I emphasized that conflicts of need were those clashes between people that had a direct effect on each one, while conflicts of value were those clashes which represented differences of beliefs, opinions, or preferences. While conflicts of values can be handled somewhat effectively with the method for conflict resolution I am going to teach you today, it is particularly effective in resolving a conflict of need. So right now I would like to teach you a six-step method for resolving conflict which you can apply yourself when in conflict with another person or to two other people in conflict with each other.

Conflicts seem to be best resolved when certain steps are followed in a specific order. We are going to take each of these steps in order, using our empathic listening/responding and empathic self-expression skills to facilitate the process.

Before explaining the steps involved in conflict resolution, I want to mention that real problem solving is not a hit-or-miss process. It is vital that all parties in a conflict find the time (when free, available and unhassled), appropriate place (quiet, undistracted), interest (all parties should agree to some extent about wanting to improve the conflict situation) and the emotional energy to invest in the process of problem solving (not when people are tired or preoccupied).

The six-step method of conflict resolution follows. Since it is lengthy, three suggestions are offered:

1. Read over the content and grasp it thoroughly so you can present it without too much recourse to reading it verbatim to the trainees.

2. As you proceed from step to step, record the step number and concept on newsprint.

3. Stop frequently for comments and questions.

Step I: Statement of Conflict as Self-Viewed

In this step, the conflict is defined clearly in terms of the behavior of the other person that is interfering with your own need. There are three components in this step that are likely to get the conflict resolution off to a good start.

      a) Begin with something positive about the other person.

      b) Express your feeling about the specific behavior you object to, and why.

Here are some examples:

-- (a) I really appreciate the way you get up by yourself in the morning, but (b) when you play the radio so loudly (c) I get very upset because I can't sleep.

-- (a) I like it a lot that you work with us in this program; you can really be depended on, but (b) it bothers me a lot when you do not stay at the activity you are assigned to because the children are then unsupervised.

During Step I you are making use of two kinds of communication skills that foster the closeness and cooperation we have worked on over the last weeks: (1) use of caring phrases, and (2) empathic self-expression ("I feel _____ about _____ because _____ ").

Step II: Exploration of Conflict as Other-Viewed

In this step, the problems as seen and felt by the other person in the conflict are surfaced. Helping another person in a conflict to clearly articulate his side of the story requires the kind of empathic listening/responding skills we have talked a great deal about. In this second step of the process of conflict resolution you will need to practice this carefully. In fact, a great deal of time may need to be spent on this step in order to help a person feel understood and motivated before you can enter fully into the problem resolution stage. This empathic listening/responding step may need to go back and forth several times as the exploration of the conflict unfolds.

> Empathic listening/responding. In this step you must be open to hear the thinking and feeling of the other party and not profer roadblocks. Do not make inferences, nor seek causes, nor drum up past examples, nor ask questions, nor give advice. Just listen and respond empathically, using the formula:
>
> So, you are feeling _____ about _____ because _____ .

Step III: Empathic Summarization and Invitation to Problem Solve

In this step there is a summary of feelings of both parties in the conflict. This step merely ties together the specific behaviors of all parties in the conflict and the feelings that accompany them. The summary makes use of the empathic listening/responding formula as well as the empathic self-expression formula:

So, you are feeling _____ about _____
because _____.

I am feeling _____ about _____
because _____.

Redefine the problem as it now appears. After both parties in the conflict have communicated their thinking and feeling to each other regarding their conflict, the problem can be redefined in terms of what is wanted on both sides in this way:

It seems that you need _____, while I need _____.

Appeal to problem solving. When both parties agree to the problem as redefined and feel understood, an appeal to find a mutually satisfying solution is made in this way:

"Let's put our heads together and come up with some possible solutions."

Step IV: Generating Possible Solutions and Choosing Best

Step IV is basically a brainstorming session. It is not a decision phase, but rather a phase where everyone is invited to think up all conceivably possible solutions to the conflict at issue. Although many ideas may seem absurd (and all ideas, including the "far out" ones, should be encouraged), realistically innovative, creative ideas are actually energized through "permission" to think freely.

It is a good idea to help a child express his ideas first and add your own later. With acceptance of the child's ideas, there is a reinforcement of his motivation to work at a solution. No ideas are to be belittled or evaluated during this stage. All ideas should be listed on paper in order to review and evaluate them when brainstorming is finished. Evaluation is the task of Step VI.

Step IV is the heart of the conflict resolution process. A solution to the conflict that is mutually agreeable needs to be decided on. As the list of possible solutions generated in this step is reviewed, there should be no "all or nothing" thinking in regard to each proposed solution, but rather an open attitude of "What am I willing to accept?" You might say, "Which of these solutions look best to both of us? Let's go through them all and see which might work out best for us."

In going through each possible solution, cross out those that are clearly unacceptable to you or the child and put stars next to those most favorable to both you and the child. Then carefully review the solutions that have the most possibilities of being mutually satisfying. In deciding on the best of the solutions considered, it is important that both you and the child feel realistically, even though not ideally, comfortable, with the decision. Honesty is vital. If you are not satisfied with a solution say: "I wouldn't be happy with that one"; or "that would still leave me feeling burdened." Probably the decision will be one where, through the process of an honest exchange of ideas and reactions, no one wins or loses, but agrees, compromises, or just goes along with the idea.

Step V: Implementing Chosen Solution

When the best solution is decided on there must be a clear understanding of the terms of the agreement. Step V has three components:

1. A statement of the solution and the commitment of both parties to make it work.

2. Terms of the solution are to be spelled out specifically:

   -- Edna is to clean her room on Saturday morning between 9 and 12. An alternative day is Friday afternoon after school between 3 and 5. Cleaning means changing sheets, vacuuming rug, dusting and clearing off desk, bureau, and table.

   -- Dad is to be home on Monday and Wednesday evenings at 6 p.m. to have supper with the children and take care of them so Mom can get to class by 7.

   -- Chores for children to do after school will be posted on the family bulletin board in kitchen. Each child's name and chore will be listed. Chores are to be completed by 5:30.

3. Terms of agreement (as illustrated above) can be reinforced through writing them down and placing them in a familiar place (posted on door, on bureau, on car dashboard, etc.)

Step VI: Follow-Up Evaluation

Decisions are like hunches. They make sense and seem logical, but the test of the pudding is still in the eating. It is important, therefore, that a plan be agreed on to review the workings of the solution in a week's time or before. The time should be specified (e.g., Monday evening at 9 p.m. in the living room). It can also be specified that a meeting can be called before that time, if needed. All involved in the problem solving must agree to the follow-up evaluation plan. At the follow-up evaluation the question is raised: "How is our decision working out?" The process of empathic listening/responding and empathic self-expression is to be used to assure that all feel understood and cooperation is reinforced.

When follow-up evaluations are adhered to they serve two purposes: (1) they correct unworkable original decisions; and (2) they reinforce conflict resolution attitudes.

I am going to pass out conflict-resolution worksheets which summarize everything I just said. They are similar to the outline on the newsprint here. Look over the sheet briefly for a few minutes.

Pass out worksheets and allow 2 or 3 minutes for this scanning.

Activity 1: Conflict Resolution

We are going to experiment now with putting the conflict resolution method into practice.

You might remember that a while back we talked about a problem between Nestor and his father. Nestor's job was to take out the garbage after supper each night. It was not an easy job because he had to walk down six flights of stairs with a huge load accumulated from a large family. He was inconsistent about his job, although reminded constantly by his father. The father became increasingly annoyed. Now, Nestor played ball every day after school between 3 and 5 and he was very good at it, dependable, and talented. He came home each day at 5 and then watched TV until supper. Dad worked from 8 a.m. to 5 p.m. each day in construction work and then battled the subway crowd from 5 to 6 to get home, so he was pretty tired. When supper was over each day, Dad went to the living room and fell asleep. Nestor went out again to play ball after supper, thus neglecting the garbage. When Dad awoke and Nestor had not taken the garbage out, Dad had to do it because the super closed the basement at 8 p.m. Nestor usually came home at 10.

What I want you to do now is to take your conflict-resolution worksheets, imagine you are Nestor's dad, and figure out how to resolve this conflict you are having with Nestor by applying each of the six steps to your situation. We will do this together. Write responses most agreed on, on the worksheet.

Take the class as a whole through this process, inviting and encouraging all responses, gently correcting misunderstandings and reinforcing correct understandings of the concepts explained in the lecture. Remember that this is the first attempt by the trainees to integrate the new skill experientially, so you may need to go painstakingly slowly, even repeating certain steps. When group has finished, praise their efforts, grasp of material and creative thinking. Suggest that it is like learning a new language: some may find it harder than others, but all can learn, mostly through repetitive practice, as in learning a new language.

Activity 2: Practicing Conflict Resolution

What I would like you to do now is to get yourself into foursomes with anyone you want to join. Do that now.

Pause and pass carbon paper out to each trainee

Here is what you are to do:

1. Look at the list of conflict of needs on this chart here Refer to newsprint and select one conflict situation to work on as a group. The group task is to apply the six-step conflict resolution method to the conflict situation you have chosen.

2. In order to do this well, each one of you in the foursome will have a specific task. One of you is to be the child in the conflict situation, and one of you is to be the parent. Another is to serve as the recorder for the worksheet, and the fourth person is to act as the facilitator, keeping everyone focused on the job at hand and keeping things moving. Child and parent will build a story about their conflict situation. In order for you to deal with the conflict situation you have chosen, you will have to know more about both parent and child. Therefore, the parent should describe his child to the others in the foursome including the kind of person he or she is together with some negative as well as positive qualities. Parents then should describe the problem they are having with their children. Then, the child should do the same thing, that is, describe the parent, including the kind of person he or she is, some positive as well as negative points of view, and finally, the problem he or she is having with the parent. Recorder and facilitator can ask questions of parent or child. Take about 5 minutes to elaborate the conflict situation story.

3. When the story is completed, facilitator will lead the foursome in brain-storming the best responses to make to each of the six steps on the worksheet. Recorder will record the chosen responses on two worksheets, so put the carbon paper between the worksheets. Everyone in the foursome should brainstorm responses, not just the parent and child. Be creative and have fun doing this, but keep to the task. You have 25 minutes for the whole process. Are there any questions? Pause Begin now.

Circulate among the foursomes, offering help as needed, gently correcting misunderstandings about the steps and praising correct applications of the method.

Please come back to the whole group now. After that workout, what I would like now is to hear some sharing of your experiences. Would some member of each group tell us the story that went with your conflict situation? Then the recorder for that group will read the responses you have written on the worksheet.

Allow about half an hour for this activity, but organize the sharing in two ways:

1. Two groups will describe their conflict situation and then read out their written responses.

2. Two or three groups will describe their conflict situation and then role-play the responses.

So after two or three groups merely describe the results of their work together, say:

Who would be willing to do a little role playing on their conflict situation? The parent and child of that group may come and sit here Get up and put two chairs in center of room and talk to each other, using the worksheet as your script.

When a group volunteers, have "parent" and "child" seat themselves and ask the recorder or facilitator to describe the conflict situation. Ask recorder to take the two worksheets he/she has recorded the responses on, and give them to parent and child. Paraphrase what the facilitator has said about the conflict situation and what the parent and child have said to further exaggerate the drama. Then let the drama begin.

Thank you for that sharing. You certainly know how to cooperate together. If time allows, repeat the role playing with a new situation Did any other group take that same conflict situation in their foursome? Show us how you handled the same conflict in your own way. Who was the parent, who the child? Come sit here. Point to seats in center of group Facilitator, describe the conflict situation of this parent and child. Pause Recorder, give your worksheets to this parent and child. Again, paraphrase what facilitator has said and let the drama begin.

Thank you for that sharing. You too have learned well how to settle conflicts between yourselves.

We have some time left. What are you feeling about what we have done today?

It is suggested that you let the following principles be your guideline in responding to trainees:

1. Accept and reflect positive, negative, or mixed feelings expressed by the group about their experience in learning this method.

2. Encourage the discouraged by saying, "You are feeling discouraged about the worth of learning this method because it seems so different from what you are used to doing. I am not surprised. It is like learning a new language. Don't give up yet, stay with it. In that way, you will have two languages for settling conflict: the one you already have and this one, too."

3. If questions about any of the steps arise, ask the other group members what their thinking is.

Today we have been speaking about conflict and a method for resolving it. Conflicts were seen as those of need and those of value. Although both kinds can be resolved through the six-step method we learned today, it is in the conflict of need category, when our need clashes with someone else's need, that the conflict resolution method is most effective. Next time we meet we are going to learn how to use this method to help other people who are having a conflict together but which does not include us in the conflict, such as two youngsters fighting or siblings arguing.

CONFLICT RESOLUTION BETWEEN SELF AND ANOTHER PERSON
- WORKSHEET -

PLACE:_____ DAY: _____ PARTICIPANTS:_____

STEP I : Statement of Conflict As Self Viewed
    (Introducing your concern)

    a) Caring statement to other person :

    _____

    b) "I" Statement
      "I feel _____
      about _____

      because _____"

    c) Clarification of Need :

      what I would like (need, want)
    from you is_____
    _____

STEP II: Exploration of Conflict as Other Viewed
  (Listen & Reflecting feeling of other by making
  1-3 "you" statements)

    a) listen
    a) "you feel_____
      about_____
      because_____ "
    b) listen
    c) make another "you" statement
    d) listen
    e) make a third "you" statement.

STEP III: Emphatic Summarization of "You" and "I"
    statements , Mutual Need, and Invitation
    and Invitation to Problem solve.

    a) Empathic Summarization
      "So, you are feeling
    about_____
    because_____ "

        and

      " I am feeling _____
        about _____
        because_____ "

    b) State both your and other persons need
      "What "you would like is_____
      and I would like_____."

    c) Invite person to resolve conflict with you.

Let's put our heads together and come up with
some possible solutions.""

STEP IV : Generating all possible Solutions:
    and Choosing Best
  1.

  2.

  3.

  4.

  5.

  6.

STEP V: Implementing Chosen Solution

    a) Plan: _____
     .Who _____
     .Does What?_____
     .Day/Time _____
     .Other_____

    b)Follow up Evaluation

     .When?_____
     .Where?_____

STEP VI: Follow up Evaluation:

    a) .Who_____
     . Did (or did not) do What?_____
     . Day/Time agreed on_____
    b)Did solution work_____
    c) Why/Why not_____
    d) If solution worked suggest that
      process and solution were good.

    Acknowledge and praise parties.
    e) If solution did not work, suggest
      process was good but best possible
      solution was not chosen. Suggest
      reapplication of process.
    f) Begin process again or reconsider
      other stated alternative from STEP
      IV.

MODULE III: CONFLICT RESOLUTION

SESSION 3: Conflict Resolution in Practice

> **Objectives:**
> 1. To review conflict resolution between self and another.
> 2. To teach the application of conflict resolution to situations between individuals and groups.
>
> **Materials:**
> 1. Newsprint.
> 2. Three copies of the script located at the end of this session.
> 3. Copies of conflict resolution between other individuals, located at end of this session.

Reviewing the Six-Step Method of Conflict Resolution

We have been learning a method of resolving conflicts that any of us could use in a variety of situations as a parent, child, teacher, student, friend, employer, employee. When we are in conflict, someone else's behavior interferes with our achieving what we want or need; or our behavior interferes with what another person wants or needs. This is called a conflict of need. Both people need to resolve the conflict between them so that the needs of both are not obstructed although they may be modified. The process for achieving this is called conflict resolution and consists of six steps:

1. Statement of conflict as self-viewed
2. Statement of conflict as other-viewed
3. Empathic summarization of both sides/Invitation to problem-solve
4. Generating possible solutions and choosing best
5. Implementing chosen solution
6. Follow-up evaluation

Let's review a conflict situation briefly. Remember Jimmy who would shower each morning between 7 and 8 a.m.? Well, you remember his father needed to use the bathroom no later than 7 a.m. in order to get out of the house by 7:45 to catch his bus. It was hard for both of them to get up before 7 because they were both tired. So they both tended to use the bathroom at the same time. Thus they clashed and had a conflict of need. I want you to imagine yourself as Jimmy's father. You want to be fair to Jimmy since you recognize that he too has a problem of getting up before you. Plan to talk to Jimmy in a way that will win his cooperation in solving this situation together.

> Take trainees through each of the steps. Help trainees formulate responses to the steps. Include a consideration of a time and place for meeting with Jimmy that will be conducive to dialogue.

Helping Others Resolve Conflict

Helping other people in conflict to resolve their differences in mutually satisfying ways is a skill worth developing since conflicts of need abound in almost every interpersonal relationship. To develop the ability to help others resolve their conflicts rationally and peacefully is a sorely needed healing skill in a world of so much brokenness.

You have learned the six-step method of conflict resolution and how you might apply this method to situations where you are in conflict with another person. You have learned that you might begin to solve the conflict by stating it from your viewpoint in an empathic, self-expressive format. The process would then shift to exploring the conflict from the other person's point of view in an empathic listening/responding format.

In situations where others are in conflict and that conflict does not involve you, empathic self-expression is not called for, but an empathic listening/responding attention is to be directed to the parties in the conflict. As each party to the conflict feels understood, a sense of cooperation in settling the conflict will be energized. The skill of the mediator is vital here in creating the climate for this healing.

Let's take an example of simple conflict resolution where others are locked into a conflict of need.

Activity 1: Dealing with Sibling Conflict

In this activity two volunteers will read from a script which you will have xeroxed beforehand. The role-play script is located at the end of this session.

Edgar and Miguel are brothers. They both have received a new and expensive toy truck from their father. This has presented a problem for them since they both want to play with it at the same time. This is what is happening at the moment. Edgar has grabbed the truck away from Miguel and Miguel has retaliated. A fight is in progress when the father enters the room.

Say to your audience, "I will need two volunteers to play the parts of Miguel and Edgar. You will read from this script." Pause for volunteers to come forward and give them the scripts.

As Edgar and Miguel and I role-play the scene I described, I would like the rest of you to be alert to the way the father is using the six-step method of conflict resolution to help his sons. Note when the transition from one step to the next takes place. We will talk about this after the play is over.

Set the scene for Miguel, Edgar and yourself. Describe the living room where the fight takes place to the audience. Make the description as graphic as possible. Direct the volunteers to start arguing, then pushing, then fighting. Tell them to do this when you get to your position in the kitchen where you are reading the paper.

| After presentation of the role play ... | Thank you, Edgar and Miguel. So this was a case where two people were in conflict and a third party served as mediator. Did you see how the father used his empathic listening/responding skills with both Miguel and Edgar? Let's go through the steps and specify how the father went from one step to the next.

| Take each step and elicit responses, paraphrasing and acknowledging the analysis of the trainees. |

Activity 2: Application of Conflict-Resolution Steps for a Variety of Situations

Please get into foursomes as you did the last time. | Pause | There are a number of things I want you to do now:

1. Think of conflict or problem situations you are having with children, in your work, or even in your own families. A recorder in your group should write down your thoughts. Be brief. Do that now for five minutes. | Pause |

2. While keeping this list for future use, I want you, as a foursome, to now pick out one of the conflicts you stated and develop a story around it. In the story describe:

   a) the kind of person each character in the story is like
   b) two good things about each character in the story
   c) tell what the conflict is between the characters and how the conflict began

   | Repeat a, b and c |

   Do this for five minutes. | Pause |

3. Now that you have the story developed, two of you in the foursome are to volunteer to be the conflict characters and choose one of the other two in your foursome to be your friend. You will go aside with your friend and talk to him about the conflict you are having. Make sure you say specifically what the problem is, how you feel about it, and why you feel this way. The listening friends are to just listen and nod their head to acknowledge that they are listening. They are not to ask questions or give advice. Do that for five minutes. | Pause |

4. Now, all of you listening friends, put together what you have heard and reflect it back to your friend in our usual way: "So, you are feeling _____ about _____ because _____." Do that now for 3 minutes.

   | Pause |

5. Now, you listening friends will change places with the other listening friend. If you were the child's friend you will become the friend of the other party in the conflict and vice versa. Do the same thing in that role: listen and nod your head to acknowledge that you are listening. After a few minutes put together what you have heard from the person and reflect it back to him/her by saying: "So, you are feeling _____

about _____ because _____." Do that for 5 minutes.

6. Now that you two friends in each foursome know the points of view and feelings of both characters in the conflict, you are in a position to help mediate their problem. You will do this together. This is the way you will do it: One of the mediators will take a copy of the conflict resolution worksheet as summarized at the end of this chapter and guide the other mediator, Mediator B, throughout the six steps. Tell him what he is to do at Step 1, Step 2, and so on. Mediator A will follow the instructions he is hearing from Mediator B, but should use the knowledge he has of both people in the conflict to help bring about a settlement. Is there any question about this? Pause So, right now, you two mediators decide quickly who will be Mediator A and who will be Mediator B. Read the instructions and begin to carry out the mediation. Decide that right now. Pause

Mediator A, take up the worksheet and begin to tell Mediator B what to do. Mediator B, just follow what you are told. Do that now for 10 minutes.

Go around and help the foursome process this task

Please come back now to the whole group. Pause It takes a lot of time to learn what we are doing. I would like to encourage you to keep at it. Is there a group who feels they have a pretty good grasp of the conflict resolution process at this point and could demonstrate what you just did in your foursome?

If no one volunteers, lead a discussion around the trainees' feelings about what they experienced in the last exercise. Lead them to consider steps in the process which they found particularly difficult. When questions are asked, throw them back for the group's consideration, saying: "What do you think about that?"

The following activity is suggested, if time allows. If not, you may want to extend this session longer to accommodate it for the purpose of reinforcing the trainees' practice of conflict resolution in other real life situations. If this is not possible, go directly to the conclusion.

Activity 3: More Application of Conflict Resolution Steps to a Variety of Situations

Please assemble again in your groups of four. The recorder in each foursome is to read through the list of conflict situations we wrote down before. Each person in the foursome, including the recorder, is to select one of the conflict situations he or she originally gave as an example. If you did not give any, select one from the list that the recorder reads to you and make up a story about it. Do that now.

Now, each of you will describe your conflict situation, in turn, to the others in your foursome. You will do this one at a time. Ask someone in your group to be the other party to the conflict and role-play with you. Having heard you describe what the conflict is, the person who role-plays with you can then adapt him/herself to that role as they see fit. The other two of you in the group are to be the mediators of the conflict. Mediator A will do the actual mediation, according to the six-step method. Mediator B will coach Mediator A as much as needed using the Conflict Resolution Worksheet. I will come around and help out. We will have 45 minutes to do this. Take 10 minutes per person for processing each of your conflict situations.

> Circulate among teams and assist in the processing of this exercise. Ten minutes before the 45 minutes are up say: "We have 10 minutes more ... begin finishing up ... please come back to the larger group now."

Let's talk for a while about your experiences. What were you feeling or what questions do you have about what you have just done?

> Reflect all feelings acceptingly. Throw questions back for the group to answer and encourage those who learn this slowly by reminding all that we are learning a new language, one that becomes a habit with time and can be carried out naturally and easily. Encourage them to stick with it and practice often.

Today we have applied the conflict resolution method to a variety of situations involving children, playing them out here and practicing the technique with one another. Many situations in which conflict breaks out involve a group context. Such groups may be families, classrooms, or street groups. The conflict resolution method works effectively in these situations as well, although many more needs are expressed. In order to understand group situations, it is necessary to know something about group dynamics. That will be the subject of our next session.

Role-Play Script for Conflict Resolution

Father:	I see you are both quite upset at each other. Tell me what the problem is.
Miguel:	I was playing with my truck and he grabbed it away from me. I had it first.
F:	So that truck is really something you enjoy playing with. You are very upset that Edgar grabbed it from you because you had it first. Is that it?
M:	Yeah! It's mine.
F:	Okay. And Edgar, what is the problem here from your point of view?
Edgar:	It's not his truck. It's our truck and he played with it all morning. He hogs things. I have a right to play with it, too.
F:	So you too enjoy that truck and want to have fun with it. I am glad that you like it; that's why I bought it for both of you. But right now you are upset that Miguel wants to continue to play with it because he has had it all morning and you want your chance. Is that it?
E:	Yeah! He always hogs things.
F:	Whether or not either of you hogs toys is another issue right now. But let me see if I have this issue straight: Miguel, you are upset because Edgar grabbed the truck away from you and you want to keep playing with it because you enjoy it. And, Edgar, you are feeling it is unfair that Miguel play with it more than you. What you both want is equal time to play with and enjoy the truck. Is that what this problem is about?
E & M:	Yes.
F:	Let's put our heads together then and figure out how each of you can get a fair share of the truck. I will write each thought down on this paper. (Take newsprint and write out each thought in full view in numerical order.)
M:	He can ask me for it nicely.
E:	He can play with it an hour and then I can have it for an hour.
M:	I can play with it until I'm tired and then he can have it.
E:	That's not fair! See how he hogs things?
F:	That's a solution you don't like at all. That's okay. Right now you can come up with any kind of solution you want; it doesn't matter if anyone likes it or not. We will vote on an acceptable solution later.
E:	I can play with it all the time.
M:	I can play with it all the time.

E: (To father) You can decide for us who will play with it.

M: We can play with it together.

E: When Miguel wants it and I'm playing with it, he can have it by paying me 5 cents.

M: (To father) You can buy another one and then each of us will have our own.

F: Okay! That's a nice list to choose from. Let's take each one and see if we can choose one that is agreeable to all of us. We will cross out the ones that are not acceptable to us and put stars next to those we like.

M: I like #1.

E: Me, too.

F: We will start with that one, then.

M: I like #2 also.

E: I do too.

F: So we will start with that one as well.

E: I don't like #3. It's not fair to me.

F: So we will cross that one out.

M: And I don't like #4, either.

F: So there goes another cross-out.

M: I don't like #5, either.

F: Another cross-out.

M: I like #6.

E: I do too.

F: I'm not comfortable with that because I want you boys to learn to settle things without me. After all, this is your problem, not mine. It would be mine only if I too wanted to play with the truck. Because I am not comfortable with this, we will cross it out.

M: I like #7, but Edgar has to play my way.

E: I don't like that suggestion at all.

F: Another cross-out, then.

M: No deal with me for #8.

F: Another cross-out.

M: Gee! Would you go along with #9, Dad?

E: That would be neat, Dad.

F:	You'd really like that, wouldn't you? But I am not able to do that.
E:	So we have two stars: #1 and #2.
E:	I don't want #1 because Miguel will think he can have it just by asking nicely anytime he wants.
F:	So, on second thought, you are not comfortable with that suggestion. So we will cross it out, unless you both want to talk about it some more.
M:	No. Cross it out.
E:	I really like the idea of me having the truck for an hour and Miguel having it for an hour.
F:	Okay! So the hour-by-hour method is the solution. How should we arrange the hour on this?
M:	Edgar can play with it when he comes home from school and then I can have it.
F:	So that means Edgar can have it from 3 to 4, and you, Miguel, can have it from 4 to 5. Then Edgar can have it again from 5 to 6. Looks like Miguel will have it on the even hours and Edgar will have it on the odd hours. How does that sound?
M:	That's neat!
E:	It's okay with me!
F:	Good! Let's check in two days to see how the solution is working for you.

CONFLICT RESOLUTION BETWEEN TWO OTHER PERSONS

- WORKSHEET-

PRESTEP: Mediator's Recognition of conflict and Feeling State, e.g. 'I see you are both very upset, angry, afraid,etc. What is the problem here?

STEP I: Statement of Conflict of Person#1
(Listen and Reflect feelings of person 1)

 1. Listening and making 1-3 'you' statements
 (e.g. 'you feel------------------------------
when----------------------becausse-------------------.'
 a) listen
 b) make 'you' statement
 c) listen
 d) make another 'you' statement
 e) listen
 f) make a third 'you' statement

 2. Clarification of need (e.g. 'what is it that you
 would like from him/her (person 2)

STEP II: Statement of Conflict of Person#2
(Listen and reflect feelings of person 2)

 1. Listening and making 1-3 'you' statements
 (e.g. 'you feel --------------------when----------
 ---------------because-------------------------.)

 a) listen
 b) make 'you' statement
 c) listen
 d) make another 'you' statement
 e) listen
 f) make a third 'you' statement

 2. Clarification of Need
 . What is it that you would like
 from him/her(person#1)?

STEP III: 1. Summarize Feelings of Person
#1 and Person #2 and restate their need

 . So you (person #1)are feeling------------
When---------------, because--------------------------,
and what you would like is--------------------'
 .'you (person#2) are feeling-----------------,
when-------------------, because-------------------------.
and what you would like is ----------------------,
---.

 2. Invite both persons to problem solve
'Let's put our heads together and come up with some
possible solutions.'

STEP IV: Generating all Possible Solutions
and Choosing Best

 1.

 2.

 3.

 4.

 5.

 6.

STEP V: Implementation of Chosen Solution

PLAN: .Who?--------------
 . Does What?-------------------
 . Day/Time----------------------
 . Other-----------------------

STEP VI: Follow up Evaluation: When-------Where__
 a) Who-------------
 . Did (or did not) do what?--------------------

 . Day/Time agreed on------------------------
 b) Did solution work? ------------------------
 c) Why/Why not?------------------------------
 d) If solution worked, suggest that process and
 solution were good. Acknowledge and
 praise parties.
 e) If solution did not work, suggest process
 was good but best possible solution was
 not chosen. Suggest reapplication of
 process.
 f) Begin process again or reconsider other
 stated alternative from STEP IV.

MODULE IV: GROUP DYNAMICS

SESSION 1: Group Life and Leadership

Objectives:

    1. To define a group concept.

    2. To teach types of group leadership.

Materials:

    1. Pads and pencils for trainees.

    2. Two newsprints prepared in following formats:

Purpose	Leader	Members	Helped Most

Authoritarian	Laissez-Faire	Democratic

What is a Group?

We have been talking at great length about conflict resolution. We will learn now to apply conflict resolution to groups. But first, without looking at the poster, who thinks they can describe the six steps? | Pause |

Activity 1: Review of Six-Step Method

Let's have another review of the six steps. This time we will go around the room. Each of you will describe the step after the one just mentioned. You can refer to the poster if you blank out. Here, _____,you begin. Describe Step 1.

> Go around the room having each participant define steps in succession.

That was terrific! It seems like you are getting better and better at this.

Many situations where conflict breaks out are in group contexts: families, classrooms, neighborhoods, gangs, and other groups. While the conflict resolution steps apply there as well, there are additional forces at work in groups that can make conflict resolution more difficult, while, at other times, even easier than conflict resolution among fewer people. These forces are called group dynamics. Therefore, we are going to learn about working effectively with groups over the next couple of sessions.

Activity 2: Helpful Group Components

I would like you to think of a group you have been in at some time that really helped you. It could be a group where you went to learn something or a group that had a task to be accomplished or a group where you went for help in solving some problems you were having—a therapy, counseling or guidance group. If you have never been in a group, think of some kind of group you would like to be in to help you learn something or get help with a concern you have. As you think of this group, I want you to consider four points. You can jot down your thoughts on your pads if you wish in order to remember them. Think of that group now. ┃Pause┃ Get in touch with the group and be in it again in your imagination. Consider these questions:

1. What was the purpose of the group?
2. Look at the leader: What is the leader doing in the group?
3. Look at the members: What are the members doing in the group?
4. What was done or said in the group that helped you most of all?

Take 5 minutes to think of the group in reference to these questions.

> Allow time for this processing. When the 5 minutes are over, hang up the newsprint and use it to record the members' ideas in the sharing which will follow.
>
> | Purpose | Leader | Member | Helped Most |
> |---------|--------|--------|-------------|
> | | | | |

Take another minute to finish up your thoughts.... What were some purposes of the groups you thought of? ┃Record on newsprint under Purpose┃

What did leaders do in groups? ┃Pause and record┃

What did members do? ┃Pause and record┃

What was done or said that helped you most of all? ┃Record┃

Activity 3: Unhelpful Group Components

Now I want you to sit back and think of a group you were in that was the opposite. It was neither helpful nor a place where you could learn. As you think of this group, I want you to consider the same four points.

1. What was the purpose of the group?
2. Look at the leader: What did the leader do in the group that was not helpful?

3. Look at the members: What did they do in the group that was not helpful?
4. What was said or done that made you not able to be helped by this group?

Take 5 minutes to think of the group in reference to these questions.

> Allow time for this processing. Prepare newsprint to be displayed with the same format as before. When the 5 minutes are over, hang up the second newsprint and use it to record the members' ideas in the sharing which will follow.

What were the purposes of the groups you thought of this time? |Record| What did the leader do in the group that was not helpful? |Record| What did the members do in the group that was not helpful? |Record| What was said or done that made you unable to be helped by this group? |Record|

> These exercises will probably articulate the main themes of a good group experience, namely, a defined purpose, democratic leadership, and mutually helpful group interaction. You will be summarizing these themes to the group and using these thoughts for your lecture.

As you can see from this sharing, it is clear that a helpful group needs to have a purpose, have a leader who the members feel is fair, understanding and invites participation, and have members who help each other. Your thinking conforms to what the experts also have to say on effective group management.

A group can be defined as two or more people who interact with each other for a common purpose under a common leadership. Three components identify the presence of a group: (1) interaction among its members, (2) a common purpose, and (3) a common leadership. If three components are not present, you have a collection of individuals, but not a group. Let's take some examples.

Activity 4: When is a Group a Group?

Take your pads and write down your answers to the following questions. Your answers are yours, not to be marked or scored. See how you do. Here are the questions:

1. Are people traveling together on a subway car going to Times Square a group?
2. Are children in a classroom a group?
3. Are tenants in a building a group?
4. Are boy scouts having a meeting a group?
5. Are mothers in a meeting with a guidance counselor to talk together about their children's problems a group?
6. Is a family meeting with a lawyer to discuss divorce proceedings a group?

7. Are people participating together in worship led by a priest, minister or rabbi a group?
8. Are we a group?

Let's take each of these examples again. | Repeat | Now give your point of view as to whether each example demonstrates a group, remembering to judge this by the presence of three components: (1) people interacting, (2) for a common purpose, and (3) under common leadership.

Go over the examples again, using the following answers as a guide:

1. No (no common interaction)
2. No (interaction is student/teacher usually, student/student/ teacher). Yes (if teacher runs class through interactional methods of teaching)
3. No (no interaction, no common leadership)
4. Yes (if the leader allows interaction)
5. Yes (assuming guidance counselor is encouraging interaction and not merely "teaching" or "giving" answers)
6. Yes (if lawyer is allowing interaction to flow). No (if lawyer is directing responses to parents and giving advice)
7. No (no member interaction)
8. Yes (interaction, common purpose, and common leadership)

Types of Group Leadership

There was a team of social psychologists working under a famous scientist, Kurt Lewin, back in the 1930's. They studied the effects of three kinds of leadership on the behavior of four groups of 11-year-old children. The three kinds of leadership were democratic, authoritarian, and laissez-faire. The authoritarian leaders gave orders and commands, planned activities, praised and criticized the children's work according to how they felt and allowed no discussion about decisions. The laissez-faire leaders gave the group freedom to do whatever they wanted, were friendly but gave no direction or suggestions to the group at all. The democratic leaders encouraged group discussion and decision-making and also contributed their thoughts to the discussions. Motion pictures were made of the groups' responses to the different types of leadership so that social scientists could determine the effects of different leadership forms on the behavior of children. From these observations, the scientists were able to discover some psychological tendencies about the part group leadership plays in determining group behavior. Here is what they found:

1. The authoritarian-led groups stirred two kinds of behaviors in the children: (a) apathy, submissiveness, and dependence of the members on the leader; and (b) rebelliousness, aggression and opposition toward the leader and the discharge of aggression toward some outside group.

2. The laissez-faire-led groups achieved very few of the goals of

the group. In fact, when the leader was absent, the children achieved more through their own leadership than with him.

3. The democratic leadership resulted in more personal, friendly, mutually helpful interactions, a mutual respect for individual differences, a group mindedness, and a steady output of work whether the leader was present with the group or out of the room.

From this study and innumerable others since that time, it seems that a general principle to follow if you want a group to achieve behavioral or task-centered goals is to provide effective democratic-type leadership. When groups really achieve the purpose for which they meet, it is primarily because of the climate created through effective democratic leadership.

Activity 5: Types of Group Leadership

I want you to imagine you are a group of sixth-graders in a classroom. You are going to go on a class trip. Each of you has an idea of a place you would like to go because you all have different interests. Think about where you might like to go that you feel would be fun, enjoyable, and relaxing. Your teacher announces that it is the time of year when class trips are planned. Tomorrow we will be talking about it. It is now tomorrow. You are the class. I am the teacher.

> You will play the part of the authoritarian, laissez-faire, and democratic leader, in that order. Arrange your words and mannerisms to conform to the different types of leadership to give the trainees the experience of all three types. Exaggerate if you wish. Allow 15 minutes for this activity, 5 minutes per leadership style.

a) In the authoritarian type, announce that we will be going on our class trip to Central Park. They should bring lunch the next day, $1.00, and baseball equipment. If any questions are asked, decide the answer but promote no interaction.

b) In the laissez-faire type, take no leadership. Ask them where they want to go. Give no direction and let their thinking freewheel at random. At the end, say it sounds like they want to go to (wherever the last person mentioned).

c) In the democratic type, give direction by following the six-step method of conflict resolution; invite their suggestions; write them down, help them discuss pros and cons, giving equal recognition and respect to each suggestion. Summarize where the thinking is from time to time; then call for a vote.

Alright, let's finish up our role playing. I would like you to react now to what you were feeling in the different types of leadership you experienced from me.

Put newsprint up in the following format:		
Authoritarian	Laissez-Faire	Democratic

What were you feeling when I was an authoritarian leader? Record on newsprint

What were you feeling when I was a laissez-faire leader? Record

What were you feeling when I was a democratic leader? Record

So, you are saying that you felt best and accomplished more when I was a democratic leader. We are going to learn about developing your capacities as effective democratic leaders to use in task-centered educational work and counseling groups.

The group skills material contained in the following session is lengthy and may take one to two sessions. If there is sufficient time left in the present session and you wish to begin the group skills session, aim to teach Skill Steps 1 and 2 as described in the following session, leaving Skill Steps 3 and 4 for the next time.

If you choose to end the session now and not begin the group skills training, go directly to the following:

We began learning today about groups: what makes a group a group (two or more people interacting with each other for a common purpose and under a common leadership), and the types of leadership (authoritarian, laissez-faire, democratic) that can be used with groups.

At the next session we will learn specific skills that will be helpful in mastering the art of effective and therapeutic group leadership.

MODULE IV: GROUP DYNAMICS

SESSION 2: Group Leadership Skills

Objectives:

1. To teach four effective group skills:

   - Attention to purpose
   - Leader-member bonding
   - Member-member bonding
   - Techniques for stimulating group interaction

2. To demonstrate the application of these skills to a simulated counseling group.

Materials:

1. Paper and pencils for trainees.

2. Handouts on "Group Process" and "Overview of Group Process" located at end of session, to be xeroxed by Trainer.

3. Newsprint prepared in following formats:

Group Skill Steps	Techniques of Group Interaction
1. Maintaining group purpose 2. Promoting leader-member bonding and interaction 3. Promoting member-member bonding and interaction 4. Stimulation of group interaction	1. Elicit feedback 2. Direct members to talk to each other 3. Explore details 4. Reinforce positive responses 5. Reframe 6. Clarify polarities 7. Establish connections 8. Interpret hidden agendas 9. Apply skills of conflict resolution 10. Summarize 11. Set tasks

---

Group Skills Based on Democratic Leadership

We have been saying that a group is two or more people interacting with each other around a common purpose. Of the three types of leadership (authoritarian, laissez-faire, and democratic), it appears that the democratic leadership elicits more positive, cooperative, and responsible responses, particularly as related to interpersonal growth.

As the leadership of the group goes, so goes the group. A hostile and abusive leader stirs up the same emotions in his group members. They will act this hostility out toward him or find others to scapegoat. A loving, accepting, but limit-setting leader elicits mutual helpfulness and controls among his group members. An effective group leader creates a climate among people where self-worth, cognitive or emotional growth, learning and mutual helpfulness come together for member satisfaction and task achievement. There are four general skills an effective, democratically oriented group leader needs to learn in order to lead a group well:

> | Put up newsprint on Group Skill Steps |

Here is a list of four basic group skill concepts we will be talking about and learning to develop through our exercises:

Step 1:   Maintenance of group purpose

Step 2:   Promotion of leader-member bondedness and interaction

Step 3:   Promotion of member-member bondedness and interaction

Step 4:   Stimulation of group opinions

> | Comment briefly on the four skills in the following way: |

Step 1:   Refers to the skill of clearly defining the purpose of the group and maintaining the group's focus on this purpose continuously.

Step 2:   Refers to the skill to develop personal bonds of relationship with each group member individually either before or during group sessions.

Step 3:   Refers to the skill to stimulate personal bonds among group members.

Step 4:   Refers to the skill to stimulate group opinions and interactions in helpful ways leading to goal achievement.

I want to teach you the skills needed in all four steps. To do this clearly, I am going to distribute a handout to you on "Group Process."

> | Distribute Handout I located at end of this module, to members. Place a handout on table next to you for reference. |

Although in practice, each of these four steps does not necessarily separate in such a logical fashion, for our learning purpose, we will be separating group process into these four steps since they represent the component parts of making and developing group life. We will learn these four steps in the following way:

1. I will ask you to refer to your handout for each step.

2. I will briefly describe the concept involved in each step.

3. We will role-play the examples on the handout in order to get a feel of the concepts in practice. Keep in mind that the leaders' interventions are exaggerated to make teaching points.

We will begin now to learn the four component parts or steps of making and developing group life.

Skill Step 1: Group Purpose

Since each step is described in the handout you have received, please place the Skill Step 1 handout in front of you. [Pause] You will notice in Skill Step 1, under Technique, that the leader has to do four things:

1. The leader has to clearly define the purpose of the group. That means that someone is keeping the group on its course. Without someone to keep the group to its focus, groups tend to wander, become fragmented, distracted, or regress.

2. Establish the basic rules. This means the leader has to spell out the basic requirements that people have to agree to in order to make a group work. People have to come regularly, be helpful, express their points of view, talk in turn, and not attack each other. Without rules, the group can become anarchic.

3. The leader has to invite the members to talk together about any concerns related to the group's purpose. They should not talk about other issues or concerns not related to the purpose of the group's existence.

4. The leader has to set limits empathically. That means that when members start changing the group's purpose or becoming disruptive in their behavior, the leader has to bring them back to the focal point by restating the group's purpose or the basic group rules.

Activity 1: Group Focus and Rules

You will now form groups of five in the following way:

> Count off from your left and go clockwise around the group: 1,2,3,4,5, ...1,2,3,4,5, ... and so on.

Remember the number I gave you and arrange yourselves in groups now. [Pause]

Look at your Skill Step 1 handout under Example. You will note that, except for the section on establishing group rules, there are five examples to illustrate each technique. You are going to role-play these examples. Use the example next to the number I gave you as your script. Read the example to yourself and then in turn imagine you are a group leader dealing with a group like the one described in your example. You can read it as it is written or say it in your own words to your group members. When your turn comes, read all the responses next to your number on both pages. Everyone will read the group rules section. Here is an example of what I mean. Pretend I am number 1 in all group examples in this group here [Indicate the group to your left] This is what I would do:

- 147 -

> Join group to your left and recite all examples preceded by #1 on the handout. Do this dramatically, especially the examples under (d) and (e).

a) The purpose of this group is to talk together about where to go on the class trip. [Pause]

b) Groups work best if certain rules are followed:

- regular attendance is maintained
- only one person at a time is allowed to speak
- everyone expresses their thoughts or feelings about the subject being discussed
- everyone helps each other out
- no physical or verbal attacks are allowed
- what we talk about here stays here [Pause]

c) What are some of your ideas on a class trip? [Pause]

d) It seems that something is going on here that is not related to this group discussion. It seems to be getting in the way of our work together here. Can we talk about this briefly in order to clear the air and get back to our focus, which is the class trip? [Pause]

e) You will have to find a way of controlling yourself. It interrupts what we are here for. [Pause]

Take turns as I did, have fun with this, exaggerate and dramatize with your group members and make your responses come alive, even if they are pre-written. Do this now for 10 minutes. I will come around and help out as needed.

> Circulate around the different groups, coaching and monitoring the process to assure its being learned.

Take 2 minutes more. [Pause] Please come back now to the larger group. Although I want to move on to Step 2 in order not to interrupt the flow from step to step, I do invite questions or reactions about what you have just done so that we may deal with it at least briefly. [Pause for responses from group]

Skill Step 2: Leader-Member Bonding

Moving on to Skill Step 2, please place that handout in front of you. [Pause] You will notice in Skill Step 2 under Technique, that the leader has to bond himself with each group member. He does this in three ways:

1. He should relate empathically with each group member through paraphrasing. That means he says in his own words what each member says. That helps each member feel the leader's friendliness and understanding.

2. He should personalize his relationship with each group member. That means calling them by name and referring to each by name often.

3. He should foster his own personal identification with each member. That means he should find things he might have in common with each member and let them know it. This helps each member feel more attached or bonded to the leader. Two ways are suggested:

   a) Share a personal interest or life situation that is similar to the group member's.

   b) Act a bit like the member in the way you talk or sit or move. That is what is meant by adopting personal or cultural mannerisms.

Activity 2: Leader-Member Bonding in a Parents' Group Role-Play

Look at your Skill Step 2 handout. You will see that there is a running script used as an example of the techniques. This script is about a group of parents meeting with a counselor to talk together about problems they are having with their children. There are six parents, four mothers and two fathers, and one leader. I will role-play the leader. I need six volunteers. Who will be Maria? Who will be Miguel? Who will be Edna? Who will play Nelson? Ruth? Anna? | Pause for responses | Please come with me into a circle in the middle of the room with your script. | Pause for this | Please take a minute to read over your part to yourself. | Pause |

What I would like the rest of you to do is be alert to the three techniques I will be using with these parents. Remember, I want each parent to feel empathically understood so I will paraphrase or repeat what they say, call them by name personally, and find something each one of them and I have in common in order for them to feel safe with me.

> Enact the role play according to the script. Be dramatic and involved. This will also help the volunteers to dramatize their parts. When the role play is completed, the volunteers should return to the larger group. Then continue, saying:

Although I want to move on to the next step, in order not to interrupt the flow, I do invite questions or reactions about this little play to deal with at least briefly.

> Pause for responses from group

Skill Step 3: Member-Member Bonding

Moving ahead to Step 3, please place that handout in front of you. In Step 3 the leader needs to help the group members bond with each other. It is through the interaction that they have with each other that the work of the group will be accomplished.

After forming personal bonds himself with each group member, the leader now has to link the members with each other and help them to help each other under his leadership. The leader does this in three ways:

1. He should remember anything one member says that is similar to what another member says and make this known to each. This is what is meant by fostering common identifications.

2. He should call attention to people's similarities through continued reference to members' personal names. That is what is meant by personalizing member bondings.

3. He can warm up the group members to each other through "ice-breaking" interpersonal exercises. This is optional, but it might be useful with inhibited groups or groups of children or adolescents where play is still a vital part of the communication process.

Activity 3: Member-Member Bonding in a Parents' Group Role-Play

Would the "parents" join me again with your Skill Step 3 handout? Pause for this response As the volunteer "parents" and I go over this script, I would like the rest of you to be alert to three techniques I will be using with these parents to bond them to each other. Look for the way I find:

- Similarities between them and refer to this verbally.
- My continuous calling of them by name.
- The warm-up exercise I use to help them get to know each each other better as people.

Enact the role play according to the script, as in the previous role play. When the role play is completed, the volunteers should return to the larger group. Then continue, saying:

Although I want to move on promptly to Step 4 in order not to interrupt the flow, I do invite questions or reactions about this little role-play to deal with at least briefly.

Pause for responses from group

Skill Step 4: Stimulation of Group Interaction

Moving ahead to Skill Step 4, please place that handout in front of you. You will notice that the leader now aims to use a variety of techniques to stimulate the group members to interact helpfully with each other. But this does not happen by chance. The leader has to learn skills to facilitate this kind of interaction. Eleven specific skills are suggested in the Step 4 handout which a group leader can use to help the group members interact helpfully with each other. These 11 techniques are:

Post prepared newsprint with 11 techniques enumerated. Do not include the definitions on the newsprint. Elaborate the definitions verbally.

1. *Elicit feedback:* This is an invitation to the group members as a whole or any one individual to respond or to react personally to a statement just made.

2. *Direct members to address each other:* This means that the leader discourages members from talking to him or through him, but encourages or directs them to talk directly to each other.

3. *Explore details:* This means that the leader helps members explain themselves with specificity and concreteness. Vagueness and abstractions are not helpful and should be concretized. Emphatic usage of clarifying inquiries is used which gets at the "what," "who," "where," and "why" of communication. Asking for examples is also clarifying.

4. *Reinforce positive responses:* This means that the leader attends to positive and helpful elements between group members and reinforces such communication through acknowledgement, praise, support, and appreciation.

5. *Reframe:* This means that the leader takes any negative comments and reformulates the words to give them a positive connotation. For example, instead of saying to a person that he is stubborn, one could say that he has an unusual ability to persevere; instead of saying that a group of teenagers are uncooperative in confronting each other, one could say to them that they are really very kind to each other in not wanting to hurt each other's feelings.

6. *Clarify the development of polarities:* This means that the leader, seeing the different points of view emerging in the group, specifically pinpoints the gamut of them in summary form. For example, "So, on the one hand many people here feel that parents should punish their children physically; others here are totally opposed to this, and few others feel both ways at different times. What about the rest of you, what is your thinking on this?"

7. *Establish connections:* This means that the leader, hearing or observing similarities between past behaviors and present ones or seeing certain relationship patterns emerging in the group sessions, suggests a connection related to a present problem. For example, a boy who talks frequently of his run-in with older women teachers, women neighbors, his older sisters and an older woman secretary in his school office, may not see the interrelational thread, the common connection in all these examples. Pointing this pattern out to him empathically works to es-

tablish connections.

8. *Interpret:* This means that the leader helps members to understand their behaviors or symptoms from a different point of view than that to which they are accustomed. Interpretation is based on seeing psychological purpose in behavior. Interpretation "suggests" an alternative way of perceiving one's situation. For example, a father who says that his son needs to be physically punished whenever he misbehaves because it is the only way to drive the devil out of him, and then talks of his own father doing the same to him, may be asked what he himself wanted from his father.

If he says he wanted his father to take him out more, play ball with him, talk to him, then it would be logical to piece this connection together by verbalizing the connection and then saying: "Could it be that your child is misbehaving in order to get attention from you in the only way he knows, while what he really wants is merely what you wanted also from your own father?" This "interpretation" aims to give the father a new way of perceiving his son's misbehavior, an alternative to viewing it as the devil working in the child.

9. *Apply conflict resolution skills:* This means bringing the group as a whole or an individual member through the six-step method of problem solving spoken of in previous sessions. This includes:

   a) problem definition as defined by one party to the conflict
   b) problem definition as defined by other parties to the conflict
   c) generation of alternative solutions
   d) choosing a solution
   e) putting the solution into practice
   f) follow-up evaluation

   It is particularly effective to concretize the conflict through role playing (sociodrama).

10. *Summarize:* In task-or-problem-centered groups, summarizing means that the salient points of the group's progress in achieving its aims and the process by which this occurs should:

    a) be reviewed at the beginning of the session
    b) be summarized from time to time throughout the session
    c) have a summary closure at the end of the session

11. *Agree on Tasks:* This means that a "contract" is made by the group members or any individual group member to carry out a specifically designated activity related to the purpose for which the group member is in the group. For example, a father in a parent counseling group agrees to play ball with his son on Monday, Wednesday, and Friday evenings from 7 to 8 p.m. in the school yard.

**Activity 4: Interactional Techniques in
a Parents' Group Role-Play**

We are going to continue our "parent counseling" group to demonstrate the use of these interactional techniques. But to make sure our "original" parents here have a chance to be observers to the techniques also, I would like to ask that other people volunteer this time for the role-playing. Who will play Maria? Miguel? Edna? Nelson? Ruth? Anna? [Pause] Please come with me into a circle in the middle of the room with your script.

What I would like the rest of you to do while the play is going on is to be alert to the techniques I will be using with the "parents" which are listed here on the newsprint. Whenever I speak, try to determine which of the techniques I am using. Then briefly look at your handout script to check your answer against the correct one listed in the Techniques column on the left. In doing this, try not to lose the flow of your involvement in observing the group's interaction.

> Enact the role play according to the script as in previous role plays. When the role play is completed, the volunteers should return to the larger group. Then continue, saying:

That was a long session, wasn't it? I would like to hear your responses, questions, comments about this ... from both actors and observers.

> Pause for responses. Allow sufficient time to process the responses so that there is closure to this exercise. Closure for this part is particularly important since many members may have, directly or vicariously, gotten in touch with some deeper sentiments within themselves through the role play. This should be expected, as role play often elicits such response.

I am going to give you another handout now which summarizes our learning experience in group process.

> Distribute Handout II: "Overview of Group Process"

This brings us to the end of our formal training in group dynamics and group skill building. Becoming effective group leaders takes a great deal of practice with supervised assistance. What we have done here, hopefully, is to open your minds to the power contained in groups and taught you the essential steps involved in helping a collection of people become a group to achieve their purpose.

You have seen how we have taken all those skills learned in previous sessions and helped the group members use them with each other, particularly the skills of empathic communication and conflict resolution.

Developing a healing community, which is the ultimate aim of this training curriculum, brings together all the skills learned previously, both individual and small group, and applies them to the building and maintaining of a large group of people who meet regularly for the purpose of mutual helpfulness. The following module -- a lengthy one -- introduces the concept of the therapeutic community, explains ways of integrating all previously learned healing skills within this large group and teaches some useful methods of stimulating healing energies in large groups of children.

Our work together for the next and final three sessions in this training curriculum, therefore, will focus on methods of building and maintaining a healing community for children.

GROUP PROCESS
Skill Step 1: Group Purpose

Keeping the group on its purpose provides the structure necessary to accomplish its aims. Without focus, a group tends to wander, go onto other themes, regress, become fragmented, and eventually dissolve. To prevent these happenings, the first task of an effective leader is to define the purpose of the group clearly and maintain its focus from beginning to end. Maintaining such a focus requires the ability to clearly articulate the group's purpose and not allow its members to change focus or be disruptive to the group process. The focus becomes real for the members when the leader invites each one to articulate his/her specific concerns regarding the group's purpose.

Technique	Examples
1) Clearly define purpose of group	1. The purpose of this group is to talk together about where to go on the class trip. (Task-centered purpose) 2. The reason we are meeting together is to figure out ways of cutting down the noise in the class. (Task-centered purpose) 3. This group is meeting to figure out ways of getting more people involved in the evening center. (Task-centered purpose) 4. We are meeting together to talk about methods of understanding and handling children's misbehavior. (Task or therapy-centered) 5. In this group we are going to be talking about becoming more aware of ourselves in order to get along better with others. (Therapy-centered group)
2) Establish basic group rules	Groups like this work best if certain procedures are followed: 1. Regular attendance is maintained. 2. One person at a time speaks. 3. Individual thoughts or feelings about a subject are allowed expression. 4. Members help each other out. 5. No physical or verbal attacks are allowed. 6. What is talked about in the group remains confidential. (Therapy group)
3) Invite members to express specific and individual concerns related to group's purpose	1. What are some of your ideas on a class trip? 2. Who has an idea about ways of cutting down noise in the room? 3. And so, you see it is important to get more people involved in our evening center.... 4. I wonder who would care to tell us something about the problem he/she is having with their children? 5. In this therapy group, it is important that you share your impressions of each other together. What are some of your impressions at this point?

4) Set limits, empathically, for:
- Members who change focus
- Members who clash with other members

1. It seems something is going on here that is not related to this group discussion. It seems to be getting in the way of our work together here. Can we talk about this briefly in order to clear the air and get back to our focus which is the class trip?
2. That thought about noise pollution is very interesting. But how can we handle noise in this classroom?
3. The two of you have a lot of feeling about abortion, obviously well thought through. However, the purpose of this group is to figure out ways to get more people involved in the evening center.
4. Maybe that concern you have about housing is something we can talk about individually, but right now, can you share more about your child?
5. That is a very interesting thought you have about politics, but what about the politics between all of you in this group, since our focus here is on your impression of each other.

- Emotional outbursts and disruptive behavior

1. You will have to find a way of controlling yourself. It interrupts what we are here for.
2. What is going on here? Why are we here?
3. I am not surprised that you have so much feeling about this, it is a controversial point and many people feel similarly. However, the reason why we are here is to discuss what we want to do about the lack of heat in this building.
4. That kind of behavior is out of place here.
5. You are restless. What is happening?
6. I am concerned about the talking on the side that is going on. Is anything wrong? Perhaps we're losing you and with good reason. Can we deal with this in order to keep you involved with us?

Skill Step 2: Leader-Member Bonding

The group leader represents authority to the group members. This position stirs up a variety of feelings in the group members regarding past authorities in their lives, including feelings of dependency, rebellion, fear, distrust, respect, antagonism, expectation, cooperation, resistance, and so on. The group members will tend to respond to the leader with similar feelings. Such feelings will interfere with the group members' ability to feel comfortable, safe, open-minded, and secure with the leader. Because these responses are individual, the leader needs to make his own individual bonding with each group member. To offset the negative effect of these "transference" reactions, each member needs to experience the leader as a friendly, fair, understanding person who in some way shares things in common with them. The group leader has to become part of a "kinship" system with members. As the group members feel this bondedness with the leader in Step 2, he can then help them form bonds with each other in step 3.

Technique	Example: A Parent Counseling Group
Communicate empathically (paraphrase)	Leader: In this parents' group we will be talking about parents' concerns while raising their children. I would like to get to know each of you, your name, a little about your children and some of the concerns you would like to hear discussed in this group. If someone would begin, we can go around from there.
Personalize people to each other	Maria: My name is Maria and I have three children, all teenagers now. My problem is with the middle one who is failing in school, has no friends, stays in his room all the time and listens constantly to rock at top volume. It's as though he is in another world. The constant sound is unbearable to me, not to mention my anger toward him. The other two are fine, but this one ....
Foster leader-member identification	Leader: So, Maria you are really confused by this boy, really puzzled, and would like to understand what's going on with him. I can particularly appreciate the volume getting to you since I too am very sensitive to sound. I have a teenager who likes volume, also.
	Miguel: My name is Miguel. I have two boys ages 7 and 11. They are good boys but they can never sit still. I get complaints from their teachers because they don't pay attention in school; they are always running and getting into things at home. My wife work nights and I work days so we can make ends meet. But these kids really wear me out. I want to know how to get them to listen to me and their teachers and behave themselves. I lose so much time going to their school that I have no time for myself.

Communicate empathically (paraphrase)	**Leader:** I am glad to meet you, Miguel. You have two boys who really give you a run for your money. But you feel now your money is running out. It is hard to manage two active boys all by yourself nights, leaving no time for yourself. I can appreciate that from my own experience two years ago when my wife was in the hospital and I had to manage work and taking care of the children by myself. I really got burned out.
Personalize people to each other	**Edna:** I'm Edna and I have a three-year-old girl. I want to know what to do about her clinging to me when I leave to go to school in the mornings. It is a real heartbreaker. She cries and carries on and I get really upset even though I've tried to explain to her that mommy has to go to school each day. You see, I'm finishing my college work in music with a major in piano and it's going really great, but lately I've been affected by Nancy's clinging. It seems to have become worse a month ago when I began staying at school each day to practice piano an extra hour for my final performance exam. I can't do this at home at night because we live in a small apartment and the neighbors have been complaining about my practicing late at night.
Foster leader-member identification	**Leader:** So, Edna, you are feeling torn between wanting to be available to Nancy, take advantage of this opportunity to finish off your music degree and be fair to your neighbors. It has particularly become a problem in the past month because you are away an extra hour each day for piano practice. Being a pianist myself and living in a small apartment I can really appreciate the problems that can be present with neighbors, especially those who knock on walls.
	Nelson: I'm Nelson and I have six children, three boys and three girls between the ages of 5 and 14. They fight so much among themselves; the young ones come running to me or my wife to say the older ones are picking on them. It is so hard to get them to cooperate together. It ends up with me always having to get out the belt to keep them in line. My wife and I went to the movies the other night to see "Ordinary People." Because we don't have those kinds of problems, it made us think how lucky we really were. We talked for hours about the picture afterwards.
Communicate empathically (paraphrase)	**Leader:** Nelson, it's good to have you with us. You too feel frustrated trying to get a lot of people living together to get along with each other. You really don't like using the belt to accomplish this but at least it works, you feel. My wife and I saw the picture too and loved it. We too sat for hours talking the same way you describe.
Personalize people to each other	**Ruth:** I'm Ruth and I live with my 16-year-old daughter. I am single so it is just the two of us. You can't tell her anything; she knows best and a suggestion to her is like giving her poison.

She will argue any point to prove she is right and you are wrong. If I say it is hot she will say it is cold... that kind of thing. Its just a running battle with her. She has had a mind of her own since she was a child, but now it's really something else.

Foster leader-member identification

Leader: I hear you, Ruth. You can't seem to win with her ... a running battle all the time and you feel punched out with battle scars. You hurt and wish for relief. I have a sister who is raising a 15-year-old daughter by herself and I almost feel I'm talking to her right now; there is much similarity.

Anna: My name is Anna. I heard about this parent discussion group from our pastor, Rev. Ortiz. I talk to him a lot. He is friendly and has given me a lot of good advice over the years. He says he knows you. I sure can use some answers because I'm ready to shoot the whole lot. I have three kids, ages 8, 10, and 11. I'm raising them by myself. Their father is no good. He left us four years ago. I don't even know where he is anymore. The kids are always fighting. I take care of my sister's kids too, three of them, ages 5, 7, and 8. She had an accident two months ago, fell out of a window and has been in the hospital ever since. So that's why I keep her kids. They all are so demanding I can't take it anymore. I hope you people have some answers.

Leader: I'm glad you're here with us, Anna, you sound really pressured, kind of desperate. Taking care of six youngsters single-handed is no small feat. This is the place to talk about these concerns, and I am pleased that you responded to Rev. Ortiz' suggestion. I have known Rev. Ortiz for many years. He is a kind man, speaks so well of his parishioners, and has a lot of very good ideas. Let him know that you are with us and say hello to him for me.

The group leader is the catalyst who helps the group members bond with each other. It is through the interaction the group members have with each other that the work of the group is achieved. The group leader uses certain techniques to assist the group members to find safety, trust, acceptance, encouragement and nurturance in each other. After forming personal bonds himself with the members, the leader now begins to link the members with each other through techniques ranging from verbally pointing out similarities to actually putting them through ice-breaking, and warm-up interpersonal exercises.

Techniques	Example: Parent Counseling Group (Continued)
Foster common identification	Leader: While each of you—Maria, Miguel, Edna, Nelson, Ruth and Anna—have very particular concerns related to your individual children,what strikes me even more are the similarities some of you share with each other. You, Maria, are concerned about an adolescent son who has withdrawn into his own world leaving you not only bewildered by such behavior, but feeling pushed out of his life as well. I think you have something in common with Ruth who has an adolescent daughter who also is in her own world and keeps her mother out. Both of you are utterly confused by such behavior and hurt. You share a lot in common.
Personalize people to each other	Miguel, you have two sons who are live wires, demanding of you all the time. Edna has a child who does the same. It is also hard for both of you to find time for yourselves. So even though it involves different children and different ages, the attention they demand and the form it takes is strikingly similar.
	Nelson, you have demanding kids, always wanting your attention, just like Edna's and Miguel's. You also have a lot in common with Anna who is raising her own three children and her sister's three. How to get six or eight people to learn how to get along with each other is a real problem which you both feel and express.
Use warm-up interpersonal exercises	Groups like this work best when people get to know each other better, not just as problems, but as people. I would like you to do this exercise now. Each of you is going to pretend you are a newspaper reporter and get to know the person next to you individually, as quickly and fully as you can. You will have 6 minutes to get to know the person. That means 3 minutes apiece. Time yourself. Do that now. Take another minute to finish up .... Each of you know different things about the person next to you now. Introduce your partner to the rest of us and tell us about that person.

Skill Step 4: Stimulation of Group Interaction

This step is the heart of the group experience. In Step 4, the leader helps the group members to interact with each other, rather than himself, in mutually helpful ways. The leader encourages open communication of ideas and feelings; stimulates and reinforces positive displays of helpfulness; maintains an encouraging group atmosphere; stimulates alternative perceptions on issues raised; and helps the members deal with difficult group members. The leader is responsible for making sure that the interaction he has stimulated in the group maintains the group's purpose whether that is a collective group goal (such as in a task-oriented group) or individual growth (as in a counseling or therapy group). Remember: leader activity in the example is exaggerated to make teaching points.

Technique	Example: Parent Counseling Group (Continued)
Elicit discussion of specific problems around group's purpose. (Step 1 technique) Reframe (use of word "challenges" as a positive articulation in place of "problems," which connotes a negative feeling)	Leader: Last week you began to get to know a little bit about each other and about the challenges you are having with your children. That's what this group is about; how to understand and deal more effectively with children. When you talk about your children be very specific and give examples.
	Ruth: The problem I am having with my daughter involves her rebellion. She won't listen to anything I say to her and that makes me furious. Her reasoning about things is unreal. This morning I tell her it's cold out, its December, not July and to wear her coat. So what does she do? She gives me an argument about me feeling the cold because I'm old and that it is like spring out. So she goes to school with a thin sweater. And this after the newscaster says it is 34 degrees out. She has no sense of things. It seems all I do with her is to react negatively constantly. What does she get out of this kind of thing with me? It's like she's programmed it.
	Maria: Well, talk about reacting, my 15-year-old son who stays in his room listening to rock day and night with his spaced-out pictures on the wall, really gets to me. At least with you Ruth, you have some kind of give-and-take exchange between yourself and your daughter, but I feel helpless about my son and can't say anything even though I feel furious. Sometimes I think it would help if I expressed my fury, but I am not very expressive that way. Sometimes, I wonder if he does this kind of thing in the hope that I will react. But as it is I just leave him alone, not wanting to make things worse.

- 161 -

Paraphrase empathically	**Leader:** So, Ruth, you are looking for a way to maintain a close relationship with your daughter. You react angrily at her and are beginning to not only see the futility of it all, but to even question your own reaction and what she gets from that.
Paraphrase empathically	On the other hand, you, Maria, are also looking for a way to maintain a relationship with your boy and you feel if you just leave him alone and not interfere, not react to his behavior, it will make things better. But again, you are beginning to wonder if he is wanting you to react to him.
Foster common identification	It sounds like the two of you have similar concerns, wanting to have good relationships with your teenagers, but trying to figure out if there is a purpose to their behavior.
Invite feedback	What do the rest of you feel about this? How do your children behave that make you say in desperation, like Ruth and Maria, "Why are you acting that way?"

Miguel: I am like Ruth, I react. They get scolding and the belt from me. Just before I came here, I asked my 11-year-old to sweep the floor and help his younger brother put his toys away for the night. Next thing, he was watching TV, deliberately not doing what I asked. He heard me. That's why I was late. I spent the next half hour trying a new tactic, sitting down with him and telling him that he has to learn to do as he is told or else he will grow up to be like some of his cousins whom we all laugh at because they are so stupid.

Anna: All my kids make constant demands on me. I'm so fed up, that I find I have become the family nag. I can't think of anything nice to say anymore, so I have become the world's expert on sarcasm. So that's what they get. I guess they like it because they keep on misbehaving.

Foster common linkages between members	**Leader:** Nelson, from what you told us the last time, you have a lot in common with Anna and Miguel. Can you share anything with either of them from your situation that sounds familiar?
Direct members to talk to each other	

Nelson: Well, Anna, you and I have six kids to take care of and I do scold them a lot for misbehavior, which helps for a few minutes, but then it gets back to the way it was. The difference for me is that I can share this burden with my wife when she comes from work, but you never seem to get any relief.

Edna: I'm different than you, Nelson. I keep my feelings to myself, like Maria. I feel that if I don't have control, and both myself and my little girl start feeling sorry for each other, we will both be stuck. So I take a strong upper hand and suffer with it. But I do believe it is the better way. But then too, I wonder about that and that is why I am here.

Continue to foster	**Leader:** Well, you all seem to be struggling with two

common linkages between members		issues: the first is your wondering why the kids are acting the way they do and the second is whether reacting or not helps. You-Ruth, Nelson, and Miguel and Anna-feel that reacting with anger and even using the belt is a way of dealing with your children's misbehavior; Maria and Edna, you believe that a better tactic would be not to react at all lest the misbehavior increase. It seems that we have two points of view on this. Can we talk more about that?
Clarify the development of polarities through empathic paraphrasing		
Encourage member-to-member dialogue		
	Miguel:	I don't know that it has to be either extreme. Sometimes I'm too tired to yell so I just close the door and soon they stop fighting. I also notice that when my wife takes my younger boy out and I am home with the older one, he will do anything to please me. We watch the ball game together and he snuggles up on the chair with me. Then when his brother comes home he wants to get on the chair too and then the fighting starts again. I get angry then, and feel so helpless that I start smacking whoever yells the loudest.
Reframe a negative articulation into a positive perspective Explain details	Leader:	You are popular with your boys, Miguel. They each want you all to themselves. What do you make of that?
	Miguel:	They are both selfish, neither one wants to give. They have to learn how to get along together. You have to punish them until they learn that lesson.
Invite further group dialogue	Leader:	What about the rest of you? What do you feel about Miguel's ideas? How does this fit in with your experience?
	Maria:	You know, I just remembered something when you were talking, Miguel. One night at supper my 11-year-old daughter was talking to the 15-year-old about some music he had on, she sounded so interested and he became very involved with her about it, even letting her into his room to listen to it later. I thought to myself: what's going on in this house? Now I have two weirdos. But now that I think of it, he really responded to her interest with such liveliness. They just enjoyed each other, just like you and your boy, Miguel, found time to just be together without demands.
Clarify connections	Leader:	Maria, it sounds like you are beginning to make some connections with why kids might misbehave to get personal attention.
	Edna:	I think patience really wins out. I hate to think how my little Cathy would react if I scolded and belted her. My mother, who takes care of her while I'm at school, has less patience than I do. She's kind of cool to her, saying that I spoil her. My mother says she has no problems with her during the day, but when I come home everything breaks down. She needs me a lot and I give her all of my attention, but she can never get enough and that's what troubles me, enough is enough. How can my mother say Cathy is fine when she leaves her a

lot just to play in the yard? But, Miguel, I
think you are impulsive with your boys, you have
to be more patient. They probably fight a lot
because they are angry at you for hitting them
so much.

- Reframe a negative
  criticism into a
  positive statement
- Establish connections
- Invite feedback

Leader: Miguel, Edna is saying you are a passionate man
who responds quickly to situations. She is
suggesting that their misbehavior might be a
reaction to being hit a lot. What do you think
of that?

Miguel: Boys have to learn to be tough, Edna, and learn
to take care of themselves and not be cry-babies.
In my family my mother always sided with my two
sisters. When I misbehaved she would say I was just
like my no-good father who left us when I was
three. That hurt a lot at first but I had to learn how
not to let things like that affect me. That's
how I survived and made my way in the world.

Edna: Miguel, your boys will begin to hate you for strap-
ping them so much. I am sorry about your past and
it sounds like you were pretty hurt by your mother's
attitude and your father's neglect, but if you stub-
bornly keep doing to them what was done to you, how
will that help?

Reframe a negative criticism
into a positive statement

Establish connections
(with past)

Leader: Miguel, Edna is saying that you have an
unusual ability to persevere, to stick to
your beliefs. Such predictability can
have a reassuring effect on children. But
she is also wondering if you might consider how your life circumstance was one
thing and their's is another. Can you tell
us a bit about the hurt you felt from your
mother and father.

Anna: I agree, Miguel. Hearing you talk reminds
me so much of my own family. My father
died when I was five and my mother raised us
on welfare, I remember how my father would
take me on his lap and sing to me, read me
stories and tell me that everything was
going to be all right. I missed him so
much after he died and used to pretend he
was still alive for years after that. Do
you remember your father?

Miguel: I was very young so I don't remember too clearly. My
older brother says he was fun to be with,
was easy-going and always picked me up and
said I was his favorite. He didn't keep
a steady job and drank, so my mother didn't
look upon him too favorably. To her, he was irre-
sponsible. But he sounded like he was
okay to me. I wish he had been around longer.

Edna: So you remember your father in a very caring way, as
friendly, not stern or impulsive. Don't you
think this is what your boys want from you?

Interpretation

Leader: Edna is suggesting that there might be a connection
between their misbehavior and wanting a different
kind of relationship with you. Could it be that the boys

| | | misbehave in order to get attention from you in the way they know best, by misbehaving, while what they really want is merely what you yourself wanted from your own father? |

Miguel: I don't know what to say to all that. All I know is that boys need a lot of discipline, really firm, because they have no control.

Acknowledge
both points of view.

Reinforce:
● establishing connections
● interpretation

Leader: Well, firm handling and discipline certainly are important. However, Maria is suggesting that another way of looking at what is going on with your boys is to see them as needing a special kind of attention from you, the kind you remember most wanting yourself from your own father.

Miguel: I don't know what I wanted from him. I don't really remember him. I told you that. I only remember what my brother told me. He sounded like an okay kind of guy to me. I just wish he would have been in my life more. I would have liked that.

Psychodrama

Leader: Put a chair in front of Miguel. Miguel, I know you don't remember your father but you have thoughts about what you might have wanted from him if he had stayed with you. We are going to pretend that he is with you now to hear you. Would you choose someone in the group to represent your father? (Pause and then direct "father" to sit in the empty chair.) Miguel, you are going to talk to your father, telling him what you wanted from him during all those years of your boyhood. "Father", you are just to listen, you will not respond in any way. so, Miguel, begin this way, "Dad, I missed you... what I wanted from you was...."

Miguel: Dad, I wanted you to just be around...to talk with me...play ball with me in the park like the other kids' fathers...be on my side when I got blamed for things. I wanted to be held when I felt lonely. I wanted advice when I felt bad about breaking into the school and stealing those typewriters with the Gonzalez boys. I wanted to know from you what I should do to get some experience with women when I was 12; I wanted to know if it was all right if I didn't. I wanted you to break up that fight I was having with Joey Rodriguez that landed me in Lincoln Hospital because I knew he would kill me, but I had to save face. I wanted you to help me feel that I was somebody and could get ahead by doing things right. You know, without you around, now that I think about it, things never went right for me. I always wanted a father just for me every day. That's all I want to tell you now.

Establish connections

Leader: Thanks, Miguel, for sharing those thoughts with your father. "Father," you can go back to your seat now. Thanks for listening to Miguel. Miguel, that was terrific. Do you see any connection between what you felt you wanted from your father and your own boys' misbehavior?

	Miguel: That really struck me. Each boy needs me for himself in special ways. I never thought about it quite that way. The older boy, Manny, is always saying to me, "Let's go to the park, Dad you and me," and I say, "We'll go on Sunday, all of us." And then he goes away and before you know it, he is fighting with his brother. That's when I get up and get the strap.
Paraphrase empathically Agree on tasks	Leader: Miguel, you say that you have two boys who need you in their own special ways. You mentioned that one of the ways Manny feels he would be special to you would be by going to the park just with you. That is one way he would feel especially cared about. If you were to be special to each boy you would need to know what kinds of things would make them feel cared about. Would you be willing to discover some special ways of being that way to them?
	Miguel: Of course!
Agree on tasks	Leader: I am going to propose a way. You are to ask each boy to make a list of ten things that you could do to show you care about him. You will sit with each boy and compose the list together. From the list, choose two of those suggested to do within the week. Pin it down specifically with each boy as to a day and time. How do you feel about that?
	Miguel: That sounds great to me. I only hope they don't want to go on a trip around the world.
Agree on tasks	Leader: it will be up to you to decide which two caring activities from the list they make would be acceptable to you in terms of time and cost. When can you talk about this list with each boy?
	Miguel: Anytime.
Agree on tasks	Leader: Make it specific. How about Monday night at 8 for Manny and Tuesday night for Eric?
	Miguel: That is as good as any other time.
Agree on tasks	Leader: But it is more planned this way. You agree to it then? And you will tell us here next week how it went?
	Miguel: I think it will really work. I feel better already, as though I got a new look at things today.
Summary (closure)	Leader: Today you have talked a lot about specific kinds of behaviors of each of your children and your own reactions to them. You have been wondering if there is a connection between their misbehavior and your own reactions. Reactions here ranged, from quite emotional such as in Miguel, Nelson, and in Anna to almost a martyr-type patience as in Ruth, Maria and Edna. It seems to have become clearer, at least to Miguel, that his boys may be looking for some of the same attention or

caring that he wanted from his own father and
that they are trying to get this through misbehaving,
the way they know best. Miguel shared some
very personal feelings with us through a pretend
play in speaking to his father. He also devised a
plan to work on during the week to get closer to
his boys in ways they really want.

HANDOUT II

OVERVIEW OF GROUP PROCESS

Skill Step	Leader Technique	Purpose

1. Group Purpose	1) Define the purpose of the group clearly.
	2) Establish the basic group rules
	3) Invite members to talk about their specific concerns relating to the purpose of the group.
	4) Set limits,empathically,
	  • on people who change group focus.
	  • on disruptive behavior.
		Establish basic group framework and group boundaries.

2. Leader-Member Bonding	1) Empathic communication with individuals (paraphrasing)
	2) Personalizing
	3) Fostering personal indentifications with each member through:
	  • sharing of personal anecdotes, examples, talents,which are similar to group members'.
	  • adopting personal or cultural mannerisms.
		Create conditions for group cohesiveness
		• security
		• acceptance
		• belonging
		• reduce emotional distress
		• increase feelings of kinship

3. Member-Member Bonding	1) Fostering common identifications and linkages among group members. 2) Personalizing member bondings. 3) Warm-up exercises.	

4. Stimulation of Group Interactions	General techniques to stimulate interactions:
	
	1) Elicit feedback.
	2) Direct members to address each other.
	3) Explain details.
	4) Reinforce positive-oriented responses through personal acknowledgement and appreciation.
	5) Reframe negative articulations into positive ones.
	6) Clarify the development of polarities and potential group factions in empathic and accepting ways.
	7) Establish connections (past or present).
	8) Interpret.
	9) Conflict resolution skills (six-step method)
	10) Summarize:
	  • during session
	  • end of session
	11) Agree on tasks
		To achieve:
		
		• group or individual goals
		• self-awareness
		• insight
		• behavioral change
		• altered perceptions
		• reduction of anxiety
		• symptom abatement
		• increase of self-esteem
		• conflict resolution
		• positive interpersonal functioning
		• stimulation of social interest
		• increased responsibility and cooperation

MODULE V: THERAPEUTIC COMMUNITY

SESSION 1: Large Group Discussion Skills

Objectives:

1. To teach the concept of therapeutic community meetings.

2. To define skills for conducting large therapeutic community sessions: large group discussion skills, subgrouping skills, theater skills, and management skills.

3. To teach large group and subgrouping skills as applied to the therapeutic community.

Materials:

Newsprint on group skills used in Module IV, Session 2.

Concepts and Techniques of Therapeutic Community

Therapeutic community meetings are large group sessions of generally 25 to 100 persons who meet regularly to share the responsibility for helping articulate and resolve problems related to the collectivity. These meetings symbolize the unity and coherence of the whole group. The "culture of the community," its ideology, is most articulated, reinforced and expressed in practice during this time. How to act, how to talk about and deal with problems, how to respond to others and how to support others' strengths, are filtered through the community's ideology. Content of the sessions is substantially interpersonal in nature, but may also be related to outside situations that affect the group: institutions, protection, health, employment, school, etc. Many of the healing qualities found in small group dynamics, flowing particularly from the experience of intimacy, can be lost in large group activities. However, therapeutic community sessions can be conducted in such a way that some degree of intimacy is maintained along with the therapeutic effects that are created through large group dynamics.

The techniques described in the small group process section are almost equally applicable to large groups. The difference between a large group and a small one, obviously, is that in the large group it becomes less possible for any one person to be the frequent giver or recipient of healing responses. Thus, while the leader of a therapeutic community meeting can use small group techniques, the intensity with which the therapy experience can reach everyone in the group through group psychotherapy skill is limited. Small group treatment skills are necessary but insufficient in a therapeutic community meeting.

There are four types of skills needed for the effective leadership of therapeutic community sessions:

1. Large group discussion skills: These are techniques derived from small group practice.

2. Subgrouping skills: These are techniques of dividing the large group into smaller units to achieve more personal discussions of an issue.

3. Theater skills: These are techniques derived from drama, ritual, and ceremony. They reach audiences or congregations in compelling ways.

4. Management skills: These are techniques that aim to keep controls over disruptive behaviors in large groups.

Today we will focus on the first two skills: large group discussion and subgrouping skills.

Large Group Discussion Skills

The techniques used in leading large group discussions are similar to those used in small group discussions which we learned in the previous sessions. They can be applied in a similar way even though the group is larger. These techniques are: Point to newsprint with listing of these techniques from previous session

1. Define the problem or issue to be discussed and maintain focus.

2. Paraphrase empathically.

3. Foster linkages among members on the basis of similar points of view.

4. Stimulate interaction through: (a) eliciting feedback, (b) directing members to address each other, (c) reinforcing social responses, (d) reframing, (e) clarifying polarities, (f) establishing connections, (g) conflict resolution skills, (h) summarizing, and (i) task agreements.

Activity 1: Large-Group Discussion
Using Small Group Techniques

Let's practice large-group discussion skills using techniques learned with small groups. Pretend you are a large group of 75 children in a day camp program. You all arrive home from the city pool late today because the train was delayed. It is now 1:30 p.m. and the Center where you stop for lunch has already distributed all the lunches. The same thing happened last week, but you let that slide. Now that the group has to go without lunch for a second time, many of you are furious. The complaint is brought to the meeting by Noreida. In the therapeutic community meeting, Noreida says: "We didn't have lunch again today. That dumb place gave away our lunch and it wasn't our fault the train was stuck." You are the community of children. I need a volunteer leader to lead the children in a conflict resolution session. I will help you do this.

When a trainee volunteers, have him sit next to you and help him conduct a conflict resolution session for this large group through the use of some small group techniques. Use of the following is suggested:

- Definition of focus
- Use of group empathy
- Conflict resolution skills

Start your trainee off in the following way by having a dialogue with him at the same time that he is also dealing with the group of children. The following excerpt is your dialogue with him. Use it verbatim.

Leader: What is the problem that Noreida brought up?

Trainee: (He repeats what Noreida said but in his own words)

Leader: So that is the problem! Say that to the group!

Trainee: (He does this)

Leader: How do you think they feel?

Trainee: (He says something about their being "angry, hungry, sad ...")

Leader: Tell them that you understand how they feel and why. That is empathy.

Trainee: (He tells them this in his own words)

Leader: You are now going to lead the children in a conflict resolution process. The basic problem, as you said, is that there were no lunches when they got to the Center. How can that be prevented from happening again? Get a lot of ideas on this. Help trainee to stimulate the generation of many ideas and write the ideas on the newsprint.

Trainee: (He asks them for their ideas on what they think could be done to prevent this from happening again and writes them down)

Leader: Go over each item with the children and have them settle on trying two possible solutions for next time. Cross out the others.

Trainee: (Follows your instructions)

Leader: Ask them how they will make sure this is done. Pin them down to a person in charge, a time, a day to do it, etc.

Trainee: (Follows your instructions)

When this process is over, thank trainee for his courage and good work. If you wish, invite another trainee to have this experience of leading a large group using small group techniques. Such a repetition will also reinforce the process of conflict resolution in a large group for the other trainees.

Subgrouping Skills

All groups can be divided into smaller units or subgroups. Groups do this naturally when people find similarities with each other. In a heterogeneous group, people will subgroup on the basis of age, sex, religion, occupation, hometown, personality, hobbies, or lifestyle (couples, singles, the divorced, etc.). In these subgroups people find support, comfort, relaxation, acceptance, intimacy, and safety. Following this natural tendency, therapeutic community meetings can also arrange that, for therapeutic or educational purposes, the larger collectivity be broken down into smaller groupings to deal with items on the agenda. Any question or problem dealt with in a therapeutic community can be productively resolved through the leader's use of subgrouping skills. Structurally, subgroups should be small groups of 5 to 7 people each, have a person in charge of the subgroup to keep order, and perhaps have a person who records ideas from the members. The leader of each subgroup regulates the discussion in such a way that order is maintained, that each person has his say, and that focus is centered on the subject.

Subgrouping skills can be used with any topic that is brought up in a therapeutic community meeting. They allow the entire collectivity to express personal feelings and points of view which they might hesitate to do in a large group or for which there might not be time. Topics can range from subjects that have relevance to the collectivity because of developmental needs or problems of living and working together. Some examples of personal problems or worries that children may bring up which can be profitably discussed at the session and identified with by the other children could include:

-- I got a bad report card. How can I show it to my father?

-- I lost my sweater and that boy has it.

-- I hate that class. The students call me names.

-- I didn't mean to break the window. It was an accident.

-- My best friend moved away. I feel lonely.

-- My grandfather died. I feel awful.

-- I always get blamed for what my sister does.

-- I want him for a friend, but he ignores me.

-- The teacher gives me too much homework.

-- We never go out anywhere.

-- I'm embarrassed to bring friends home. My mother's always drunk.

-- Mom and Dad are always fighting. They're talking of divorce.

The following exercise will demonstrate the use of subgrouping techniques around a specific problem brought up by a child who complains about mistreatment by his teenage counselor.

When personal confrontations or complaints about specific community members are articulated in a session, it is necessary before applying the subgrouping technique to see if a dialogue between the two can resolve the issue. If it cannot, breaking the group into smaller units to generate ideas, which are then shared with all, can be highly effective for the two in conflict. If the original dialogue between the two settles the matter, it can still be useful to keep the subject open for further consideration by the community members. The exercise to follow will demonstrate this latter point.

Activity 2: Large-Group Discussion
Using Subgrouping Techniques

After the lunch problem was resolved in your group of 75 children, Mark brought up a problem he had this morning with a counselor, Paul. Mark complained that Paul had hit him because he did not come out of the pool on time. Many of the children have been complaining about being smacked around by counselors when they disobey orders. They feel mistreated, so Mark's complaint is something other children have experienced as well. Mark has just brought up this complaint to the therapeutic community session.

I need three volunteers: a group leader, Mark, and Paul.

When three trainees volunteer, have them sit in a small group in the middle of the room. You sit next to the "group leader" in order to give him instructions about what to do. Let him know that you will be doing this with him. Then ask the other two if they understand their part. Ask them to describe what happened as the story was presented. Then proceed to help the group leader deal with the conflict between Mark and Paul by your having a dialogue with the leader about what he is to do with them.

Leader:	So, Mark is feeling bad about Paul twisting his arm this morning. Say that back to him and ask him what happened.
Trainee leader:	(Follows your instructions)
Mark:	(Responds with his own story)
Leader:	So what did you hear Mark say?
Trainee Leader:	(Repeats to you what Mark said)
Leader:	Say that back to him, but use the formula we learned, "You are feeling_____about_____ because_____." And then say, "Is that it?"
Trainee leader:	(Follows your instructions)
Mark:	(Agrees or corrects leader's statement)
Leader:	Paul is also feeling something and has his opinion about the event. He is feeling angry at something Mark did. Say that back to him, and ask him what happened.
Trainee leader:	(Follows your instructions)
Paul:	(Reports his story on the event)
Leader:	So, what did you hear Paul say?
Trainee leader:	(Repeats to you what Paul said)
Leader:	Say that back to him using the formula, "You are

	feeling_____about_____ because_____." And then add, "Is that it?"
Paul:	(Agrees or corrects leader's statement)
Leader:	So, here we have two people in conflict who are upset at each other for good reasons. Help them to talk to each other one at a time. You will serve as a mediator. Tell them that there are two rules: (1) one person at a time talks and (2) no insulting or name calling is allowed. Then say to them: "Talk together right now in a way that can help settle this. I will stay right here to help out if you need me."

The simplicity of the above dialogue should not be discounted as ineffective. It appears in at least half, if not more cases, to be highly effective as a way of settling surface conflict through mediation. If, after several minutes, the conflict is spiraling further, it may be necessary to set controls on the dialogue. An effective way to do this is to intervene and say to the trainee group leader:

Leader:	They are having a hard time of this, aren't they? Ask Mark what he wants from Paul. And then tell him to say that to Paul. Then ask Paul what he wants from Mark and tell him to say that directly to him, also.
Trainee leader:	(Follows your instructions)
Leader:	Repeat to both of them what you heard each one saying he wanted from the other. Then ask them if they would be willing to do this.
Trainee leader:	(Follows your instructions)

If Mark and Paul are unwilling to settle this conflict tell the group leader to say to them that he is going to get the larger group to help out because they are stuck. If they have settled the conflict, tell the leader to tell them that what they did took a lot of courage and he has to "really hand it to them."

Trainee leader:	(Follows your last suggestion)
Leader:	So you see, Mark acted like a hero in bringing up his problem with Paul here in this big group. And Paul too had courage to stick with finding a solution that would help him as well as Mark. So you see, one way of stopping someone from hurting someone else is to help them talk it out together as you did with them. But you know sometimes that doesn't work. They can't settle it even when you serve as their mediator. In that case you could invite the whole community of children to express their thoughts on the matter. I am going to do that now myself as a way of showing you how you can do the same thing. I want you to stay right here next to me, as you have been doing, pretending you are me as I go through this. Working side by side with someone who knows something is a great way to learn to do what he does. Let me show you what I would do with the children.

Tell the trainees that they will now pretend they are a community of children or counselors who are going to develop some ideas on what they could do if someone physically hurt them and they were afraid that person was going to keep on doing this. Tell the trainees that while they will go through this experience as a group of children and counselors in this exercise, they should also be aware of the technique of subgrouping you will be using, since you are trying to teach them how they can use this technique in their own practice with children and counselors.

Sometimes people hurt children. Sometimes they mean it and sometimes they don't. I wouldn't be surprised if you had some ideas about what you could do if someone hurt you and you were afraid they would keep on doing so. It could be someone at home, at school, or in your neighborhood. This is what I want you to do. You are going to form into little groups right where you are. Here is a group 1-2-3-4-5-6; here is another group 1-2-3-4-5-6.

Continue this arranging until all trainees are in a subgroup. Everyone now belongs to a little group within this big group. These little groups are called subgroups. I want one person in each subgroup to be in charge. You decide who that person will be. The person in charge is to keep order, to make sure that everyone has a chance to talk, and to keep the group on the subject.

This is what you will talk about together in your subgroups. Tell the people in your group about a time when someone hurt you or pushed you around. Tell them what was done to you and what you did about it that helped or didn't help, and if it is still bothering you.

Who can say in their own words what I have just said? Pause for paraphrasing So, form your subgroups into a small circle now. Remember to put someone in charge. Pause for this process to take place Come back to the whole group now. Who would like to share some of the thoughts expressed in your small groups? Wait for responses from the "children" in each subgroup as they report their ideas. Use empathic paraphrasing and bonding skills during these presentations. You also might want to itemize the ideas on newsprint to get across the main idea that there are many ways in which the problem of children being hurt can be dealt with and has, as a matter of fact, been dealt with by children. At the end of this sharing, summarize the ideas and praise the children for their wonderful ideas and for sharing.

Ideas generated in the above technique should further give Paul and Mark a rich source of alternatives to choose from in resolving an unresolved conflict.

Today we have talked about the use of therapeutic community techniques to help children learn ways of settling problems, either personal ones or those that concern all of them in the community. We talked about using some of the skills we learned in dealing with small groups and applying them to the larger group of the community and we learned how to subdivide the larger group into smaller units, called subgroups, for the purpose of getting everyone's input in a personal way to come to bear on a problem. We learned then how to feed back the input of all the members to the larger group through the technique of sharing. I would welcome your questions, comments and even any feelings that might have been stirred as a result of our work today.

Allow ample time for some discussion of the trainees' experience in today's session. If emotional issues are raised, you may want to make an empathic statement and ask if others might have felt this way too, thereby encouraging the sharing of similar concerns.

MODULE V: THERAPEUTIC COMMUNITY

SESSION 2: Theater Skills

Objective:

To define and teach four specific theater skills to be used in therapeutic community contexts:

- Warm-ups
- Ritual
- Gestures
- Storytelling

Materials:

1. Small pieces of paper and a box.
2. Newsprint prepared in following formats:

Warm-Ups
1.
2.
3.
4.
5.

Rituals	
Words	Actions

Theater Skills

We have begun to talk about the concept of therapeutic community, a large group context where sometimes 25 to 100 people meet regularly to share the responsibility for helping resolve interpersonal problems or problems related to their community life together. We talked last time about the use of small group techniques applied to the larger group context; about the technique of dividing the larger group into smaller units called subgroups where issues could be discussed more intimately; and, finally, the technique of sharing the issues talked about in the subgroups with the community group.

Today we are going to continue to learn other effective techniques to use in therapeutic community interchange. The techniques we will be learning today are derived from social life, theater, and ritual. I call them merely theater skills.

Theater skills include all those methods that attempt to positively involve large groups of people in an emotional experience directly or vicariously. Large groups of people assembled together are similar to audiences or congregations where drama, suggestion, ritual, and ceremony take place. These theatrical or ritual forms of expression are powerful communication vehicles that reach and heal people in profound ways.

There are five specific theater skills that can be used effectively in leading therapeutic community meetings where the goals are interpersonal changes and social conditioning:

1. Warm-up

2. Ritual

3. Gestures

4. Storytelling

5. Sociodrama (role playing)

We will be considering the first four of these today, leaving sociodrama for the next session.

Warm-up

Warm-ups are like "icebreakers." They provide initial interactions in social and fun ways. They stimulate the mind or body to be fully responsive. Joggers walk before running; jockeys walk their horses before a race; ballplayers limber up with practice catches; weight lifters begin with calisthenics. Warm-ups are necessary preparations of the body or mind to achieve full responsiveness. Groups are like that too. A fully responsive group is a group that has properly warmed up. This is done through actions or exercises designed to increase the involvement of group members. There are many ways to stimulate the group's energy level for involvement. They all tend to create a sense of cohesion or a feeling of oneness between the group members. Here are some ideas.

Activity 1: Warm-Ups as a Theater Skill

Take newsprint and write "Warm-Ups" at the top, followed by five numbers:

Warm-Ups
1.
2.
3.
4.
5.

Listed below are some techniques of warm-up. As you present these techniques to the trainees, write the concept next to the corresponding number on the newsprint (e.g., introductions would be written next to #2 on the newsprint). Explain the concept by demonstrating the example given in the text below. At the end of this listing, ask the trainees if they can add other warm-ups they may know. Add these to the list with a number next to them in succession. Here is the list. Remember, only itemize the technique, not the example.

Technique	Examples
1. Hospitality or Welcoming	Greet each member at door, welcome the person by word, handshake, embrace, or taking of hands. Words of welcome and pleasure are exchanged.
	"Eric, I am so glad to see you again. I enjoyed being with you so much last week and looked forward to your being here again today." Smile, make eye contact, and shake Eric's hand warmly. Turn to people nearby. Shake hands with them and get to know their names, work, and interests.
2. Introductions	Escort these people to join another small group standing on the other side of the room. Shake hands with them, introduce everyone, and tell them what you know about the persons you brought over.
3. Exercises	Ask the group to exercise with you. Stand up and stretch up, down, out, back, and front. Bend to right, left, front, and back.
4. Singing, Clapping, Joking	How many people know "He's Got the Whole World in His Hands"? Good, most of you. Who knows how to lead? Who would like to lead? Here, you look willing. Let me sit with you and we'll do it together. I need all the help I can get.
5. Bonding	How many people here know two people in the room? Three people? Five? Half? All but one? All?
	How many people here are between 10 and 20 years old? Between 20 and 30? Between 30 and 100?
	How many people here are: musicians, poets, carpenters, mothers, fathers, grandparents, lovers, cheaters, loafers, magicians, etc.?
	How many people here are brothers? Sisters? Only children? Adopted?
	How many people here have dogs, cats, birds, monkeys, hamsters, roaches, mice, elephants?

Can you add other warm-ups to the list? | Pause for responses and add them to list | Now, what I want you to do is team up with a partner.

> As trainees are doing this, prepare small folded papers with a number on each, depending on the number of warm-up items on the newsprint and the number of trainee pairs. If there are five trainee pairs, write out five slips of paper with a number on each; if there are ten trainee pairs, write out ten slips of paper with a number on each. Put papers into a box and have each trainee pair take one paper. When they receive their papers say:

The number you have corresponds to the warm-up technique with the corresponding number on this newsprint. Work together in your pair to develop a small scene or skit to demonstrate your particular warm-up technique to the group. Remember the warm-up is to help certain people in this group or the group as a whole to feel relaxed and involved. Do that now. If you need help, call me over.

> Allow about 5 minutes for these skits to be developed and then lead each pair in a demonstration of their prepared warm-up

Ritual

A ritual consists of certain words or actions performed repeatedly and in a precise manner to express a belief in something symbolically. Because of the absolute sameness of the ritual at all times, ritual provides a sense of security, safety, sacredness, and meaningfulness. Such experiences can also provide certainty and a sense of protection, especially to persons who are experiencing chaos and uncertainty in their real world.

In therapeutic communities, ritual includes all those words and actions that enable people to feel a sense of specialness and significance in belonging to the group and that are always predictably present to symbolize such specialness.

Ritualistic words and actions can be powerful transmitters of therapeutic acceptance since they are given unconditionally to each member of the community whether in good standing or not. I would like to compose a list of ritualistic words and actions together with you which you can begin to think about using with members of a group you are involved with, even your own family, in order to create a profound sense of specialness or belongingness.

Activity 2: Ritual as a Theater Skill

> Take newsprint and write "Rituals" at the top and divide into the following columns:
>
> | Rituals | |
> |---------|---------|
> | Words | Actions |
> | | |

Here are some thoughts to help us develop words and actions that will convey the effects of ritual. I will give you the main category. You will try to think of ways that people express that category ritualistically and

I will fill it under words or actions on the newsprint.

1. What are some ways that people customarily greet each other? (Examples: Good morning, Welcome, How are you today?)

2. What are some ways that people greet each other religiously? (Examples: The Lord be with you, God go with you.)

3. What are some ways that different cultures express affection? (Examples: Kissing on both cheeks, kissing on the hand, kiss of peace, hugging.)

4. What are some titles that people use to convey respect and power? (Examples: Doctor, Father, Reverend, brothers and sisters.)

5. What are some actions that people use to indicate respect for others? (Examples: Bowing of the head, kneeling.)

6. What are some blessings that people give to their children or their subjects? (Example: Traditional Latin peoples' blessing to their children, "Dios te bendiga.")

7. What are some games and songs of childhood that employ repetitive words or actions that are followed without questioning their logic? (Example: Simon Says; Fine, fine, superfine)

8. What are some techniques used in education that teach children through rote? (Examples: The teacher says to the whole class: "The reason we are here is to learn from each other." He then turns to the children on the right side of the room and says, "Why are we here?" The children respond, "To learn from each other." The teacher then turns to the children on the left side of the room and says, "Why are we here?" The children say, "To learn from each other." The teacher then says to the entire class: "Why are we here?" The class responds, "To learn from each other.")

9. Are there any other rituals that people use to convey their messages that we have not included?

Gestures

Gestures are any movements of the body, particularly the hands, that symbolize or emphasize an idea, sentiment, or attitude. Gestures make ideas and feelings visual. They add to the messages we communicate in words. Gestures are very powerful vehicles of communication; many times more powerful and effective than words.

Activity 3: Gestures as a Theater Skill

Let's practice gestures without words. Who can:

1. Welcome a group of people warmly?
2. Express an idea with anger?
3. Say hello to someone across the street?
4. Tell someone to stop doing something?
5. Tell a motorist he has a long way to go yet?
6. Suggest other gestures?

Storytelling

Storytelling has been a method of communicating ideas, morals, and sentiments since the beginning of time. The stories depicted through drawings in caves during the Stone Age; fables, parables, myths, and novels are all indicative of the power of storytelling in peoples' lives. Dreams, reflecting the deepest part of our personalities, are sometimes presented to us by our minds as stories, metaphorical expressions of our inner selves.

Jesus told stories to multitudes of people as a way of influencing their perspective on life, affirming their dignity, and kindling their curative powers of faith and hope.

When you tell a story, people listen, become mesmerized, identify with the heroes, ponder the story's message, and gain new insights. Storytelling in large groups superficially entertains, but can substantially convert and change lives. Storytelling is a theater skill that lends itself to large audience participation. Storytelling in large groups involving member participation can be done in two ways. The first is by telling a prepared story and then inviting a discussion around it such as: "What was that story saying?" You can invite the ideas of people from the group as a whole or divide the group into subgroupings, as we learned last time, to talk about the meaning of the story.

The second way of storytelling is to have the group develop the story once you have begun it. We will practice both techniques. Although you will be as the children listening to the story, keep alert to my technique so that you will be able to do the same thing with your groups.

Activity 4: Storytelling as a Theater Skill

Story 1:

I want to tell you a story:

One day a man decided to leave his village. He was uncertain about where to go, but he planned to stop at every village he passed and ask what it was like to live there. One particular village had a small square in its center. The square was bordered by shady trees and under one of them sat an old man. The traveler went up to him and asked, "Old man, can you tell me what it is like to live here? I am looking for a new village and I am wondering if this could be it." The old man answered, "Well, that is a difficult question. Tell me first what it was like where you came from." The traveler told him a woeful tale of insensitive, unfriendly, cold villagers who were lacking in the decencies one would expect to find in a small community. There was little kindness and almost no compassion. The old man listened and when the traveler had finished his sad description of his former village, he said, "The people in this town are the same way." The traveler shook his head with great discouragement and walked away.

Some time later a second traveler entered the same village and encountered the same old man under the tree. This new visitor was the brother of the first traveler and had lived in the same village. "Old man," said the brother, "can you tell me what it is like to live here? I am looking for a new village and this may be the place." The old man replied, "Well, that is a difficult question. Tell me first what it was like where you came from." So the brother told him how sad he had been since he left his old village. There, he said, the people were gracious and friendly, filled with compassion and kindness. They had often gone out of their way to help and he felt fortunate to have lived there. The old man listened and when the brother had finished praising his former village, he said, "The people in this town are the same way."

> Take the group through a discussion of the story by asking them: "What did the old man mean?" Do this in either of two ways: by large group discussion or by subgrouping and sharing.

Story 2:

Here is another story:

Once upon a time there were two children, Miguel and Anna. Miguel was 10 and Anna was 8 years old. They lived with their mother and grandmother on the top floor of an old building on Beck Street. They had no heat in winter and no water in the summer. The neighborhood was dangerous and the buildings around them were always being burned down. One day Miguel and Anna's mother decided ... what? Who thinks they know...?

> Invite the group to develop the story. Affirm, recognize, and paraphrase each comment, developing the story that the group creates. Ask questions such as: "And then what do you think happened?" Or say: "That is true. How well you know this story!" Or: "Please go on. You know so much about what happened to the father." "Yes, they made it through the tunnels and out of the city." And so on. When the story seems to be over, conclude it positively and ask the children what they thought the message of the story was.

Today we increased our repertoire of skills in leading therapeutic community sessions by introducing concepts and techniques from theater. Such ideas included warm-ups, ritual, gesture, and storytelling. These techniques are part of a total repertoire of skills that can be effectively used in leading therapeutic community sessions.

When we meet next time we will consider and practice a very powerful form of therapeutic communication which invites large audience involvement. It is called sociodrama or simply role play.

MODULE V: THERAPEUTIC COMMUNITY

SESSION 3: Sociodrama

Objectives:

1. To define and teach the art of sociodrama for use in therapeutic community contexts.

2. To elaborate specific techniques proper to sociodrama: role reversal, doubling, and soliloquy.

Sociodrama

We have been learning about techniques that can be used in conducting community therapy sessions with groups anywhere between 25 and 100 people. We have talked about using small group techniques, subgrouping and some theater skills, namely, warm-ups, rituals, gestures and storytelling. Today we will learn a powerful theater-derived technique called sociodrama.

Sociodrama is a derivative of psychodrama, a method of psychotherapy developed by Jacob Moreno in 1921 in Vienna. In psychodrama a person is helped to explore and resolve his personal conflicts through acting them out rather than by just talking about them. Sociodrama takes group conflicts and problems and enacts them in drama for educational or therapeutic purposes. These conflicts are not uniquely personal as those expressed in psychodrama, but have a group theme pertinent to all members of the audience.

Sociodrama is an action method of exploring alternatives and more effective approaches to resolving a group problem. Any topic or problem can be the subject of a sociodrama: it can be a topic chosen by the leader or the group members; it can relate to the developmental needs of a group in general; or it can be a dramatic representation of a real problem the group is experiencing. Whatever the topic, the problem is presented in play form. It is not a sit-and-talk discussion.

Sociodrama is made up of four parts:

a) *Introduction:* The problem is described either by the leader or by a member of the group. The problem may be imaginary or an actual one that the group is experiencing.

b) *Preparation:* A cast of characters similar to those described in the introduction is named and described. If the problem is a real problem that a person or group is having, the sociodrama should not be a direct portrayal of it, but should be handled metaphorically; that is, by preparing a skit which is like the problem but a little different too, so as to keep a quality of "play" in the presentation. The following skit demonstrates this idea. Volunteers are requested or appointed to fill the different roles and a setting similar to the one described in the introduction is named and described. When the actors know the roles they will play and the problem to be acted out in their roles, the stage is set for action.

c) *Presentation:* The actors improvise the play with little or no help from the leader.

d) *Discussion and sharing:* The audience is invited to respond to the play, give their opinions, express their feelings about the plight of the players, and suggest ways of resolving the problem situation other than the way portrayed. Suggestions are made for alternative solutions, and these may then give rise to additional role plays depicting the same problem handled differently.

I am going to take you through an experience in sociodrama. Although you will act as the children in the role play, keep alert to the techniques I have described and will continue to describe to you throughout the session so that you can begin to do the same thing with your own groups.

Activity 1: Sociodrama

I would like to introduce a problem for us to role play in order to illustrate the four parts of sociodramatic role playing. Here is the idea of the *Introduction:*

There is a group of 75 children meeting in a therapeutic community session. A problem is brought up by a counselor named Angel. He says that when the children are on their way to the pool, they have to walk through a neighborhood with abandoned buildings and deteriorated walls. Many children climb up on the walls and will not obey the counselors' instructions not to do that. Because of the danger involved, this situation has created a conflict between the children and their caretakers.

So, the problem that I have introduced to you is a real one that this community of children is having. Let's go on to show how this can be arranged in order to prepare the scene for the play. Actors need to volunteer and be briefed on the parts they will play and the setting has to be described in such a way that it can be seen in the imagination of the audience. Here is the *Preparation:*

Let's pretend that there is a group of children and counselors on a trip to the zoo and they have to pass through a neighborhood with abandoned buildings. The same problem occurs between these children and their counselors. We need three counselors and six children. Who will volunteer? Pause Will one of the counselors describe to the rest of us what this street looks like, where the abandoned buildings are, and where the deteriorated wall is. Pause How high is the wall? Show us with your hands. What is in front of it, in back of it, where does it begin and end? Anything else you want to say about it? So, you children will climb up and down on the wall in this play; and you counselors will try to stop them. The play is almost ready to begin, now that the preparation has been made for the play and it is ready to be enacted.

Note how we have changed the originally presented problem to one similar to it by changing the place they are visiting and saying that it is another group of children and counselors. What follows now is the *Presentation;* that is, the actors improvise the play, carrying out their roles as they think best. Direct the actors to commence their play. Stop the play after the point of conflict has been made and both children and counselors have demonstrated the power struggle between them.

The play has been presented, highlighting in visual form the conflict that was brought up by Angel. It is important that recognition be given to all the actors. The audience is now asked to respond to what they have witnessed and experienced. This is the *Discussion and sharing* part.

Thank you for a fine presentation of this problem. I am wondering what some of the group's ideas might be as to why the children would not listen to the counselors and what ideas you might have to encourage them to listen?

Take the group through a "generation of solutions process," para-phrasing each suggestion as you go along. When solutions seem to center on one or two common themes that sound workable, throw these final solutions into role-playing also. Bring volunteer actors to the center of the circle and describe the new action they will take with the uncooperative children. Follow the same format of intro-duction, preparation, presentation, discussion and sharing for each new sociodrama. When all sociodramas depicting various solutions to the problems are played out, a final discussion could elicit shar-ing in the following way:

Those plays were really excellent. How did you children feel when the counselors corrected you the first time? How about the second and third times? What might the rest of you have felt as the children climb-ing on the wall and the way you were treated in those different scenes? Why do you think the second or third solutions were different from the first?

Sociodrama is a very powerful tool to bring about behavioral and atti-tudinal changes. Role playing in which people are encouraged to act out their thoughts and feelings results in releasing blocked-up feelings, developing sensitivity to other people, understanding their own feelings more deeply, gaining insight, learning social skills, and developing creativity and spontaneity.

There are two thoughts I want to emphasize that are important to remember as you use sociodrama. The first is to remember that the effec-tiveness of sociodrama depends on the play remaining a play. Although the content may depict real life, the scenario is not necessarily one in which the real life of a person in the group is being directly and consciously exposed. Real situations and real names are not used. Both become fictional in the play. Keeping the play in the realm of metaphor buffers anxiety, prevents anyone from losing face or esteem, lowers defensiveness, and keeps the process of problem solving on a cognitive, rational level. No one is blamed, accused, or judged . . . after all, it's just a play! Keeping the play as a play enables therapeutic effects to take their course naturally. This is the reason why, in the example above, the situation depicted was not the pool described by Angel but the zoo. A "different group" went to a "different place" with a "different counselor." Yet the message of the play remains clear to all.

The second thought refers to the choice of the role players. Generally, role players are asked to volunteer, but there are many times when a socio-dramatist will deliberately choose certain children to play certain parts for healing purposes. Here are some suggestions:

a) Cast aggressive children in shy roles

b) Cast shy children in aggressive roles

c) Cast neglected children in roles of receiving

d) Cast popular children in unfavorable roles (they can "take it")

e) Cast unpopular children in roles where they shine

f) Cast problem children in non-problem roles

g) Cast "parental children" in roles of being parented

In casting characters this way, healthy functioning roles will be experienced by ego-deficient children; nurturance and self-enhancement will be felt symbolically by deprived children; and children who rarely experience psychological pain will experience those feelings thereby developing empathy.

Three Basic Sociodramatic Techniques

There are three specific techniques that socio- and psychodramatists use to enhance the effectiveness of their approach. They are used during the presentation of the role play. These techniques are role reversal, doubling, and soliloquy.

Role reversal as an action in which two people in a discussion change places with each other and continue their discussion from the other person's point of view. Role reversal helps a person to understand what it feels like to stand in someone else's shoes. There are two forms of role reversal: (a) two-person dialogue role reversal and (b) one-person role reversal.

a) *Two-person dialogue role reversal:* Two people in a conflict change places and continue their dialogue. While it is *highly suggested* that the conflict between two persons be enacted metaphorically, the conflict *may nonetheless be* enacted directly between the parties in conflict. Thus, the examples that follow below can be understood either way. For example, if a child has a dispute with a counselor, the scene can be played out with the actual counselor and the actual child. From time to time in the presentation, the child and counselor are asked to change places and continue the dialogue in the new role. The child is encouraged to see things from the counselor's point of view and the counselor from the child's point of view. A good time for the leader to call for a change of places is when an important question or point is brought up by one or the other.

Activity 2: Role Reversal

Let's play role reversal now. I need two vounteers: one to play a child, William, and one to play a counselor, Danny. ⌈Pause⌉ Thank you. I would like to brief each of you on your part separately. Danny, would you go outside while I brief William? Then you will come in to be briefed and William will wait outside. ⌈You will now be talking to William, but in front of the audience so they can hear as well.⌉

Here is the situation. William, remember the time when you were going to the pool and you had to pass by that bad neighborhood with those deteriorating walls? Well, you will remember that Danny did not want you to climb it because he was afraid you would get hurt. But you didn't think that way. It was fun and exciting to you, and you had a chance to show the others what courage you had. A lot of other kids were doing it too and no one had gotten hurt. Besides, you felt that your counselor was no fun, so you might as well make some fun for yourself. You are going to try to convince Danny that it is not dangerous because you want to have the fun of climbing the wall. Any questions? Okay...you go outside now and have Danny come in.

⌈Pause⌉

⌈To Danny:⌉ Here is the situation. Remember the time when you were going to the pool   and you had to pass by that bad neighborhood with those deteriorating walls? William wanted to have some fun and excitement by climbing up the wall, but you were afraid he would get hurt. You had an experience with another child who fell off a wall and broke his legs and had to stay in the hospital for six months. You also saw signs that said: "Danger: Condemned Wall." You noticed that many cement blocks were loose or missing and looked as if they would fall apart with just a touch. You were also aware that if anything happened to William you could be fired or sued. You are going to convince William not to climb the wall because of these reasons. Any questions? Okay . . . tell William to come back in.

And so, here are . . . the street, the wall, the bright sun, the children, the counselors . . . and the two of you. Play this out now in your own way. I will ask you from time to time to change places. That means that you, Danny, will switch to William's part and William to Danny's. You will do this by saying the last sentence of the other person. I will help you.

As the scene goes on, say "change places" as the conflict emerges more and more. Do this frequently throughout the five minutes of the total play. When the points have been made, cut the scene and then elicit reactions from the actors about the parts they have played.

Thank you for that wonderful play. Superb! How did you feel when you changed places? Was it easy? Hard? Did you have any change of heart as you got to be in the other person's shoes? What particularly impressed you in this play?

> Allow time for these questions to be processed and then go on as described below

b) *One-person role reversal:* This type of role reversal takes place when a conflict a person is having with another person is played out by having one person assume both roles. However, a substitute person can fill in for the opposing person. This substitute does not develop counterarguments but merely quotes the last line uttered by the role-playing person whenever the roles are reversed.

Activity 3: One-Person Role Reversal

Could I have two volunteers to demonstrate one-person role reversal? Pause Thank you. We will call you Nancy and you Martha. Nancy, you are upset that your child, Ileana was climbing on the wall. You feel as Danny does. You come back from the pool and are furious at Ileana and discouraged as well because she will not listen to you. Ileana was climbing the wall for the same reasons as William. Martha, you will merely pretend you are Ileana. Whenever I say "change roles" you will do that and then repeat to Nancy the last sentence she said. You will say nothing more in the play.

Here are two chairs. Nancy, you sit here and Ileana, you sit there. Talk to Ileana now, Nancy, and tell her what you feel and what is on your mind.

> Have Nancy switch roles frequently and get into Ileana's chair when she plays Ileana. Whenever roles are reversed, the last line spoken is to be repeated by Martha who is pretending to be Ileana. That is all Martha does in the role she is playing. After this "dialogue" is enacted for five minutes, cut the scene.

Thank you, Nancy, for a really excellent portrayal of this conflict. How did you feel when you were Nancy? Ileana? When you changed places? Was there any part you began to feel a change of heart in either role? What particularly impressed you about this experience? How about you, Martha, do you have anything to add?

Doubling is an action in which a person who thinks he really understands what a character is thinking or feeling, but not expressing, stands next to him and expresses it for him as though he were that person. For example, a teenager says to the counselor, "You're always picking on me." The counselor says, "You give me no choice, you are always in trouble." A double for the boy could say, "This guy is always hassling me. Why doesn't he get off my back and make life easier for himself and for me?" A double for the counselor could say, "What do I do with this guy? He can't be talked to or reasoned with. I feel stumped, helpless." Unexpressed feelings are thus expressed by the doubles, which further amplify the feelings that the characters are experiencing but perhaps aware of. Doubles give empathic support and insight to their characters, enabling therapeutic movement to flow. If doubles do not perceive the thinking or feeling of their characters accurately, the characters should promptly indicate this.

Activity 4: Doubling

You may recall our training sessions on empathic communication. Doubling is just that. We get in touch with what another person is feeling and then pretend to be that person. However, instead of saying "You feel _____ about _____," the double dramatizes this as though he were the person and says instead "I am feeling _____ about _____."

Let's go back to the scene between Danny and William. Would you mind acting again, Danny and William? Remember the point in your play, Danny, when you said _____. Recapture a certain point for Danny that you feel would lend itself to good doubling And William, you said _____.

Recapture a certain point for William as well. You both will do that scene again. Can you get into it now?

Lead Danny and William through some moments of this re-enactment and then cut the scene. Then address yourself to the audience as follows below.

What is Danny thinking or feeling? Wait for responses. When there is a particularly good response invite that person to come to the center and double or Danny. What is William thinking or feeling? Wait for responses. When there is a particularly good response invite that person to come to the center and double for William.

To Danny's double: Here, in doubling for Danny, stay slightly to his back, but in a way that he can see you; you will act and gesture as he does, become like him. Do that now. Pause

To William's double: Here, you do the same for William. Become William in the same way. We are going to pick up the scene again. You doubles, imitate whatever your characters do. Put into words whatever feelings/or thoughts they are leaving unexpressed. I will help you.

Follow doubles and ask them what they think their characters are feeling. Tell them to say this out loud, "I am feeling _____ about _____." After five minutes of this, cut the scene.

Thank you, Danny and William and the doubles, for that lovely performance. Did anyone else feel similarly as these doubles?

Elicit different responses from audience, asking them to pretend they

- 191 -

> are one of the doubles and put their responses into a doubling format: "I was feeling _____ about _____."

Soliloquy is an action in which the main character is given "time out" during the play to think through his thoughts out loud.

Activity 5: Soliloquy

Let us imagine in the drama between Danny and William that Danny remembers William saying that he, Danny, is no fun to be with; that he is boring and wants to walk only with his girlfriend anyway, so there is no point in walking with him. Danny remembers William saying this with a great deal of feeling. It left him speechless. Let's pretend this scene has just transpired. Danny's thoughts are many, but he feels flooded. He feels defensive and yet sees some truth to what William has said. However, he cannot deal with his own flood of feelings right now. He needs time out to recenter himself.

Leader: Danny, take a walk over here with me. Let's cross the street. You were really struck by what William said. Tell me what's going on in your mind. What are you thinking?

> Encourage Danny to speak out on his thoughts and feelings as you walk with him. Serve as an empathic reflector, paraphrasing his statements. Reinforce his insights and help him to develop new approaches to resolving his conflict with William on the basis of his "time-out" thinking. When enough soliloquizing has transpired, lead Danny back to the scene with William. Invite William to come back into the scene and sit with Danny.

To Danny: Why don't you talk to William now? Share some things with him that you've thought about.

> Direct this process of dialogue between the two of them. Double, if appropriate, or invite doubles from the audience. You can bring this to closure soon after by saying what follows below:

We have to finish this up in a minute or two. Danny, finish up your discusssion with William by saying something that feels comfortable for you. Pause William, finish up your discussion with Danny by telling him something that feels comfortable for you. Pause Why don't the two of you quietly tell each other again what it is that you would like from each other?

Review

We have talked of sociodrama as having four parts:

1. The *Introduction,* where the problem situation is described.

2. The *Preparation,* where the actors are chosen, the parts they will play are clearly outlined, and the setting is set up and described. If the introductory problem is a real one for the group

or anyone in it, make the preparation similar but a little different to keep the quality of play.

3. The *Presentation,* which is the enactment of the play.

4. The *Discussion and sharing,* which is the audience's response to what they have seen. In this part a number of themes may be encouraged:

   a) People may be encouraged to share the parts of the play that had particular meaning for them.

   b) People may respond to the question: "Was there anything in this situation that reminded you of something in your own life?"

   c) Players may tell how it felt to play their parts.

   d) The leader may reflect the theme and open it up for further consideration (e.g., friendship, loyalty, justice, loneliness, drug abuse, misbehavior, etc.)

We have also learned three techniques to enhance the effectiveness of sociodrama:

   1. *Role reversal,* where we change places with someone else.

   2. *Doubling,* where someone else expresses our real feelings for us.

   3. *Soliloquy,* where we take "time out" within the play to talk to ourselves out loud in order to figure something out.

Activity 6: Role Play — Putting It All Together

Let's try to put all of this together. I want you to get into groups of six. [Pause] I am going to introduce a problem situation to you. Then I want you to prepare a small role play in your group, volunteering whatever characters you want to create for it, setting the scene, and then deciding on how you want to resolve the problem. After your preparation, you will present your play to the rest of us. When all the plays have been presented, we will have a discussion. This will give you the experience of going through the phases of sociodramatic role playing. Try to use at least one psychodramatic technique (role reversal, doubling, or solioquy) in your presentation. But don't worry about it. Have fun putting it together.

Here is the Introduction: There is an eighth-grade student who is remaining in the class after the lunch period. This student has dropped a pen in the back of the room and is looking for it. The teacher thinks everyone has left the class, so he also leaves. The teacher forgets to lock the door. The student sees an interesting book in the back while looking for the pen, gets distracted by it, and sits there quietly on the floor reading it. In about five minutes, the door opens and two other students tip-toe into the room and start rifling through the teacher's desk. The student in the back sees them and does not know what to do -- it has happened so suddenly. The student sees them take a set of keys from the desk and move out of the room quietly. They are not aware that they have been observed. Class begins again in the afternoon. The teacher is distressed and asks if anyone knows anything about the keys. The teacher explains that it is the only set he has. They are the keys to the teacher's locker, car, and home. The teacher lives in the neighborhood. The student who witnessed the scene does not know what to do. If the student tells, he will be beaten by the thieving students because they are notorious in the school. If the student does not tell, the teacher will suffer and the thieves will score a victory.

Brainstorm in your groups about what the student should do. Then prepare a role play showing this solution in action. Be creative. I will come around to help, if needed.

> Allow 15 minutes for this preparation. Help out as needed. Then have the play presented. After all the plays are presented, have a discussion about the struggles they had in deciding what they might do in this situation. Themes such as those below could be discussed.

A. What is the responsibility of one who witnesses an injustice?

B. What would happen in a neighborhood or a family where everyone just minded their own business?

C. When do you mind your own business and when do you not?

D. What would make it easier to take responsibility for something difficult to do?

E. How do you decide what to do?

F. Is self-respect worth getting a beating?

G. Some people have died to bring justice about. What do you think about that? Would you die for an ideal?

Today we have been talking about and been engaged in sociodrama, a powerful theater skill in which actual or universally experienced problems which people face can be presented in action rather than through mere description, and solutions found through their enactment.

We have talked about three basic techniques used in sociodrama, namely, role reversal, doubling, and soliloquy. We concluded our session today by having you form groups of six and putting together these different concepts into an action sociodrama of your own. I encourage you to keep doing this among yourselves, to start doing it with your children, to read more about this technique and have your practice observed by someone skilled in this art who can help you develop it further.

We have been talking over the past several sessions about specific healing techniques that can be applied with large groups. Whenever large groups assemble there is a danger of fragmentation, regression, and breakdown of controls. Next time I would like to talk about therapeutic management skills which can provide the kind of limit setting needed to enable a group to keep ego forces under control in order for the work of the healing community to achieve its purpose.

MODULE V: THERAPEUTIC COMMUNITY

SESSION 4: Management Skills

Objectives:

1. To teach four verbal techniques for the therapeutic management of large groups:

   - Hospitality
   - Co-responsible action
   - Empathic communication
   - Confrontation

2. To teach seven non-verbal techniques for therapeutic management of large groups:

   - Eye contact
   - Silent technique
   - Touch and physical proximity
   - Arrangement of healing dyads
   - "Sh-sh-sh" utterances
   - Gestures
   - Acknowledgement of helpers

3. To conclude the training curriculum.

Materials:

1. Newsprint.

2. Original newsprint from orientation session depicting trainees' expectations.

Communication(C)	Behavior(B)	Why(W)

Management Skills

We have been talking for several sessions now about techniques to use for the building of a cohesive and helpful therapeutic community. We have considered large group discussion skills, subgrouping skills, and theater skills. We have spent a great deal of time on theater skills which included warm-ups, ritual, gestures, storytelling and sociodrama. Helping groups work through their common problems and conflicts through enactment of them in play form include role playing, role reversal, doubling, and soliloquy.

Today we will be concluding our training sessions on therapeutic community as well as our overall training curriculum. In the training session today we will learn to develop skills for the therapeutic management of large groups.

When large numbers of people assemble together, there inevitably is the problem of management. How do you assure that behavior will be compatible with goals? There are rules that govern people's behavior in churches, conventions, courtrooms, school assemblies, football games, classrooms, rock concerts, and concert halls. When rules and their enforcement are clearly understood, management controls mob psychology. When rules or their enforcements are fluid, ill-defined, or vaguely understood, the regressive forces of group life can take over with consequent chaos. Management techniques are needed in therapeutic community meetings to assure that the purpose of the session is accomplished.

Therapeutic community meetings are not meetings where a large number of people meet just to express themselves. They have clearly articulated goals, namely, interpersonal problem solving around issues related to living, working, and getting along together. To this end a variety of small and large group therapy skills are employed. In the process of using these skills, fragmentation or regression of the group -- a phenomenon natural to large groups -- easily occurs. Management skills counteract these tendencies. Expressions of fragmentation are seen in such forms as talking out of turn, side talking, subgrouping for private reasons, developing heated arguments, taking group focus off course, playing, sleeping, attacking, insulting, clowning, not cooperating, and so on.

There are several verbal management techniques that are effective in maintaining the external order or controls needed to move the group in therapeutic or educational directions. Without order, neither healing nor learning is possible. Verbal techniques are those in which words are used to influence and control external order. These verbal techniques include hospitality, co-responsible action, empathic communication, and confrontation.

Hospitality has already been mentioned under theater skills as a warm-up technique. It is the friendly, welcoming gesture to friends and strangers alike in bonding. When people are personally welcomed, especially by the group leader, the group representatives, and fellow members, a symbolic tribal cohesion on a baisc primitive level is experienced, allowing defensiveness and aggression to be neutralized. Loyalty, cooperativeness, and friendliness emerge through hospitality. Indeed, hospitality is probably the most powerful of the management techniques. How you are received at the door determines much of what happens after that. This is true in welcoming company into your home, congregations into a church, children into a classroom, employees into a workplace, and so on.

Activity 1: Hospitality or Receiving Another

I want you to lean back, close your eyes, and for a little while think of some time when you visited someone -- a friend, family members, anyone -- and you were welcomed so warmly that you felt really special. Get in touch with that experience. [Pause] As you think of that situation, picture the person's action and words toward you. How do they physically approach you, what do they do, what do they say? Pick up all the details you can in their actions and words and remember them. [Pause]

Now come out of your reverie and join us again. I want you now to get into groups of five. [Pause] Share your thoughts together for 5 minutes on your remembrance of being treated with hospitality. [Pause for 5 minutes] What I want you to do now is to select one of the examples you shared in your group and prepare a short role play to demonstrate for the whole group. Do that now. [Allow 10 minutes for this activity and then call for the presentations]

Co-responsible action is a form of control in which the members of a group understand and accept that they have the permission, the right, and the responsibility to maintain the order needed to achieve the goals of the group. Controls are understood as a co-responsibility. This involvement needs continual support and reiteration because of the tendency, promulgated through traditional institutions such as the family, schools, and bureaucracies to leave responsibility for control to the authority. In therapeutic communities, the natural capacities of all people to exercise their influence on each other extends to controlling each other's behavior as well. Social peer pressure is a powerful source of managerial influence. As a group leader in a therapeutic community or a classroom when requesting that members quell a disruption, the leader could say:

- There is a disruption going on. Would you help each other take care of it? (Then wait!)

- I am waiting for you to take care of this disruption. (Then wait!)

- Help each other. (Then wait!)

- I see something that has to be taken care of. (Then wait!)

Activity 2: Control of Disruption Through Co-Responsible Involvement

I want you to sit back, close your eyes and think of a time when you have assisted or supported others in controlling a disruption such as a fight, a heated argument, a conflict and so on. Remember the incident, your words, your actions. If you cannot think of anything personal that you got involved with, think of someone else whom you observed who did something like this. Do that now for a few minutes. [Pause]

Please start coming out of your reverie now and get into groups of five again, the same group or another. Share your remembrances. [Pause] What I want you to do now is to select one of the examples you shared in your group and prepare a short role play to demonstrate for the whole group. Do that now. | Allow 10 minutes for this activity and then call for the presentations |

Empathic communication, as we have discussed throughout the training, can be applied to large groups and small groups. You will remember that empathic communication means the ability to express what another person is feeling or what you are feeling in order to understand or be understood. You will recall that when you want to convey that you understand what another person feels, you say, "You are feeling_____ about_____ because _____." When you wish to convey how you feel in order to be understood, you say, "I am feeling _____ about _____ because _____." Empathic communication, a healing technique, is also used for managerial purposes.

Here are some examples of empathic communication used as a managerial skill:

1. A student interrupts a lesson or a group member interrupts the treatment session. The leader says, "It bothers me a lot when you talk out of turn because I lose my train of thought."

2. A group member monopolizes the discussion. the leader says, "I feel uneasy when you talk too long because I know others would like to respond."

3. A group member is sleeping. The leader says, "I really feel defeated when you sleep while I talk because I really worked hard last night to get these thoughts together to give to you."

Activity 3: Control of Disruption Through Empathic Communication

a) I want you to sit back again and close your eyes and think of a time when you were in a group where there was a disruption. Maybe it was a fight that broke out or people interrupted what was going on. Perhaps someone monopolized the group talk or there was so much noise from outside that it was difficult to concentrate and so on. Remember the event, the feeling you had and why you felt this way. In remembering this event, see if you can put the experience together in such a way that you can make a brief statement that goes: "I felt (name feeling) about (name the event) because (why it bothered you so much.) Do that now.

| Pause for a few minutes |

Please start coming out of your reverie now and get into groups of five again. Share with each other what your remembrance was and the statement you developed to explain the event, your feeling and the reason it bothered you so much. | Pause for 5 minutes | What I want you to do now is to select one of the examples you shared in your group and prepare a short role play to demonstrate for the whole group.

b) Please assemble into the larger group again now. I want you to think of a time when a friend of yours interrupted a group you were in with him and you wanted to help your friend not to get into trouble. So you told him that you understood or agreed with the way he felt about the situation and his reason for it. You said this to him quietly or out loud in front of the group. You supported his feeling, but also tried to discourage him from disrupting. Think of such a time now for a few minutes. ｜Pause｜

Please start coming out of your reverie now and get into groups of five again. Share your remembrances with each other. ｜Pause for 5 minutes｜ What I want you to do now is select one of the examples you shared in your group and prepare a short role play to demonstrate how your empathy with your friend helped him to control his disruptive behavior. Do that now.

Confrontation is direct leveling with an individual, a subgroup, or a group in which behavioral disturbance is dealt with in direct limit-setting ways not open for discussion. Confrontation needs to be used in a firm, clear-cut manner that communicates a no-nonsense message, yet it is not done in a way that could stir up opposition, belligerence, or hostility. Confrontation may be transmitted in the following ways:

-- That's quite enough over there... Knock it off!

-- Cut it out... that's not why we're here!

-- What's going on over there? What has that got to do with our being here?

-- That game looks like fun, but we're not here to play that game. Put it aside.

-- Why are we here?

Activity 4: Control of Disruptive Behavior
Through Direct Confrontation

I would like you to think of groups that you have been a part of, including class groups, in which disruptions were handled effectively and fairly by direct confrontation by the group leader or teacher.

Think of words the leader or teacher used to bring about order in such a way that no one felt put down or antagonized. After you think of such a situation, we will write down these phrases on the newsprint. ｜Pause for few minutes｜ Who can share a particular memory and the confrontation strategy used by the leader or teacher? ｜Post newsprint and write in trainees' responses｜

Non-Verbal Management Skills

We have been talking so far about techniques that use words to manage disruptions in a group. Equally powerful are a number of non-verbal techniques for managing group disruptions. Non-verbal techniques are methods using actions or gestures by themselves or together with words to influence and control external order. These non-verbal techniques are: eye contact, gestures, arranging healing dyads, the silent technique, physical proximity, touch, "sh, sh, sh" and acknowledgement of helpers.

Eye contact, as hospitality, can reach a person in bonding ways unless prohibited by cultural mores. The eyes are said to be the windows of the soul. People speak of having been touched by the way a person looks at them. In looking and being looked at, we spiritually enter a person. When eye contact is made in a warm, human way, a basic primitive feeling of fusion is experienced, powerful in its capacity to heal and neutralize aggression. In therapeutic communities, eye contact should especially be made by the leader with each member on entry into the group and during the beginning of the therapeutic community session itself. Again, a sensitivity to the cultural meaning of eye contact should be kept in mind.

In order to develop competence in using eye contact as a management skill through the bonding it engenders on a relationship level, I would like you to begin to develop comfort in using this bonding skill with each other. You should feel relaxed and natural as you rehearse eye contact with each other. Do the same thing with the children in your care. This will promote bonding with them and help to control disruptive behavior.

Activity 6: Practice of Eye Contact

a) Please turn to a person near you and form a twosome. Pause I want you to take two minutes just to practice looking into each other's eyes. You can smile, look briefly away, then come back. Look carefully into the person's eyes, discover their color, the feeling they convey. Or you can merely relax, looking into the eyes of the person, trying to imagine the feeling that those eyes might be expressing. Pause Now come back to the whole group. How did you feel doing this?

> Elicit the many reactions to this exercise: reactions of anxiety, self-consciousness, embarrassment, comfort, understanding, pleasure, etc. Spend needed time on this, then continue.

b) From where you are, look around and make eye contact with each member of the group. When your eyes meet someone else's at the same time, nod, smile and go on.

Arranging healing dyads means pairing troubled children with other children who have a good influence on them in order to arrange the milieu in such a way as to make use of naturally existing forces of healing and management. Some children respond to age mates with particular sensitivity; others to those who are older; some respond to the same or opposite sex better. Whatever the case, group leaders should observe who those people are whom a child responds to most, and arrange the structure of the group to allow for such healing dyads.

Activity 7: Capitalizing on Special Relationships for the Control of Disruptive Behavior

I would like you to think of situations in your own personal life where you were in an anxious or threatening circumstance and the presence of a special friend enabled you to relax and even gain positively from the experience. How was this person related to you? How old were they? What did they say or do that helped you and why did you do what they wanted? Do that now for a few minutes. ☐ Pause ☐

Come out of your reverie now. I would like to invite anyone to share a remembrance of a special friend and how that friend enabled you to come through that bad time.

☐ Pause for this sharing ☐

Now, what I would like you to do is relax and think of some children you have known who responded to certain other children in ways that seemed remarkable to you when, at the same time, these children did not respond to offical people they were supposed to, such as teachers, parents, clergy, and other authorities. You might think of children you knew when you were a child, friends you had or children you have been working with in the present. Who was the person whom the child responded to, how old were they, what did the person say or do for the child that was helpful, and why did the child do what the other person wanted? Get a memory going on this task now for a few minutes. ☐ Pause ☐

Come out of your reverie now. I would like to invite anyone to share a remembrance of the child you were thinking of and how that person the child responded to enabled the child to come through a bad time.

☐ Pause for this sharing ☐

What were the similarities between the situation you thought of in your own personal life where the presence of a special friend helped you come through a bad time and the situation of a child you thought of who had the presence of a special person who enabled him to also come through a bad time?

☐ Pause for this discussion ☐

So you see, calling upon people who have a special kind of relationship with a person whose behavior is disruptive within a group is a very powerful method of managing the disruption therapeutically.

Gestures are powerful visual indicators of messages. Joined with spoken words or used by themselves, they echo primitive ways of communicating, natural to that very early time when humans did not understand words but depended on body communication to connect with the world.

Activity 8: Practice of Gestures

I am going to read a list of expressions that can also be understood in action as well. What I want you to do is communicate the meaning of the words in gesture but to say nothing verbally.

- Hello!
- I love you!
- Watch out!
- Stop that!
- What's going on here?
- That's great!
- Come here!
- Don't talk to me!

I would like you now to try your hand at other non-verbal gestures. Let's see if the rest of us can guess what your message is. Who would like to try this?

> Encourage as many trainees as possible to experiment with this invitation. If the group is shy, look around for natural gestures already taking place such as body postures, eye movements, yawns, etc. Point these out in positive, even humorous ways and ask the trainees what these natural gestures might mean.

There are several other non-verbal methods for therapeutically managing disruptions in a group which I would like to mention briefly now as we come to the end of this session. These are:

- The silent technique
- Acknowledgement of helpers
- The "sh, sh, sh" technique
- Touch and physical proximity

Silent technique: Using silence communicates clearly that you are waiting for the group to bring itself to order. Silence accompanied by a bowed head usually brings about a group response of order fairly quickly. Many group members, however, interpret this as anger on the part of the leader. So, it is a good idea when first meeting with the group to inform them that when you do not speak and lower your head, it does not mean you are angry; it means that you are waiting for them to bring themselves to order. This statement has to be made from time to time, in order to reinforce your message. Otherwise, many group members will go on believing that your silence and bowed head means you are angry with them. When order is restored through this technique, look up and continue the session in a friendly manner.

Acknowledgement of helpers: In order to create a climate whereby all are encouraged to help maintain order, a system of recognition of those who take such responsibility needs to be established. When individual members take charge of quelling disruptions in helpful ways, immediate acknowledgement should follow. This can be done either in non-verbal forms of acknowledgement such as hand gestures showing recognition and through smiles, or it can be done through verbal forms of acknowledgement such as praising, saying thank you, encouraging others to support the actions of the helpers, and by describing the personal effects on the group and oneself as a result of the action taken by a helper.

Sh, sh, sh: Children, especially, can learn very quickly that quietly uttering the famous "sh" as in "shoe" can bring more quiet and order in two seconds than all the loudly proclaimed "shut ups" and "be quiets" that could be yelled for an hour. But this takes training and practice. When joined with hand gestures, "sh's" are quite effective.

Touch and physical proximity: Earlier in our training program, we talked about the significance of touch in healing. Touch was seen as taking the forms of holding, rocking, stroking, cradling, massaging or leaning side by side. It was also pointed out that sensitivity to the reaction of touch should be observed since many people can become hyperactive and even sexually aroused through being touched. Touch was described as most effective therapeutically when it is a nonexploitative, nonsexual, nurturing action between two people, one of whom takes the responsibility for comforting the other in a parental way.

With persons who are so troubled that control of their bodily and verbal behavior is extremely difficult for them, positioning someone next to them -- someone who has a positive or influential relationship with them -- enables their anxiety to be settled sufficiently to quell their disruptions. Sometimes this is due to the comforting effect of this person's presence; sometimes it is due to the fear of incurring the other person's displeasure. When physical proximity is combined with touch, powerful primitive forces of bonding, mothering, and comfort are communicated which create a feeling of safety, thus neutralizing feelings of aggression.

In the ways described above, both touch and physical proximity become not only vehicles of healing, but approaches through which disruptive behavior is calmed as well.

Today's session on methods for therapeutic management of large groups stressed a number of verbal and non-verbal techniques related to the maintenance of the external order or controls needed when a large group convenes, in order to lead the group in therapeutic or educational directions.

Conclusion of Training Curriculum

Today's session also concludes our training curriculum. You may remember that in our original orientation session I asked you to think of three specific concerns you had related to dealing with children that you would like to consider as goals for yourself during this training period. I asked you to write these down on pads, then meet in small groups to talk together about your goals and have a recorder summarize them for sharing within the whole group. I then wrote down your goals or expectations on newsprint according to whether your goal was to learn better communication (recorded under the letter C); or whether your goal was to learn how to deal more effectively with behavior (recorded under B); or whether your goal was to gain understanding about why children behave in certain ways (recorded under W).

Here is the original newsprint as it appeared in this format:

Post original newsprint as it appeared in this format:		
Communication (C)	Behavior (B)	Why (W)

As you review the newsprint, I would like you to consider the goals you specifically set for yourself at that time and, if you wish, share with the whole group whether these goals were met. If they were not met, would you share this disappointment and what you think might have helped here? If your goals were met, would you say how this was accomplished and give an example of how you viewed things or dealt with behavior before the training and how you see or do things differently now? Pause for this sharing

Ending a long term training course with "co-travelers" is also a time to leave each other - at least in the way we have been together here. This is also a time of separation.

Take sufficient time to allow feelings of separation to be expressed and dealt with. Also allow trainees' methods for maintaining ties with each other to be expressed and supported. Some trainees may even pass a paper around for names and addresses to be written. Support this action but also make sure no one feels they must share this if they do not wish. When sufficient time for expressions of separation has been given, wish the trainees success and bring the session to an end.

Appendix

FAMILY CIRCLE
as Vehicle of Therapy

Therapeutic
Techniques

I. Introduction

Welcome

Hello to all of you, my brothers and sisters, sons and daughters. It is good to see all of you again and to be with you here.

Definition of purpose

This is Unitas, a program that helps children to help each other and learn better ways of getting along together. We do this in two ways: through talking together, as we are doing now, and through play, after we talk.

Description of structure

Unitas is arranged as a big family, made up of little families from the whole neighborhood. Who here comes from Fox Street?... Beck?... Kelly?... Longwood?.... Southern Boulevard?.... Where else?...

Boundaries

I would like to see where each little family here begins and where it ends, where its boundaries are. Do that now. [Pause] that is beautiful; thank you for helping each other. Every family is clear to me now. As I look around [*leader does so, pointing to each family*] I see Eric, the elder, and his large family. I see James and Eric, the younger, and their family together with Nestor and Wilfred, the uncles. Over there, I see Edna's family together with David, an uncle, and Carmen, an aunt. [*Leader points to and names all familes present.*]

And when all these individual families are put together, they are called ... (the children, in unison, exclaim "an extended family").

Exhortation on family hierarchy

As you know, all the little families are made up of mothers and /or fathers, young men and women 16 years of age or older; aunts and uncles 14 to 16 years of age; and younger brothers and sisters. Each family is to take care of its members. The mothers and fathers are in charge of the families. The aunts and uncles help out the mothers and fathers by taking care of the older brothers and sisters. The older brothers and sisters help out by taking care of the younger brothers and sisters. Everyone has a part to play in their family.

Exhortation on value of family life

To have a family that you like to be with is important. Sometimes you can't get this in your own family at home. But that's no big deal. Even if you are not happy with your family at home -- and that's okay -- just make your little family here be like a family for you to help you feel happy.

II. Bonding maneuvers

I want you to learn how to talk together as a little family and get to know each other better. Here is a task. I want each little family to form a circle right where you are. Then I will tell you what to do. Do that now. [Pause] Now, each of you is to describe to the sisters and brothers in your family one or two things you learned in school today. Mothers and fathers, help your children share this with one another and remember our rule: everyone gets a chance to speak their mind, but only one person at a time. I will come around to each family to help out. Do that now. [*Pause; allow 15 minutes for this bonding task.*]

Invitation to collaborate in therapy

I would like to make eye contact with each of you. As I go around, look at me as I look at you. If you have something you would like to say to anyone here, or to the whole group, raise your hand when I come to you. Do not speak your thought when you raise your hand. Wait until I go around the whole circle and then I will call on you. In that way I will know how many people want to speak today.

Bonding with leader through eye contact	Leader does this, going around the whole circle, gesturing to and looking at each person. As each hand is raised, the leader smiles and says, "Eric, one; Vicky, two; Sam, three..." and so on. At the end of this activity, the leader invites each person to speak in turn. The leader encourages helpful interaction as each child speaks of a problem, as in the following example where Joey presents a problem concerning friendship.
III. Presentation of problems	Does anyone else have a pressing concern they need to bring up today or can we attend fully to Joey's problem now? Pause
Statement of rules	Before we begin, let me remind you of the rules of helping: (1) Pay attention. (2) When you speak, give your point of view and the reason why you think as you do. (3) Help keep order here. (4) There is no physical or verbal hurting allowed.
Empathic communication	Joey is feeling discouraged because he would like to make a friendship with a boy in his neighborhood, but the boy seems to ignore him even though Joey smiles, says hello, holds the door for him and does other nice things. Did anyone else ever have that happen to them? Pause I can see many of you have. So, Joey, you have many people here who understand your problem.
Format of subgrouping	The question here, then, is what can Joey do to try to win that friendship. I want you to team up with some people sitting near you, in teams of five, and try to figure out what Joey can do to win that friendship.
	Leader goes around structuring groups of five and repeating the task, encouraging dialogue and priming the dialogue in shy groupings. Allow time for subgroup discussion.
Praise of social behavior	Please come back to the whole group now. Pause It was hard for you to come back to the whole group again. You were so involved. It is a pleasure to see this. I would like to ask you to share some of the ideas you have developed in your small groups with each other. The question was this: There is a boy in Joey's neighborhood whom Joey wants as a friend. But by the boy's actions, Joey thinks he does not like him. We don't know if that is so. What can Joey do to try to win his friendship?

IV. Application of problem-solving dialogue	Yvette:	He should find out if the boy wants to be his friend. He can ask him.
Empathic paraphrasing	Leader:	So, he could be straightforward. Go to him and say, "We've seen each other around for a long time. I'd like to be your friend. Do you want to be my friend?"
		Let's make a list of your ideas on the board. Yvette is giving the first suggestion: Ask him straight out!
	Linda:	If he doesn't want to be friends, forget about him.
	Leader:	Another thing that could be done is to forget about the whole thing. Sometimes what you have to do is say to yourself, "Look, I've tried. I have enough going on in my life. It may be nice to have him for a friend, but I don't need him if he doesn't want to respond to me." And then forget about it. That's a very valid thought. So, the second suggestion is:

		Forget about the whole thing!
	Lucas:	You can be nicer to someone and then they'll know you want to be their friend.
	Leader:	What Lucas is saying is that sometimes if you are very, very nice to someone, it finally gets through to them. Some people have to be hit over the head before they believe something.
		We have three thoughts going now: Be straightforward. Forget the whole thing. And be nicer. Terrific! What are some other ideas to add to our list?
	Eric:	You can play with him on the block. You can act like he does in games and say things like, "Wow! You got a homerun."
Clarification	Leader:	Terrific idea! You are really mentioning two things in your suggestion. One of the things you're saying is to go to him and say, "Hey, you want to play ball?" You don't even have to ask, you can just throw the ball his way and say, "Catch." You are also suggesting that he act a little bit like the other person. That can make someone feel comfortable with you. Can you give an example in your own life of acting like someone and making that person feel comfortable with you?
	Eric:	Well, boys like to hang around boys, not girls. that's what I do. He shouldn't stick around with girls so much. (Snickers and side comments from the group.)
Reframing negative comments into positive equivalents	Leader:	Okay... so a boy might feel comfortable with girls but a friend he wants may not. So if you want his friendship hang around with guys when that person is around and he will feel good being with you. So we can add: "Hang around with friends of your own sex." That means boys might feel more comfortable with boys, and girls with girls. But in reality it certainly is OK for boys to feel comfortable with girls and girls with boys. It's not better or worse, or right or wrong. Everyone has their own preferences and that's cool.
		So, putting down your two thoughts would go like this: Invite the person to play a game. Hang out with boys if you want a boy friendship; with a girl if you want a girl friendship.
	Susan:	Joey could do the same thing to the boy that he does to him and not treat him differently.
Empathic paraphrasing	Leader:	You mean if the friend is holding the door for Joey, then he shouldn't say thank you either. Treat him like he treats you. If he's tough, you be tough too. If he's nice, then you be nice. That's really a good suggestion. We'll write it down: Treat as you are treated.
	David:	You could make an appointment to talk to him when he has some free time. He might be busy.

	Leader:	Great. Instead of leaving it to chance, tell him you would like to talk to him. "When's a good time?" you might ask him. So another suggestion for our list is: Make time to be together.
	Ray:	You might do something you like together.
	Leader:	You could find out about something you are both interested in. That's a really nice thought. Can you develop that more?
	Ray:	Like a hobby.
	Leader:	So, you could work on something you are both interested in. That could bring you closer together.
	Elena:	Maybe the boy heard some things about Joey from others that made the boy turn against him, so he doesn't want to hang around with him.
Encouragement	Leader:	A fascinating thought. Maybe there is some gossip going around and the boy has heard these things. But the things he has heard may not be true. But he bases his decision on the gossip and not on facts. Let's put that down on our list as: Set the facts straight.
Bonding		How many of you have ever had that happen? (Show of many hands) How many have had gossip make people stay away from them? (Show of hands) So, this idea of gossip really hits home with many of you. Could we have a few more thoughts before we close the list?
	Anna:	Maybe he wants to be his friend but he wants to be tough about it and not show it.
Encouragement Clarification	Leader:	Do you hear this terrific thought she said? Who can put what Anna said in their own words? Each person says things in their head in their own way.
	Cathy:	Some people don't want to say they want to be your friend. They just want to be tough about it.
Encouragement of direct interaction	Leader:	Could you put in your own words what Cathy just said?
	Mark:	I don't know what she said.
	Leader:	Thank you for letting us know that. What part of what she said didn't you understand? Can you ask her?
	Mark:	The part about his wanting to be tough. I didn't understand that.
	Leader:	Say that to her.
	Mark:	I don't understand what you mean about being tough.
	Cathy:	A boy might want to be the leader of the street. He might not want others to think he has favorite friends. If he's friendly, then people might think he's soft.

Empathic communication	Leader:	Sometimes people, especially guys who express themselves in friendly warm ways, might make people think, but wrongly so, that they are not a man. So a guy may think he has to be tough so people won't get the wrong idea. But inside he really is a warm sensitive person, but won't let anyone know this. So he acts tough on the outside. Is that your idea about toughness, Cathy?
	Cathy:	Yes, lots of guys I know are that way.
	Mark:	I understand now.
Clarification of an opinion through sociodrama	Leader:	I think maybe that is the opposite for Joey. He seems to be a warm sensitive guy who lets his feelings be known. So it could be that the guy wants to be Joey's friend but he may not know how to show it, except by being tough. What we're saying is that in making a friendship it could help to become a little like the other person in order for him to feel comfortable with you. Let me show you what I mean by a little play.
		(Leader chooses a volunteer, Tito. He and the leader sit in the middle of the circle.) I would like Tito to pretend he is in my office. I want to make him feel comfortable with me, by becoming a little bit like he is. (The class is instructed to look carefully at what goes on between Tito and the leader. It is a non-verbal role play. Leader mirrors all actions of Tito. When Tito cups his chin with his hands, leader does the same; when Tito stretches, leader does too, and so on.)
	Leader:	What did you observe?
	Eric:	I saw two people not talking; it seemed to feel lonely.
	Linda:	There was communication, but not in words.
	Nelson:	You were doing what Tito was doing.
	Leader:	All your thoughts were right on target. How do you think using the same mannerisms as Tito was the same as the suggestions that Joey act "tough"?
	Linda:	When he is around that boy he could imitate the way he walks or acts and then the boy won't feel strange with him.
	Leader:	That's right. To make a friendship, you might have to change a little of yourself. When you want to find a treasure, you have to work at digging for it.
Summarizing and affirmation of group's insight		So, here we have a fine list of your thoughts on actions a person could take to make a friendship. We developed these ideas from a situation Joey brought up about how to make a friendship with a neighborhood boy. There are lots of ideas to choose from. That's what we've done today. I really appreciated the ideas you have shared with me and each other. They are terrific. I also feel there have been some other ideas many of you who have not spoken have been thinking. They are equally terrific.

		But time has run out. While these thoughts are for everyone to use in making friendships, certain suggestions on the list will appeal more to some of you than to others. Joey, I was wondering if you would be interested in considering some of these ideas to use with the friend you have talked about with us today. Would you mind telling us next time which suggestions you feel might work for you?
	Joey:	That's OK, but I don't like the one about acting like he does.
Closure	Leader:	That's OK, too. What we'll do next time is go through the list and cross out the ones you don't feel comfortable with and think about trying out two or three others. So, that's the plan for next time. But for now, it's time to play together.

SUGGESTED READINGS

Adler, Alfred.   *What Life Should Mean to You.* New York: Capricorn Books, 1958.

———   *The Problem Child.* New York: Capricorn Books, 1963.

———   *The Practice and Theory of Individual Psychology.* Totowa, N.J.: Littlefield and Adams, 1969.

———   *The Science of Living.* New York: Doubleday-Anchor Books, 1969.

———   *The Education of Children.* Chicago: Henry Regnery, 1970.

Almond, Richard.   *The Healing Community.* New York: Jason Aronson, 1974.

Ansbacher, H. & R. Ansbacher (eds.)   *The Individual Psychology of Alfred Adler.* New York: Harper and Row, 1967.

Bettelheim, Bruno.   *A Home for the Heart.* New York: Alfred E. Knopf, 1974.

Campbell, Joseph.   *The Power of Myth.* New York: Doubleday, 1988.

Carkuff, R. and Berenson, B.   *Beyond Counseling and Psychotherapy.* New York: Holt, Rinehart and Winston, 1967.

De Mello, Anthony.   *Song of the Bird.* Chicago: University of Loyola Press, 1982.

———   *Wellsprings.* New York: Doubleday, 1984.

———   *Taking Flight.* New York: Doubleday, 1988.

———   *Awareness.* New York: Doubleday, 1990.

———   *Contact With God.* Chicago: University of Loyola Press, 1991.

———   *The Way to Love.* San Francisco: Sierra, 1992.

Dinkmeyer, D.; Pew, W.; and Dinkmeyer, D.   *Adlerian Counseling and Psychotherapy.* Monterey, Calif.: Brooks/Cole Publishing, 1979.

Dreikurs, Rudolph.   *Fundamentals of Adlerian Psychology.* Chicago: Alfred Adler Institute, 1953.

———   *Group Psychotherapy and Group Approaches.* Chicago: Alfred Adler Institute, 1960.

———, and Soltz, V.   *Children: The Challenge.* New York: Hawthorne, 1964.

———   *Psychodynamics, Psychotherapy and Counseling.* Chicago: Alfred Adler Institute, 1967.

———   *Psychology in the Classroom.* New York: Harper and Row, 1968.

Egan, Gerard.   *The Skilled Helper.* Monterey, Calif.: Brooks/Cole, 1975.

Erikson, Eric.	*Identity and the Life Cycle.* New York: Norton, 1980.
Feldman, Christina and Kornfield, Jack (eds.)	*Stories of the Spirit, Stories of the Heart.* New York: Harper, 1991.
Frank, Jerome.	*Persuasion and Healing: A Comparative Study of Psychotherapy.* Baltimore: Johns Hopkins University Press, 1973.
Frankl, Victor.	*The Doctor and the Soul.* New York: Vintage Press, 1973.
———	*The Unconscious God.* New York: Simon and Schuster, 1975.
———	*Man's Search for Meaning.* New York: Simon and Schuster, 1984.
Freud, Sigmund.	*General Selection from the Works of Sigmund Freud.* (John Rickman, ed.) New York: Doubleday, 1957.
———	*The Ego and the Id.* London: Hogarth Press, 1927.
———	*New Introductory Lectures on Psychoanalysis.* London: Hogarth Press, 1933.
———	*Group Psychology and the Analysis of the Ego.* London: Hogarth Press, 1933.
———	*The Problem of Anxiety.* New York: Norton, 1936.
Gordon, Thomas.	*Parent Effectiveness Training.* New York: Peter Wyden, 1974.
Gottlieb, Benjamin.	*Social Support Strategies.* Beverly Hills, Calif.: Sage, 1983.
Guerney, Bernard.	*Relationship Enhancement.* San Francisco: Jossey–Bass, 1977.
Haley, Jay.	*Changing Families: A Family Therapy Reader.* New York: Grune & Stratton, 1971.
———	*Problem Solving Therapy.* San Francisco: Jossey–Bass, 1976.
Hammond, D. C.: Hepworth, D. H.; & Smith, V. G.	*Improving Therapeutic Communications.* San Francisco,: Jossey–Bass, 1977.
Hoffman, Edward.	*The Drive for Self: Alfred Adler and the Founding of Individual Psychology.* New York: Addison–Wesley, 1994.
Jacobs, Michael.	*D. W. Winnicott.* Beverly Hills, Calif.: Sage, 1995.
Jones, Maxwell.	*The Therapeutic Community.* New York: Basic Books, 1953.
———	*Maturation of the Therapeutic Community: An Organic Approach to Health and Mental Health.* New York: Human Sciences Press, 1976.

Jung, Carl.	*Modern Man in Search of a Soul.* New York: Harcourt, Brace and World, 1933.
———	*Memories, Dreams, Reflections.* New York: Random House, 1961.
———	*Man and His Symbols.* New York: Dell Publishing, 1964.
Kohut, Heinz.	*The Restoration of the Self.* New York: International Universities Press, 1977.
———	*How Does Analysis Work?* Chicago: University of Chicago Press, 1984.
Minuchin, Salvador.	*Families and Family Therapy.* Cambridge, Mass.: Harvard University Press, 1974.
———	*Family Therapy Techniques.* Cambridge, Mass.: Harvard University Press, 1978.
———	*Family Healing: Tales of Hope & Renewal from Family Therapy.* New York: Free Press, 1993.
Nowen, Henri.	*Genesee Diary.* New York: Doubleday, 1976.
———	*Way of the Heart.* New York: Harper, 1981.
———	*Lifesigns.* New York: Doubleday, 1986.
———	*Letters to Mark About Jesus.* New York: Harper, 1988.
———	*Beyond the Mirror.* New York: Crossroads, 1992.
———	*With Open Hands.* Notre Dame, Ind.: Ave Maria Press, 1995.
———	*Here and Now.* New York: Crossroads, 1995.
Olmstead, Michael.	*The Small Group.* New York: Random House, 1957.
Olson, David (ed.).	*Treating Relationships.* Lake Mills, Iowa: Graphic Publishing House, 1976.
Orgler, Hertha.	*Alfred Adler: The Man and His Work.* New York: Capricorn Books, 1965.
Redl, Fritz & Wineman, David.	*The Aggressive Child.* New York: Free Press, 1957.
Rogers, Carl.	*Client Centered Treatment.* Boston: Houghton-Mifflen, 1951.
———	*Psychotherapy and Personality Change.* Chicago: University of Chicago Press, 1954.
———	"The Concept of the fully functioning person." *Psychotherapy: Theory, Research and Practice,* 1963, 1 (17).
———	*Man and the Science of Man.* Columbus, Ohio: Charles Merrill, 1968.

———, and Wood, John.	Client–centered theory." Chap. 7 (pp. 211–258) in *Operational Theories of Personality*. New York: Brunner/Mazel, 1974.
Rossi, J. and Filsead, W. (eds.)	*The Therapeutic Community*. New York: Behavioral Publications, 1973.
Rueveni, Uri.	*Networking Families in Crisis*. New York: Human Sciences Press, 1979.
Satir, Virginia.	*Conjoint Family Therapy*. Palo Alto, Calif.: Science and Behavior Books, 1964.
Shah, Idries.	*Wisdom of the Idiots*. England: Redwood Press, 1970.
———	*The Hundred Tales of Wisdom*. London: Octagon Press, 1978.
———	*Way of the Sufi*. New York: Penguin, 1990.
———	*Tales of the Dervishes*. New York: Penguin, 1993.
Slavson, S. R.	*Re-educating the Delinquent Through Group and Community Participation*. New York: Collier Books, 1954.
Speck, Ross & Attneave, Carolyn.	"Social Network Intervention." Chap. 25 (pp. 416–439) in C. Sager and H. Kaplan (eds.), *Progress in Group and Family Therapy*. New York: Brunner/Mazel, 1972.
———	*Family Networks*. New York: Vintage Books, 1973.
Sweeney, Thomas.	*Adlerian Counseling*. Muncie, Indiana: Accelerated Development, 1981.
Thich Nhat Hanh.	*Miracle of Mindfulness*. Boston: Beacon Press, 1976.
———	*Being Peace*. Berkeley, Calif.: Parallax, 1987.
———	*Interbeing*. Berkeley, Calif.: Parallax, 1987.
———	*For a Future to Be Possible*. Berkeley Calif.: Parallax, 1993.
———	*Blooming Lotus*. Boston: Beacon Press, 1993.
Yalom, Irvin.	*The Theory and Practice of Group Psychotherapy*. New York: Basic Books, 1975.

www.ingramcontent.com/pod-product-compliance
Lightning Source LLC
Chambersburg PA
CBHW080248030426
42334CB00023BA/2737